Business Models

FOR DUMMIES®

A Wiley Brand

by Jim Muehlhausen, JD
Founder and President, Business Model Institute

FOR DUMMIES®
A Wiley Brand

Business Models For Dummies®

Published by
John Wiley & Sons, Inc.
111 River St.
Hoboken, NJ 07030-5774
www.wiley.com

For general information on our other products and services, please contact our Customer Care Department within the U.S. at 877-762-2974, outside the U.S. at 317-572-3993, or fax 317-572-4002.

For technical support, please visit www.wiley.com/techsupport.

Wiley publishes in a variety of print and electronic formats and by print-on-demand. Some material included with standard print versions of this book may not be included in e-books or in print-on-demand. If this book refers to media such as a CD or DVD that is not included in the version you purchased, you may download this material at http://booksupport.wiley.com. For more information about Wiley products, visit www.wiley.com.

Library of Congress Control Number: 2013935679

ISBN 978-1-118-54761-8 (pbk); ISBN 978-1-118-61252-1 (ebk); ISBN 978-1-118-61267-5 (ebk); ISBN 978-1-118-61275-0 (ebk)

Manufactured in the United States of America

10 9 8 7 6 5 4 3 2 1

About the Author

Like most entrepreneurs, **Jim Muehlhausen** has an eclectic background, ranging from CPA to franchisee, attorney, business owner, consultant, franchisor, public speaker, university professor, and book author.

While still attending the Indiana University School of Law, he became the youngest franchisee in Meineke Discount Muffler history (1987–1991). After successfully selling that business, Jim founded an automotive aftermarket manufacturing concern. During his nine-year tenure with that business, the company achieved recognition from Michael Porter of the Harvard Business School and *Inc. Magazine* in the IC 100 Fastest Growing Businesses.

Fifteen years ago, he found his true passion, serving as a consultant, business coach, and advisor to hundreds of businesses. During his 5,000+ one-on-one consulting sessions with business owners around the globe, Jim realized that while all business issues look unique, they rarely are. Most businesses are working to seize the same opportunities and overcome the same obstacles. To help business owners share best practices and stop learning from the "School of Hard Knocks," he wrote the well regarded book *The 51 Fatal Business Errors and How to Avoid Them* (Mulekick Publishing).

His ongoing research led to the discovery of fatal business error #52: You can't outsmart, outhustle, or outmaneuver a weak business model. The more he studied business models and worked with business owners, the more convinced he became that business models were the key to a great business.

In 2009, he founded the Business Model Institute, which is devoted to the innovation and study of business models. Jim writes several articles for the Institute each year as well as contributing to publications such as *Inc., The Small Business Report, Entrepreneur, BusinessWeek,* and various business journals. He also speaks to associations, groups of business owners, and corporations about business model assessment and innovation.

Dedication

This book is dedicated to my clients who have graciously shared their businesses with me over the years. Without their candor, support, and great depth of business knowledge, this book would not be possible. I am honored to work with these talented men and women who openly share their business experience, skills, and vast knowledge with me. Much of these experiences are included in this book and I cannot thank them enough for the honor of being included in their lives. Thank you for the privilege of working with you.

Author's Acknowledgments

When you read a book it's easy to assume it's the brainchild of the writer. Nothing could be further from the truth. It takes a village to raise a child and it takes a small army to write a book. This book is no different. A talented army of people made this book possible.

This book tackles dozens of theories, constructs, and concepts. Jak Plihal, Huss Sadri, and Michael Jones all contributed ideas and input toward the book. Any publishers looking for the next great business book should contact Merryck Leigh and Steve Shaer. Both of them served as brainstorming partners, sounding boards, and trusted confidants during the creation of this book. I cannot thank them enough.

I'm a business thinker, not a writer. Laurie Davis was instrumental in turning my thoughts into well punctuated, readable content.

The entire team at Wiley is due immense credit. Stacy Kennedy saw the need for this book and made sure it got published. Jennifer Moore helped craft the initial chapters and I can't thank my editor, Sarah Faulkner, enough. Sarah was a joy to work with on all the tough edits — pushing to make the book its best with a deft and likeable manner.

Thanks to my team at the Business Model Institute for all their work behind the scenes. Huss Sadri and Sue Lee researched facts and stories for the book. Stefanie Keffaber and Christopher Loch deserve praise for helping get the Institute off the ground in its early days. Without their hard work, there would be no Business Model Institute.

Many clients and business owners I have met in my travels provided real-world examples to make concepts come to life. Thanks to them for opening up their businesses to me. Without this real-world content, I would not have had the opportunity to create the concepts and principles in this book.

Thanks to my family and friends for the support and patience provided as I wrote this book on a tight timetable. The greatest thanks go to my wife Beth who always has been the wind beneath my wings. Her intellect, insight, and patience have been vital to my success. Thanks sweetie!

Publisher's Acknowledgments

We're proud of this book; please send us your comments at http://dummies.custhelp.com. For other comments, please contact our Customer Care Department within the U.S. at 877-762-2974, outside the U.S. at 317-572-3993, or fax 317-572-4002.

Some of the people who helped bring this book to market include the following:

Acquisitions, Editorial, and Vertical Websites

Project Editor: Sarah Faulkner

Acquisitions Editor: Stacy Kennedy

Assistant Editor: David Lutton

Editorial Program Coordinator: Joe Niesen

Technical Editor: Rita Gunther McGrath, PhD

Senior Editorial Manager: Jennifer Ehrlich

Editorial Manager: Carmen Krikorian

Editorial Assistants: Rachelle S. Amick, Alexa Koschier

Art Coordinator: Alicia B. South

Cover Image: © iStockphoto.com / VOLODYMYR GRINKO

Composition Services

Project Coordinator: Patrick Redmond

Layout and Graphics: Jennifer Creasey, Joyce Haughey

Proofreaders: Barbara Arany, John Greenough

Indexer: Steve Rath

Special Help
Jennifer Moore

Publishing and Editorial for Consumer Dummies

> **Kathleen Nebenhaus,** Vice President and Executive Publisher

> **David Palmer,** Associate Publisher

> **Kristin Ferguson-Wagstaffe,** Product Development Director

Publishing for Technology Dummies

> **Andy Cummings,** Vice President and Publisher

Composition Services

> **Debbie Stailey,** Director of Composition Services

Contents at a Glance

Table of Contents

Introduction

I've enjoyed the privilege of working with hundreds of business leaders, from both big and small companies, on an intimate level. These business leaders have shared their hopes and dreams, successes and failures, and the inner workings of their businesses with me.

Through the course of these interactions I came to discover there wasn't necessarily a correlation between education, intelligence, or hard work and success of the businesses. I found many successful business owners who were quite lazy. I found high school dropouts who created highly successful businesses. I also found intelligent, well-educated, and hard-working business leaders who failed to translate these qualities into business success.

I asked myself, "If these traits aren't the foundation of business success, what is?" The answer is the business model. Education, intelligence, and hard work are all applied to a business model. Applying these qualities to a weak or failing business model is like throwing good money after bad in the stock market.

After the realization that the strength of the business model is at the core of a business's success, I began to focus on this vital area. After years spent collecting real-world case studies, I created both a business model framework and a business model evaluation tool. I share both of these items with you in this book.

By the end of this book, I hope you'll agree that I have demonstrated the importance of your business model as well as provided you with the necessary tools to create and innovate the best business model possible.

About This Book

The purpose of *Business Models For Dummies* is to demonstrate the importance of a business model, show you how to create a structured business model, recognize when it needs a tune-up, and innovate your model via proven methods.

At this point, it may seem like an overwhelming task. Don't worry. By the end of this book you'll have a variety of tools to assist you in constructing or redesigning a business model.

My goal for this book is to add the concept of business models into the strategic discussions of all businesses. To me, the business model is at the core of profitability and should be at the core of strategic planning discussions and business plan documents. I hope the conversations and tools provided in this book give you the opportunity to do just that.

Much of the mystery surrounding business models is due to the lack of discussion surrounding business models. This book aims to increase the body of work in the area of business models, adding structure and process, so that businesspeople can better understand the role of the business model.

This book should be used as a reference. You don't need to read the chapters in order from front cover to back, and you aren't expected to remember everything. The book is created in module format, so you can read only one chapter or jump from chapter to chapter.

Conventions Used in This Book

All *For Dummies* books employ similar conventions for a sense of continuity and familiarity. This book includes the following conventions:

- ✔ Web addresses appear in a typeface called monofont. If the URL wraps to a second line of text, type the address exactly how it's presented. Hyphens are inserted only when they're included in the web address.
- ✔ **Bold** text indicates keywords, phrases, or concepts.
- ✔ When a new term is introduced, it appears in *italics* and is followed by an explanatory phrase or sentence.
- ✔ Because businesses sell both products and services, I refer to the product or service being sold as product for simplification's sake.
- ✔ I've tried to mix use of gender terms throughout this book. If I haven't done so evenly or appropriately, my sincere apologies.
- ✔ There's no effective synonym for *business model*. I'm sure the phrase business model is repeated many times throughout this book. To some extent, it can't be helped. However in many situations I've shortened "business model" to simply "model."
- ✔ CEO, owner, businessperson, business owner, and entrepreneur are used interchangeably throughout the book.

✔ A direct, sometimes sarcastic style. I've found business leaders to be a direct, no-nonsense group. My style is very similar. Sometimes you may find my style to be a little "in your face." My apologies if it's too much so. This direct style has served me well with business leaders.

I also enjoy a good laugh, and my humor can take on a sarcastic tone every now and then. I enjoy the humorous side of business and don't have a problem poking fun at certain aspects of it. Like anyone making jokes, sometimes they fall flat. Sorry if my humor isn't as funny as I think on some occasions.

What You're Not to Read

The main text is full of relevant and helpful tips, ideas, lists, and specifics for creating and improving your business model, so don't miss a word. I believe that businesspeople learn best through relevant examples and case studies, so I've tried to include lots of them. If you're one of those people who doesn't need case studies, feel free to skip them because you'll probably have learned what you need from the previous text.

The sidebars — those gray shaded boxes containing information — are supplementary and relevant, but not absolutely imperative to the business-model discussion. You can skip these bits of information without missing any key points.

Foolish Assumptions

Business models are such a broad topic that I had to make several assumptions in order to keep the book at a lean 360 pages. I assume that

✔ You're a person looking to create a new business model or improve an existing one.

✔ You have a basic understanding of general business concepts such as marketing strategies, pricing, operations, management, human resources, and the many other aspects of running a business.

✔ You're looking for a leg up on the competition via a better business model.

✔ You're a creative thinker. After all, you were creative enough to focus on your business model.

✔ You're an innovator. You're ready, willing, and able to innovate your business to incorporate the business model improvements I discuss in this book.

✔ You can be objective about your own business model. It's very difficult to see your own model objectively, but in order to get the most out of this book you'll need to recognize the strengths and weaknesses of your model so you can improve it.

✔ You realize that business model innovation is a process, not an event.

How This Book Is Organized

Business Models For Dummies is organized into five parts. Each part can be easily read by itself, and you'll feel fully informed on that topic without any other background. Check out the following overview and then dive in wherever your individual interest may be.

Part I: Getting Started with Business Models

Part I of this book discusses the business model in general. What is a business model? Why does your business model matter? How do you define a business model? What's the difference between a business model, a business plan, and competitive advantage?

This portion of the book gives you an understanding of a business model on the conceptual level. As you move through the different sections of the book, you dive into greater detail and begin working on creating your new business model.

Part II: Creating a Winning Business Model

Part II gets down to the nuts and bolts of a business model. I show you several tools you can use to brainstorm and structure your business model. Using the business model framework from the Business Model Institute, I divide a business model into three overarching areas: offering, monetization, and sustainability.

These three areas are broken down into eight distinct components:

- ✔ **Market attractiveness:** Picking the best market to sell your product to.
- ✔ **Unique value proposition:** Creating a unique product with powerful benefits that's highly differentiated in the marketplace.
- ✔ **Profit model:** Creating innovative ways to maximize revenues and profits from your differentiated offering.
- ✔ **Sales performance model:** Even the better mouse trap needs to be sold. Creating a proven and repeatable sales process to complement your strong offering.
- ✔ **Ongoing competitive advantage:** Creating a business model that keeps competitors at bay and your profits high.
- ✔ **Innovation factor:** Every company needs to innovate. This area rates your model's ability to innovate versus the competition's.
- ✔ **Pitfall avoidance:** Many great business models have been destroyed by overreliance on one customer, government regulations, lawsuits, or freaks of nature.
- ✔ **Graceful exit:** This component affects only mid-size and small businesses but is vitally important. Far too many small businesses create a model that's overly dependent upon the owner. These business models are difficult to exit. Designing a business model that allows for a significant payday or graceful exit is imperative.

Within each of these eight components, I discuss the following:

- ✔ How to best design your model with the component in mind
- ✔ Advantages and pitfalls
- ✔ Case studies relevant to each area
- ✔ Relevant personal insights

By the end of this part you should have a clear understanding of the strengths and weaknesses of your business model by using the quick and easy scoring mechanism I provide.

Part III: Dealing with Change

There's only one thing needed to turn a good business model bad — time. Just like water eroding a rock, time will erode your business model. Don't worry. This part discusses how to spot an eroding business model as well as how to fix it. You discover how many everyday business problems are really symptoms of an underlying business model issue. I show you that business model erosion is a reality and how to use innovation to not only rectify this erosion but also improve your business model.

Part IV: Business Model Innovation

Part IV dives into the innovation process. I show you where and how to begin the innovation of your business model as well as discuss several proven innovation techniques. You find out about the power of disruptive innovation and how to leverage it for the benefit of your business model.

For the brave at heart, I include chapters on advanced business model innovation and discuss my most profitable tricks. Certainly one size does not fit all, but if you can implement one of these advanced business model innovation techniques, you could make millions. After all, these aren't my tricks; they're the tricks I've observed my clients putting to work. These clever businesspeople innovated their business models over decades to come up with powerful tactics like crowdsourcing, virtualized sales processes, and offering insurance to your customers.

Part V: The Part of Tens

Every *For Dummies* book contains this part, which features a few entertaining and informative lists of tens. Turn to Chapter 23 to gather inspiration from the success stories of other businesses as well as some humorous takes (at least I hope they're humorous) on everyday business situations.

This part includes lists of highly successful business models, signs your business model may be in trouble, unique sources of innovation, and phrases you should never use with a banker or venture capitalist.

Icons Used in This Book

If you peruse *Business Models For Dummies*, you'll see little pictures, or icons, in the margins. These icons spotlight the following helpful information and key ideas:

This icon indicates the presence of a specific opportunity to improve your business model knowledge or your business model itself.

Don't skip over this icon. It indicates you're about to discover some pearls of wisdom designed to keep you from making costly mistakes.

With the last name like Muehlhausen, you can imagine what my nickname was as a kid — Mule. I have a direct, in-your-face style that works for many businesspeople. I also can be a bit of a contrarian. When you see this icon, I'm sharing a bit of contrarian wisdom or perhaps getting in your face a bit.

When I have the opportunity to make a point by using an actual example learned in the trenches of real businesses, I do so. Businesspeople tend to learn best from examples that closely tie to their own businesses. When you see this icon, you'll find a real-world case study illustrating the concept.

This icon calls your attention to concepts you want to remember. With so many moving parts to a business model, I want to make sure you catch the most important parts.

Where to Go from Here

If you feel like you have a good understanding of the business model concept, jump straight to Part II where I discuss the breakdown and scoring of a business model. To me, Part II is the most important section of the book. Because the study of business models is relatively new, you probably don't have a business plan template or an outline of a strategic plan. In the business-model world you're stuck doodling on the back of a napkin. Part II fixes this problem by giving you a structure for your business model and a quick scoring mechanism.

Ultimately, I believe you'll benefit from reading the entire book because your business model will be in need of innovation at some point. You'll need to know how to sniff out weakness in your model and fix it before your competitors can exploit the weakness. Parts III and IV show you exactly how to do this.

I hope you'll incorporate business models into your ongoing business planning and strategy sessions. Ten years from now this tactic will be commonplace; by incorporating the business model as a core strategy today, you'll be ahead of the game.

Part I

Getting Started with Business Models

For Dummies can help you get started with lots of subjects. Visit www.dummies.com to learn more and do more with For Dummies.

In this part . . .

✔ Find out what a business model is and why it's important. Understanding the business model concept — and how it differs from a business plan — gives you the best chance at success.

✔ Discover how business models interrelate with other business concepts, such as business architecture and profit formula.

✔ Look at examples of companies that use various business models. Learn lessons from the successes of companies like Amazon and Starbucks and from the trials of companies like Kodak and Blockbuster.

✔ Ditch the traditional business plan in favor of a business model plan. A great business model is always a winner.

Chapter 1

What Is a Business Model and Why Does It Matter?

In This Chapter

▶ Examining advanced business planning, also known as business models

▶ Speeding time to profit with a better business model

▶ Discovering why governments, families, churches, and businesses all have a model

▶ Predicting the future of business models

So what is a business model anyway? Is it the way you make money? Yes, in part. Is it competitive advantage? Yes, in part. Is it your business plan? Not really. Simply put, a *business model* is your profit formula. It's the method you use to acquire customers, service them, and make money doing so. I like to break down a business model into three primary areas: Offering, monetization, and sustainability. What is your offering? How will you monetize the offering? How will you sustain it?

Your business model creates not only the formula by which you make money, but also the strategic context of the organization.

Simply put, a business model is the framework of rules and "moral" imperatives within which the business operates. It provides the strategic context for both the long and short term. It defines and articulates strategic intent, which then becomes the common focus and driver among all levels of strategic management (**M**ission, **O**bjectives, **S**trategy, and **T**actics). The combination of these four becomes the compass and laws by which the organization navigates and the glue that holds it all together.

Many managers believe that all they need is a business plan, but business plans are at best reactive. In today's turbulent environment, the best way to be proactive is to have a strong business model. This book outlines an accessible way to refine the essence of your business and build it into a durable and superior model.

History of Business Models

The notion of a business model may be relatively new, but the study of business in general has been going on for centuries. The notion of a business plan has been around since the late 1800s. Since then, business planning has grown from a mere notion to a science. Colleges offer courses in business planning. Software and templates have been created, and the general business public is well skilled in the practice.

Next came the concept of entrepreneurship. If you look at the rise of entrepreneurship, you see that it's grown from a vague concept in the 1960s to a major discipline in which you can now get a business degree. If you talk to recent college graduates about careers, a significant and growing percentage of them want to work for an entrepreneurial company or want to start a company of their own one day. Never before has entrepreneurship been celebrated the way it is today — both in the real world and in the academic world, where special programs and degrees are offered in entrepreneurship.

The study of business models can be called "advanced entrepreneurship." The business model picks up where entrepreneurship leaves off and will, I believe for reasons that are becoming increasingly apparent, become the next wave of interest within the business community.

Business Models Are a Hot Topic

Aside from simple evolution in business thinking, business models are a hot topic for one reason — speed profit. There used to be an old saying in business, "It takes 15 years to become an overnight success." The gist of this saying was that a business owner needed to toil in anonymity for 15 years before becoming tremendously successful. Today, business moves much faster, and tremendous profitability can be achieved almost overnight.

Fifteen years ago, Mark Zuckerberg, founder of Facebook, was in middle school. Most people had never heard of Google or Amazon, and Spanx undergarments weren't even a glimmer in Sara Blakely's eye. Today all these entrepreneurs are billionaires. Commerce is worldwide and moves significantly faster, creating better opportunities for better businesses. There's simply no need to slog it out for 15 years.

As businesses became very successful quickly, people started to ask, "How can this happen?" The only logical answer was superior business models. With financial stakes resembling lottery winnings, business models gained more and more attention.

Business models aren't a fad. A strong business model is at the heart of a strong business and is the key to its profitability. Business models take all the complexity of a multibillion dollar business and boil it down to an easy-to-communicate profitable essence.

Who Needs a Business Model?

Why is a business model suddenly necessary? People have operated successful businesses for centuries without a business model — or have they?

Sun Tzu is widely believed to have provided Napoleon with a quantum shift in thinking, which led to the development of the model through which Napoleon's early successes were won. It's argued that when he moved away from the fundamentals of his business model and started to rely heavily on plans that didn't take into account the sustainability of his actions, he was defeated. The one thing Sun Tzu espoused loud and often was to consider all aspects and influences of the job at hand. This concept elevated management to a high art. Sun Tzu believed it was critical not only to lay a great plan but also to be flexible and make excellent decisions when things became fluid.

Whether you're an army general or a donut shop owner, every organization has and needs a business model. Schools have business models. Not-for-profit organizations have business models. Families have business models. Even governments have business models.

Take the example of capitalism versus socialism. Just like the business model determines the operational context of the business, capitalism or socialism determines the operational context of a society. One could argue that capitalism has proven to be a more successful business model for governments than socialism.

Extrapolated to the next level, one could argue that communist societies didn't shift to capitalism for ideological or humanitarian reasons but shifted to a more effective business model for a government.

For your organization to operate at maximum effectiveness, an up-to-date and innovative business model is a necessity.

Value of a Business Model

If you search the Internet you can find many lists ranking the value of top brands such as Coca-Cola, Starbucks, and McDonald's. According to these lists, the value of these brands is in the billions. The goodwill of these brands has tremendous value, but the brand alone is worth far less than the brand integrated into a strong business model.

A business can profit in many ways. I can start a lawn mowing business, walk across the street, and charge $25 to mow my neighbor's yard. The business would profit but wouldn't enjoy a strong business model. I could add experience and working smart to the equation and profit a bit more. I could even write a business plan to increase the profitability. But this business model is very limited. In order to create a powerful lawn mowing business, I must add a good business model on top of these other criteria. I call this concept the *profit ladder.* Figure 1-1 shows this ladder.

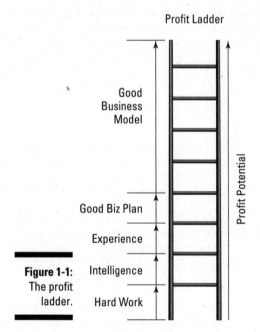

Profit Ladder

Good Business Model

Good Biz Plan

Experience

Intelligence

Hard Work

Profit Potential

Figure 1-1: The profit ladder.

As you can see, the greatest amount of profit is created via the strength of the business model. Hard work, experience, and planning alone can't create an extremely profitable business. You must also have a business model that complements your efforts.

No better example of the value of a business model exists than the growth of franchising. After all, what are you really buying if you buy a franchise? You're buying a proven business model. Here's a brief history of franchising in the United States:

✔ In 1898, William E. Metzger of Detroit became the first official dealer/ franchisee of General Motors Corporation (GM).

✔ In 1899, Coca-Cola sold its first franchise.

✔ In 1950, fewer than 100 companies used franchising in their marketing operations. By 1960, more than 900 companies had franchise operations involving an estimated 200,000 franchised outlets.

✔ In 1986, the U.S. Department of Commerce estimated that retail sales by franchised establishments represented 34 percent of all retail sales.

✔ According to a survey conducted for the International Franchise Association's Educational Foundation, as of 2001, there were more than 767,483 franchise-related businesses.

✔ Studies indicate a new franchise business opens approximately every five to eight minutes of each business day, and that franchises are, on average, more profitable than company-owned locations.

✔ Scott Shane, author, venture capitalist, and professor of Entrepreneurial Studies at Case Western Reserve University, observes that some 71 percent of start-ups will have gone out of business by year ten. According to the U.S. Department of Commerce, 95 percent of all franchises are successful.

Franchising continues to grow in popularity as entrepreneurs recognize the business model as the core of business success.

Future of Business Models

No one would have imagined the creative business models of today just a few decades ago. No one knows what the business models of tomorrow will be, but here are a few safe bets.

Increased sophistication

Just like entrepreneurship has advanced due to increased emphasis and study, so will business models. As educational institutions add business model study to their curriculum, business models will become more sophisticated. Additionally, as the entrepreneurial community recognizes the value of business models, increased focus outside the classroom will make business models improve at a greater pace than today.

More virtual goods

The Internet may seem like it's been around forever, but the Internet is still a baby. Consumers are still getting used to the purchase of electrons versus the purchase of something you can hold in your hand. Virtual goods commerce is still in its infancy. Even successful companies like Facebook have only scratched the surface of selling virtual goods, relying on old-fashioned billboards (albeit electronic) for the bulk of their revenue.

The business models of tomorrow will find creative ways to develop and sell virtual goods. With instant worldwide access to these goods, a successful virtual product has the ability to make billions in a few days. Imagine a product as hot as a Cabbage Patch doll or Beanie Baby being sold virtually on the Internet.

Intellectual property protection

As the sale of intellectual property and virtual goods becomes more commonplace, look for entrepreneurs to find better ways to protect their valued property. Hopefully, governments will realize the need for protection of ideas in a knowledge-based economy and accelerate this process. Even if governments fail to assist entrepreneurs, they'll find creative ways to leverage worldwide access to sellable intellectual property.

Leveraging transparency

Ask Best Buy, Target, or car dealers how they feel about transparency. You better duck because they'll probably throw something at you. How would you like to be Best Buy, spending millions to display television sets for potential customers only to have them scan the barcode into Amazon's price check and purchase the same TV online?

Information is plentiful and easy to access today. This abundance of information creates a transparency for businesses that's unprecedented. Everything from employee pay, vendor cost, rent, annual profits, and competitor pricing is instantly available. This scourge of transparency is killing many retail business models and making life difficult for many others.

The successful business models of tomorrow will find a way to leverage this transparency rather than fight it. Amazon benefits from pricing transparency while Best Buy suffers because of it. This form of leveraging transparency is rudimentary compared to what you'll see in the future. Successful business models will do more than just offer the lowest price. These models will harness the wealth of information to the benefit of all parties — not just the vendor offering the lowest cost.

The power of efficient operators

Because information is so readily available to customers, the most efficient operators in a market will enjoy expanded benefits. Business models designed to be more efficient, not just cheaper, than the competition will be well known to all potential consumers.

The successful business models will gain efficiency through innovation, not cost-cutting. Amazon is more efficient than many retailers not because it sells on the Internet but because its business model doesn't use retail locations in conjunction with the Internet. Walmart gained competitive advantage in the 1980s by leveraging technology that lowered logistical costs and passed the savings on to consumers — that's a business model. For instance, the use of crowdsourcing can create significant efficiencies in a business model, making the company the most efficient operator. (I address crowdsourcing in more detail in Chapter 20.)

You say business model, I say tomahto

As the old saying goes, "You say tomato, I say tomahto." Businesspeople tend to speak their own jargon, much of it specific to particular industries or occupations. This specialized vocabulary often leads to confusion and the conflation or outright misuse of terms. A business school professor may define a term one way, and a group of business owners in a specific industry may define it another way. Here I give you a list of terms that people often conflate with *business model* and a brief explanation of how each term differs:

✔ **Business architecture:** This term refers to a part of an enterprise architecture related to corporate business, and the documents and diagrams that describe that architectural structure of business. Business architecture discusses the functional structure of an enterprise in terms of its business services and business information.

✔ **Business foundation:** This term is typically used to describe the key asset of the

(continued)

business. This could be an invention like the Xerox copier, an excellent physical location, special talents of the owner, or a way of doing business, as in the case of Virgin Airlines. A business model incorporates the business foundation but adds additional elements.

✔ **Business plan:** Many components of a business plan are present in a business model. In particular, the marketing elements overlap extensively. However, the business plan is designed to demonstrate the viability of the business enterprise and covers many operational and financial aspects not present in a business model.

The following terms are subcomponents of a business model:

✔ **Customer generation model:** Okay, you can generate lots of customers. Can you make money from them? Can you keep them long term?

✔ **Competitive advantage:** A business model is more encompassing than your competitive advantage. You can have competitive advantage but fail to turn it into a solid business model.

✔ **Competitive strategy:** The long-term action plan designed to create and increase the company's competitive advantage over rivals. How you'll beat the competition is important, but you need to have a great product and sales strategy in order to do so.

✔ **Revenue model:** Your revenue model is the method you use to create sales without regard to how profitable they may be. Your revenue model may create sales that are unprofitable, or the model may work fine today, but can it be sustained?

✔ **Profit formula:** Your profit formula determines the methods and amount you profit when you make sales. This is an important part of your revenue model. However, you can have an excellent profit formula but fail to lure buyers.

✔ **Strategic advantage:** A strategic advantage is the most powerful weapon in a company's arsenal — think of Coke or the Starbucks brand, the best corner location in town, or a website's lower cost structure than brick and mortar competitors. Many turn-of-the-century steel mills were located in Pittsburgh because of the strategic advantage the local three rivers created. However, you can have a strategic advantage like the best location, but without a strong offering and monetization, you still don't have a strong business model.

✔ **Value proposition:** Your value proposition explains why your offering is worth more to the customer than what you're charging as well as why the customer should value your product over competitors' offerings. You can have a strong value proposition but target the offering at the wrong customer segment, have an inadequate monetization formula, or fall prey to pitfalls.

Chapter 2

Business Models Defined

*I*f you ask 100 people to define the term *business model,* you'll hear 100 different answers. That's because the concept behind business models is complex, and the process of creating a comprehensive, effective business model is more than just having a great idea. A business model takes the great idea and transforms it into a profitable enterprise.

In this chapter I flesh out the concept of a business model and distinguish business models from other popular business concepts. I show you how to harness the power of your business model to effectively execute your business plan by creating a business model plan. And I demonstrate the power of a superior business model to help your business outperform others inside and outside your industry.

Beware the fine line between business model and strategy. The two terms are often confused, because your business model is part of your overall business strategy. Suffice it to say there are different levels of strategy and you need a specific strategy to implement each portion of your business model. Simply put, your business model focuses on value creation and outlines what you'll do that offers value to your customers. Strategy focuses on how and why you'll create and capture that value.

The business model is *what* you'll do, and strategies and tactics are *how,* but sometimes my discussion drifts across this blurry line between business model and into business strategy. I've chosen to do so without distinction because, without touching upon the necessary strategies and tactics, the discussion would be incomplete.

Following the Recipe for a Successful Business Model

In its simplest form, a business model is your profit formula. It's the method you use to acquire customers, service them, and make money doing so.

Every business has a business model, even if nobody ever bothers to write it down. That's because the business model is the basic structure of the business — what service it provides or what product it creates or sells to make money.

Generally, business models focus on the creation of profitable revenue and the delivery required to keep the revenue flowing. Most operational, finance, and human resource issues are peripheral to the creation of profitable revenue, and so they're separate from the business model. Here are some examples of business models in action:

- ✔ Domino's Pizza focuses on inexpensive pizza, delivered fast. Jimmy John's has used a similar model in the sandwich business.

- ✔ Toyota began the push of manufacturers leveraging lean manufacturing in order to produce better quality cars at a lower cost. After Toyota proved the model successful, many other companies followed Toyota's lead.

- ✔ Walmart strives to consistently lower purchasing and operating costs and then pass the savings on to consumers. As this business model wooed customers away from established retailers, many retailers and non-retailers have imitated Walmart's model.

- ✔ Zappos.com did what most thought impossible. Zappos created an online business where physically handling the product was important, and virtualized it online. Zappos has set a new standard of online customer service by allowing customers to have several pairs of shoes delivered to their door; try them on in the convenience of their home; and send any or all of them back at no charge.

- ✔ Dollarshaveclub.com has ignited a monthly club business model craze for everything from the monthly delivery of socks and t-shirts to baby clothes and feminine hygiene products. Even Walmart has jumped onto the monthly club bandwagon.

- ✔ Zipcar competes with other car rental companies by renting cars by the hour in busy metropolitan areas for quick trips. Cars can be returned to any Zipcar drop-off location.

- ✔ Crowdspring.com uses a unique business model for graphic design by leveraging crowdsourcing. Rather than pick vendors based upon the quality of their previous work, the customer posts how much she will pay for the project and vendors actually complete the design. Low resolution samples are shown to the buyer, and then a winner is chosen.

Your secret sauce for making money

At its most basic level, your business model is the formula that allows you to make money. You can think of it as the combination of everything you do — your secret sauce — to provide your customers with value and make a profit doing so. The more differentiated and proprietary your combination is, the more profitable you'll be.

Set yourself apart through differentiation

Differentiated business models offer customers products, services, or other value that stands out from the competition. Consider the following examples:

- **BigBelly Solar** doesn't just make trash containers; BigBelly's trash containers harness solar power to compact trash five times more than a typical container. This ability allows cities like Chicago, Philadelphia, and Boston to collect trash far less often and save fuel, manpower, and vehicle wear and tear.
- **Camp Bow Wow** offers more than kenneling or dog sitting. Dogs play together much like children at recess. Customers pay a premium for their dogs to have a good time rather than be cooped up all day.
- **The Huffington Post** is an Internet-only news outlet.
- **Southwest Airlines** offers customers more direct flights than other airlines, plus they have a fun-loving staff. Operationally, Southwest flies only 737s to keep operating costs at a minimum, doesn't use fee-based outside reservation systems, and uses a faster boarding system with no assigned seats.
- **Tesla** makes only high-performance electric automobiles.
- **Walk-In Lab** doesn't accept insurance. Instead, the company provides low-cost medical testing to the uninsured.

Make your model difficult to copy

A proprietary business model is a differentiated model that's difficult or impossible for a competitor to emulate. Typically, proprietary models create methods to

- **Deliver products and services better, cheaper, or faster through a business process known only to that company.** Examples include the following:
  - Toyota's lean manufacturing process.
  - Appliance retailer H.H. Gregg's radically realigned retail and operational systems to allow for same day delivery.
  - Walmart's heavy investing in technology during the 1980s to create a logistical system that brought goods to market significantly more cheaply than its competitors.

✔ **Create a closed ecosystem where ongoing use of your product is highly-desirable or required.** A powerful ecosystem attracts new customers and discourages old customers from leaving. Here are some examples of successful closed ecosystems:

- The iTunes ecosystem (iPad, iPhone, iCloud) that created a proprietary business model for Apple.

- Amazon's Kindle, which created a large library of books on the proprietary format, making it difficult for customers to purchase any other product.

✔ **Find a way to serve customers others thought were unprofitable.** Consider the following:

- Vistaprint attacked the micro business printing market thought unprofitable by most competitors. The combination of an Internet sales process and large-scale combining of orders allowed Vistaprint to grow rapidly in a contracting market.

- Microfinance company SKS (`http://www.sksindia.com`) lends small amounts to remote villagers in India. At the end of 2011, the company had outstanding loans of $925,844,433 to more than six million active borrowers. Because SKS lends money to those whose only lending option is loan sharks, the company can charge a much higher interest rate than banks charge large corporations.

- SafeAuto offers minimum coverage to drivers the big insurers deem too risky and financially unstable to cover.

✔ **Do business in way competitors thought was unprofitable or impractical.** Your business model can be well-protected if your competitors think you're nuts for trying. Here are some business models that had competitors shaking their heads:

- For decades, Southwest Airlines served second-tier cities at second-tier airports and insisted on flying only Boeing 737s. Most large airlines were happy to let Southwest serve these less-than-desirable markets with their small airplanes. However, as cost pressures continued to grind upon the industry, it became clear that Southwest had spent 20 years creating a low-cost model that the large airlines can't duplicate or compete well with.

- FedEx started as a Yale business school project for founder Fred Smith. Everyone, including Smith's professor (who gave the project a C), thought delivering packages overnight was an awful idea. Not dissuaded, Smith pursued the concept and spent years building the infrastructure to deliver packages efficiently and quickly. By the time it was clear that overnight package delivery was a good business model, Smith had a ten-year head start.

- Nearly every computer maker attempted a tablet computer and failed. It was well known that tablet computers were a niche product for hospitals and a select few customers. Apple ignored the gloom and doom and launched the iPad anyway. The product was a huge success and left competitors scrambling to create their own tablet computers.

✔ **Create a product or service that's patented, trademarked, or difficult to duplicate.** Consider these examples:

- The Xerox 914 copier used a proprietary process to duplicate documents. It's quite possible that Xerox wouldn't have grown to become a Fortune 500 company if it had simply sold the 914 machine outright. Renting the machines was a much better business model. It cost Xerox around $2,000 to build one machine. Instead of selling it, Xerox rented the machines for $95/month plus five cents per copy for each one over the first 2,000/month. Large customers like General Motors were copying up to 100,000 documents per month (that's a $4,995 rental per month).

- NoChar (nochar.com) makes an unpatented polymer that turns nasty liquid spills of anything from diesel fuel to nuclear waste into a solid. The proprietary product isn't patented because the company doesn't want to reveal the formula, even to the patent office. NoChar has built a successful business based on a product their competitors simply can't figure out how to copy.

- Skilled professionals want to benefit from this advantage. Becoming the absolute best in your field creates a product or service that's difficult to duplicate. If you're having brain surgery or a cavity filled, you want the most talented person performing the function. The same holds true for any skilled trade. People always want the best, and they're willing to pay a premium for it.

DuraFlame burns the competition

Most proprietary business models are simply a series of excellent business practices well-executed. In the late 1960s, California Cedar Company needed a way to discard shavings from its pencil factory. Through research and development, the company discovered a process to turn these unwanted scraps into the DuraFlame log, a product that today generates $250 million in annual revenue. However, California Cedar Company didn't stop at the invention of this product. The true genius of the business model wasn't how to make the first artificial log; it was using waste to make it. In the 1970s, sawmills had to *pay* to haul off their sawdust. California Cedar went to virtually every sawmill on the Pacific coast and significantly undercut their sawdust waste hauling contract in exchange for a long-term commitment. California Cedar created a business model in which it was paid to accept its primary raw material.

Same industry, different business models

McDonald's, Wendy's, and Burger King are all in the fast-food hamburger business. However, the three burger joints have very different business models. Because of their different business models, the methodologies, psychologies, ideologies, and profit formulas of these businesses differ greatly.

Each of these burger businesses uses a different "secret sauce" — not on their burgers, but on their business models. For instance, McDonald's owns more corner lots than any other company in the world. Clearly, its business model entails acquiring valuable real estate in addition to selling hamburgers.

Wendy's focuses on freshness and more upscale customers than McDonald's mass customer approach, and Wendy's charges accordingly. Wendy's business model focuses on maximizing margin per customer. Like McDonald's, Wendy's is currently focused on a single brand. In the past, Wendy's grew its business by adding new brands, such as Tim Horton's, Baja Fresh, and Arby's. Eventually, Wendy's sold or spun off these businesses.

In recent years Burger King has struggled with its business model and place in the market. Many years ago, competitors took away Burger King's primary differentiator of making their burgers exactly the way customers want them ("Hold the pickle, hold the lettuce"). Now Burger King is struggling to find a business model that works. Burger King recently closed hundreds of stores and fell to third place behind McDonald's and Wendy's in sales despite having thousands more stores than Wendy's. It seems that Burger King's issues are with its own business model and not the hamburger business in general. While Burger King has struggled, several other hamburger chains have thrived; examples include Red Robin, Rally's, Checker's, In-N-Out, and Five Guys.

How your business model sets you apart from the competition

Your business model is at the core of your business's ability to make profit. Many of the factors that differentiate your business flow directly from your business model. For instance, Walmart and Target sell similar products to similar customers. However, their business models differ significantly.

At the core of Walmart's business model is its "always low prices" promise. To deliver on this promise, Walmart must maintain low costs in all aspects of its business:

- Low-cost employees
- Low-cost health insurance

✔ Low-cost real estate

✔ Low-cost purchasing by creating custom products or beating up vendors for the best deal

✔ Logistical efficiencies that lower costs

Walmart's business model aims to be the low-cost provider. The company's desire to provide goods at the lowest cost cascades into many aspects of its operations. Because the chain is focused on the lowest cost, its stores may not be as modern or attractive as those of Target, and its products may not be as trendy as what you can find at Target. Walmart also has a reputation for paying lower wages than Target. The company's business model decisions keep costs at the absolute minimum but have caused significant human resource issues, including potential unionization, lawsuits, and negative publicity. Walmart's business model dictates that keeping costs low always comes first.

Target, on the other hand, has chosen a business model that can be summed up as cheap chic. Target spends its organizational energy trying to find hip but inexpensive products for its customers. Of course, Target must remain cost competitive, but the niche it has carved out doesn't require that it charge the lowest possible cost on all items. The money that Walmart makes with sheer volume of transactions, Target makes in high margin per item. I can only imagine how much the $10 potato peeler with the designer handle in a choice of trendy colors actually costs Target.

Just like Target and Walmart, your business model differentiates you from the competition. The stronger your business model, the stronger your ability to make outstanding profits.

Comparing Business Models to Business Plans

Many businesspeople mistakenly believe that a business plan and a business model are one and the same. Your business model is the core concept upon which you build your business plan. Therefore, your business model should be a significant portion of your business plan. Many business plans gloss over the business model in favor of lengthy financial projections and operational details that go along with business plans. Without a solid business model, these projections and details are premature.

This section highlights the strengths and weaknesses of typical business plans and offers suggestions for incorporating all the elements of a business model into a good business plan. You can use the resulting business model plan to more accurately predict the success of your company than you can with a business plan alone.

The elements of a good business plan

Table 2-1 lists the components of a traditional business plan and describes their purpose. Without incorporating the aspects of the business model into a business plan, traditional business plans are incomplete.

Table 2-1	Elements of a Business Plan	
Section	*Purpose*	*Weakness*
Executive summary	Summarizes the key points of the business plan, including a brief description of the product, market opportunity, and funds sought	None
Background information	Explains the history of the concept, purpose, and management team	None
Marketing plan	Explains the marketing methods, segments, and so on	Can presuppose the value proposition, marketability, and ability of product to generate profitable sales
Operations plan	Shows management expertise and operational systems	Spends significant energy explaining how company will deliver on sales that may never happen
Financial plan	Shows expected profitability of the company under various scenarios	May assume sales targets will simply happen when more proof is needed to show how sales will occur
Risk analysis	Explains potential risks and how they'll be mitigated	None

All the sections of a business plan that I list in Table 2-1 are important in the running of a business. However, none of these areas *creates* a good business. Instead, these areas sustain a good business. To create a good business, you need a good business model.

Mark Zuckerberg, founder of Facebook, admitted during a *Business Insider* interview that Facebook didn't have a business plan early on. Zuckerberg was also quoted as saying that, "Startups don't need or have the time to write a business plan." Don't take Zuckerberg's tip as permission to shortcut the planning process. Facebook had a well-developed business model and some early success in the marketplace. Perhaps Zuckerberg should rephrase his statement in the following way, "If you're having sales and operational success — in other words, if your business model has been proven to work — you don't need a business plan."

Business plans don't cover everything

Most entrepreneurs already know that they need a solid business plan to be successful. They know this because the first step to funding any business typically requires handing over your business plan to a banker or investor.

Bankers love business plans in large part because they can skim the executive summary and jump right to the financials. After all, bankers love numbers. Numbers aren't squishy and subjective like branding and competitive advantage. Numbers are objective. Bankers can run ratios and complex analysis on numbers. Having cold, hard numbers makes bankers feel that their loan is secure.

Unfortunately, anyone who has read more than ten business plans knows that many of them are nothing more than pie-in-the-sky guesses. Here's why: the typical business plan presupposes the existence of a strong business model. If the business model on which the plan is based is flawed, the marketing plan and operational execution spelled out in the business plan are meaningless.

Having a bad business plan or even no plan doesn't mean that your business will fail.

During research for his book *Hearts, Smarts, Guts, and Luck* (Harvard Business Review Press), author Anthony K. Tjan's team interviewed and surveyed hundreds of successful entrepreneurs to ask them what it took to build a successful business. The team unearthed several surprising findings, including that 70 percent of the entrepreneurs who had a successful exit from their business (in other words, an IPO or sale to another firm) didn't start with a business plan.

Instead, these entrepreneurs started with what Tjan calls the Heart. These businesspeople didn't start with a piece of paper or an elaborate plan. They started with a feeling and corresponding action for their authentic vision. Clarity of purpose and passion proved to be more important for these entrepreneurs than spending time writing about an idea.

Augmenting the business plan

An excellent business plan can't fix a flawed business model. Don't think of your business plan as the all-encompassing concept, vision, marketing plan, execution strategy, and financial plan for the business. Instead, think of your business plan as the execution plan for your business model. Your business plan shows potential backers how you'll make your business model work operationally, managerially, and financially.

Too much of a business plan is spent explaining *how* the business model will work instead of *why* it will work. In order to create a successful business, you need a solid business model and a good business plan.

Every businessperson has seen lousy business models that became business plans and, subsequently, businesses that failed. On the other hand, try to name a business with a great business model that failed. In fact, you probably know a super-successful business owner who never had a business plan, was completely disorganized, never finished high school, and didn't work very hard. How do you explain his success? Simple: He had a great business model.

A year ago, I met an ambitious young man with a dream to start a cookie baking company. His friends loved the cookies he baked and suggested he create a business plan for a cookie company. The young man enlisted the help of a consultant to create a business plan for the venture. Working together, they created a professional and well-formatted business plan.

When the young man handed me the plan and explained his vision for the company, I had a hard time biting my tongue. He had given no thought to his business model. His cookies were completely undifferentiated from competitors. The only difference between his cookies and the hundreds of competitive offerings was that he baked these cookies. Without a solid business model, no business plan will make his venture work.

The young man could have differentiated his business model in many ways. He could have found a unique niche — such as micro-sized cookies, Tabasco flavored cookies, gluten-free sugar-free cookies, or funky Ben & Jerry–type flavors, just to name a few options. He could have found a unique distribution angle, such as teaming with bicycle courier companies or mobile food vans. Any business model other than "my chocolate chip cookies are better tasting than theirs" would have been better.

Creating a business model plan

A business model plan combines the components of a business plan with business model analysis. This document augments or substitutes for the traditional business plan and has the following basic layout:

- ✔ **Background:** Follow the traditional structure of the business plan for this section.

- ✔ **Breakdown of the business model into the crucial areas:**

- Market attractiveness (see Chapter 6)

- Unique value proposition (see Chapter 7)

- Profit model (see Chapter 8)

- Sales performance (see Chapter 9)

- Ongoing competitive advantage (see Chapter 10)

- Innovation factor (see Chapter 11)

- Avoidance of pitfalls (see Chapter 11)

- Graceful exit from the business (see Chapter 12)

✔ **Operational overview:** Follow the traditional structure of the business plan for this section.

✔ **Financial analysis, including proformas:** Follow the same format as a traditional business plan with additional emphasis on justifying your sales projections rather than the "we will sell this much because I said so" method.

✔ **Risk analysis:** Some risk analysis is covered in various sections of the business model analysis. Risks related to marketing are covered in the marketability sections. Competitive risks are covered in the competitive advantage section and so forth. Eliminate the duplication and focus on presenting a brief overview of the general market risks — such as economic recession, government intervention, and so on — rather than the company specific risks. The company specific risks are addressed by the business model.

✔ **Business model score:** This section is optional. To add weight to your self-evaluation of the business model, you can have a Certified Business Model Analyst score your model on a scale of 0 to 100. See Chapter 13 for details.

Traditional business plans gloss over important aspects of the business model. Figure 2-1a shows the minimal inclusion of the business model in the business plan.

As you can see in Figure 2-1b, the business model garners much greater attention in a business model plan. The graph shows the increased emphasis on the business model in the business plan.

The advantage of a business model plan over a business plan alone is the increased focus on how the business will create profitable revenue streams and the decreased focus on how the business will operate when it's generating revenue. If you focus on what matters — profitable revenue — the rest tends to take care of itself.

You can download a sample business model plan at http://businessmodel institute.com/BusinessModelPlanSample.pdf.

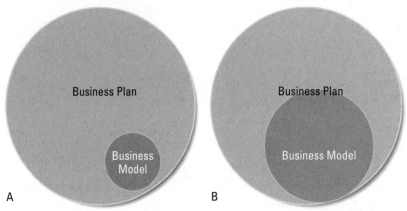

Considering your competitive advantage

Competitive advantage allows a firm to perform at a higher level than others in the same industry or market — or with anyone competing for the customer's limited budget. Competitive advantage can serve as a powerful catalyst for your business. Competitive advantage allows you to outsell, outprofit, and outperform others in the same industry or market. When you're analyzing the strength of a business, if you look only at competitive advantage, your analysis will be incomplete.

People often mistakenly use the term *competitive advantage* as a synonym for the term *business model.* The reality is that competitive advantage is a portion of your business model, but not all of it. A business model is more encompassing than your competitive advantage. For instance, you can have excellent competitive advantage but still have a weak business model. If Starbucks decided to maximize coffee poundage sales by lowering the price of a cup of coffee to $0.50, its competitive advantage may rise slightly. However, the lower price would result in a significantly different, and worse, business model for Starbucks.

Obtaining your competitive advantage

According to Michael Porter, the Harvard professor responsible for the concept, competitive advantage is obtained through cost leadership, differentiation, and/or focus.

Cost leadership means your firm has the ability to deliver similar goods or services as your competitors for a lower cost. This doesn't mean a lower sales price, but a lower cost of goods sold. If your firm has the ability to deliver a widget at a cost of $8 and it costs my firm $10 to deliver a similar widget, you have a cost advantage. If your cost advantage is the best in your industry, you have cost leadership. You can gain cost leadership in countless ways; here are just a few:

- **Access to natural resources:** China's stranglehold on rare earth minerals or cheap labor
- **Scale:** Walmart can buy Pampers cheaper than anyone else
- **Vertical integration:** Intel designs, fabricates, and markets chips
- **Technological leverage:** Many analysts attribute Walmart's rise in the 1980s to technological superiority in logistics
- **Proprietary processes:** Rolls-Royce uses a secret metallurgy process to make super-durable jet engine blades

Differentiation means that the customer feels your product has superior and different attributes than the competition. Customers pay much more for a cup of Starbucks coffee than for a cup of joe at the diner because they view Starbucks coffee as a differentiated product. Many times, you can charge extra for the differentiated attributes of your offering, creating additional margin. Businesses can create differentiation by using any of the following tactics:

- **Superior branding** (Coach, Tiffany's, Rolex)
- **Unique supplier relationships** (Eddie Bauer Edition Ford Explorer)
- **First mover advantage** (iPad, Walkman, Crest toothpaste)
- **Location** (remember the retail mantra "location, location, location"?)
- **Scale** (not many companies can build an airplane or a skyscraper)
- **Intellectual property** (iPod circular controls, Hemi engines, Intel Inside)

You can also gain competitive advantage through your focus. A business can't serve too many masters. You can translate intense focus on a market, niche, or attribute into a significant advantage. Examples include the following:

- Tesla's focus on only electric automobiles
- Taiwan Semiconductor's exclusive focus on fabrication
- Amgen's focus on biopharmaceuticals (rather than all types of drugs)
- Starbucks' focus on coffee rather than becoming just another restaurant
- Amazon's initial focus on books
- Rally's focus on drive-through hamburgers
- A doctor's focus on heart surgery

Enhancing your competitive advantage

To fully leverage a strong competitive advantage, you must shore up the other aspects of your business model as well. In the following sections I detail several other factors that a strong business model must take into account. As a savvy businessperson, you must go further than competitive advantage analysis and explore all aspects of the business model. By doing so, you can unleash the maximum potential of the business.

Innovation

You need to take into account your company's ability to innovate in order to fully evaluate its business model. Without innovation, your competitive advantage will weaken or disappear. Currently, iPad sales are outstanding. However, would you make a large bet that Apple continues to dominate this market for ten more years? Without future innovation, competitors will catch Apple and eat into its market share. Not that long ago, BlackBerry had a dominant share of the cellphone market. A few years later, BlackBerry was teetering on bankruptcy.

Customer segments

What customer segment will the product attack? Competitive advantage is somewhat generic in regard to who the customer will be. It assumes that you'll find the right one. However, chasing the wrong customers or market segment can destroy an otherwise solid business model.

Targeting your competitive advantage to the right customer or market segment makes a big difference, as the following examples demonstrate:

- ✔ Motorola had a product well-suited for the military market in the Iridium satellite phone, but the company blew billions trying to market it to nonmilitary consumers who were unwilling to buy a $3,000 phone.

- ✔ The U.S. military took five years to purchase 50,000 Hummers. In 2006 alone, General Motors sold 70,000 nonmilitary Hummers to the public.

- ✔ After NASA was exposed for purchasing $129 pencils for space missions, Paul Fisher took it upon himself to invent a pen that would write in space. He succeeded, calling his invention the Space Pen. For many years, Fisher sold his pen to NASA for $4 (it cost him $1.98 to manufacture). However, the market for the space pen as a collectible item turned out to be much larger for Fisher. The pen sells many more units today for $20 than it did to NASA for $4.

- ✔ Ivan Getting conceived of the GPS system in the 1950s. It took nearly 50 years and $12 billion to create a system for tracking military personnel, missiles, ships, tanks, and the like. The consumer electronics industry sold more than 1 billion GPS-enabled devices in just 15 years.

Pricing

What will you charge for the product? How high or low will the margin be? The answers to these questions are critical factors of the business model, but they aren't addressed directly in competitive advantage. For example, Amazon has competitive advantage in its ability to distribute product conveniently and efficiently. However, what will happen when Amazon is forced to charge sales tax and prices rise? What would happen if Amazon focused on the convenience of the online experience but charged 15 percent more than brick and mortar competitors? No one knows the answer, but these factors would affect Amazon's competitive advantage.

Ability to sell

Without a proven and repeatable sales process, most business models fail. Unfortunately, the world doesn't care if you have a better mouse trap. All products and services must be sold. It's easy to forget this inconvenient truth as you look at the long line outside the Apple store with customers clamoring to buy. However, don't forget all those iPhone and iPad commercials on television, the publicity, paid product placements on shows like *Modern Family,* and countless other efforts to drive demand. All these things help to create that long line of eager buyers.

In order to finalize the marketing process, someone must purchase your product. A solid sales and marketing system must be used to realize the full potential of your offering.

During the late 1800s, two companies had the patent to Jell-O but failed to create a sales methodology that worked. The product you know as Jell-O failed twice as a business model. Jelly molds were very popular during the Victorian era, but gelatin was sold in sheets and had to be purified. This was very time consuming. In 1845, Peter Cooper, builder of the first American steam engine, obtained a patent for powdered gelatin. This clever idea was never successful.

Cooper gave up on the idea and sold the formula to a cough syrup manufacturer, Pearle B. Wait, for under $100. Wait's wife had the ingenious idea to add flavors to the unflavored gelatin and to name the concoction Jell-O. However, Wait couldn't make the business model work. Two years after purchasing the formula, Wait sold the business to a neighbor, Orator Francis Woodward, for $450.

The rest is history. Despite significant competitive advantage, Wait was unable to perfect the sales and marketing portion of the business model, but Woodward excelled. Unable to get grocery stores to stock the product, Woodward printed thousands of cookbooks featuring Jell-O recipes and deployed armies of door-to-door salespeople to give them away. Days later, hundreds of would-be Jell-O buyers descended upon grocery stores, most of which didn't have any Jell-O in stock. The stores quickly acquiesced and stocked their shelves with Jell-O. Three years after purchasing the Jell-O formula, sales reached $250,000 (approximately $6 million today).

The lesson of Jell-O is that a great business model requires more than just competitive advantage.

Potential pitfalls

Competitive advantage doesn't take potential pitfalls into account. I like to call this factor the *Taser test*. Taser pioneered the stun gun business, holds many patents, owns the best brand in the business, and gets sued for $1 million nearly every week. Taser has a good business model despite this pitfall. However, if you look only at Taser's competitive advantage without regard to pitfalls, Taser's business looks much more attractive than it actually is.

Continuity

A significant issue for mid-sized and small businesses is the ability to operate without the day-to-day input of the owner. If the business falls apart without the owner in the building, the business model is weak and the owner will never be able to sell the business.

Tom has a business that nets him $900,000 per year. The business has significant competitive advantage as witnessed by its profitability. However, the instant Tom stops showing up, the business nets $0. Many doctors, lawyers, accountants, architects, and other professionals face the same issue. The competitive advantage of these businesses is strong, but the business model still needs some work.

Chapter 3

Business Models Come in Many Different Forms

A business model is like a lump of clay that you can mold into many different shapes and sizes. This pliability is a powerful feature, enabling entrepreneurs to craft their models to fit their business needs. Yet, despite all this potential for variety, all business models have a set of shared characteristics. These commonalities are what set business models apart from other business tools, such as business plans, strategic plans, and operational plans.

This chapter focuses on what all business models have in common. After you have the basics down, I use examples to show you aspects of all business models as well as a list of many common types of business models. By considering these examples, you can begin the creative process you need to develop your business model.

Common Aspects of All Business Models

Whether your business model is cutting edge or based on 100-year-old principles, all business models answer the following questions:

✔ **What problem are you trying to solve?** People don't need a new widget; they need the new widget to solve a problem. No one asked for an ATM. Customers wanted additional banking hours. The ATM solved this problem. Start with the job the customer is trying to accomplish, but without a good solution. These unserved or underserved markets provide the best opportunity for a great business model.

✔ **Who needs this problem solved?** The answer to this question is the customer you'll be serving. In the case of the ATM, the market is very large — everyone with a bank account. In the case of pet cloning, the market is much smaller — people with $50,000 who loved their deceased pet enough to recreate it.

✔ **What market segment is the model pursuing?** A *market segment* is a group of prospective buyers who have common needs and will respond similarly to your marketing. Nike makes shoes for many market segments, among them running, basketball, aerobics, and hiking. Traditional marketing focuses on demographic segments while modern marketing focuses on buyer behaviors.

✔ **How will you solve this problem better, cheaper, faster, or differently than other offerings?** Duluth Trading Company offers "ballroom jeans" that offer extra room in the right places so you can crouch without the ouch. Clever, unique offerings like these are superior to a better mousetrap.

✔ **What is the value proposition?** What problem do you solve for the customer in relation to what you charge to fix it? Ballroom jeans have a clever niche and solve a problem for a defined segment; but if the price is $250 per pair, the value proposition would be weak. Your product solves a problem for the customer. Hopefully, the customer values the solution and will pay you much more than it costs you to make the product. The larger this spread, the greater your value proposition.

✔ **Where does your offer place you on the value chain?** Many creative business models — like Skype, ProFlowers, and eBay — have redefined the value chain by eliminating or shifting the partners that contribute to the final offering.

✔ **What is your revenue model?** Factors such as how you'll charge for the product, how much you'll charge, and which portions of your offerings will be the biggest money makers all determine your revenue model. For instance, most airlines have radically changed their revenue models to charge for items that used to be bundled into the ticket price, effectively making them free. Items like checked bags, extra legroom, in-flight food, and even carry-on bags now generate billions of dollars in revenue for airlines.

✔ **What is your competitive strategy?** You don't want to just jump into the shark tank. You need a plan to differentiate yourself from competition — via marketing, sales, and operations — that allows you to effectively outshine the competition

✔ **How will you maintain your competitive edge?** After you distance yourself from competitors, how will you hold off their attempts to copy your winning strategies? The best business models create barriers to maintain their hard-earned competitive advantage.

✔ **What partners or other complementary products should be used?** Henry Ford was famous for creating companies to make everything included in his cars. Toyota relies on a partner network to engineer and manufacture most of the components for its cars. Savvy relationships with partners can enhance your business model.

✔ **What network effects can be harnessed?** If you owned the only fax machine, it wouldn't be worth much because you couldn't send or receive a fax. Network effects enhance the value of everyone's purchase when the network of users grows. Nightclubs and Facebook rely on their large network of users to increase the value of their offer.

The best business models aren't merely an idea. A great business model solves problems for customers creatively and generates more profit than was previously thought possible.

Business Models in Their Simplest Form

You have an overwhelming number of factors and concerns to consider when creating a business model. It can be daunting. Don't worry. By the end of this book, you'll have an understanding of all the inner workings of a business model and their interrelationships.

In the meantime, here's a simple three-part method to break down a model:

✔ **What is the offering?** Are you selling roses on the side of the road or fractional use of private jets? Why do customers need your offering? How is it different from customers' other options to solve their problem? Are you selling your product to the best market and in the best niche? Chapters 6 and 7 walk you through the basics of creating a powerful offering.

✔ **How will you monetize the offering?** Twitter has a powerful offering providing hundreds of millions of users valuable communication tools. However, Twitter has struggled to turn this offering into sales. You must have more than just a product people want. You must be able to charge a price that generates significant margin and be able to sell it. Sharper Image was a company whose products were priced at a level that afforded high margins; however, not enough customers bought them. You must be able to execute your sales strategy in order to complete the monetization of the offering. Chapters 8 and 9 discuss making money with your business model.

✔ **How will you create sustainability?** Blockbuster Video had an exceptionally profitable business model for nearly two decades, but the company was unable to sustain it. Factors such as maintaining/growing competitive advantage, the ability to innovate, and avoiding pitfalls affect the sustainability of the business model. See Chapters 10, 11, and 12 for an in-depth discussion of sustainability.

Examples of Business Models

There are business models hundreds of years old and those only a handful of years old, such as Internet freemium models. Some of the most profitable companies didn't invent new business models; they borrowed a business model from another industry. The Gillette razor and blades model has been highly profitable for Hewlett-Packard's inkjet printer business and Verizon's cellphone business. The cheap chic business model works for Trader Joe's in the grocery business and IKEA in the home furnishing business. Sometimes, one little tweak to an existing business model can yield powerful results in a new industry.

Table 3-1 shows a partial list of common business models. These examples should get your creative juices flowing as you begin to create your business model. Review the list for small ideas you can work into your model rather than copying a model lock, stock, and barrel.

Table 3-1	Types of Business Models	
Type of Model	*Description*	*Example Companies and Products*
Razor and blades	Consumer purchases a low-margin item like a razor handle or inkjet printer. Sale of necessary consumables such as replacement blades or ink are sold at a very high markup.	Gillette, Hewlett-Packard printers, Kuerig coffee makers
Inverted razor and blades	Initial purchase has a high margin, but consumables are sold at a low margin to entice initial purchase or contrast to razor and blade competitor.	Kodak inkjet printers, Apple iPod & iTunes combination. Apple makes very low margins on iTunes but high margins on hardware.
Cheap chic	Marketing of stylish but inexpensive merchandise. Typically allows for high margins because merchandise sells at low price points but has an expensive feel.	Target, Trader Joe's, IKEA
Bricks and clicks	Extension of in-store shopping to include online ordering with in-store pickup or items found exclusively online.	BestBuy.com, local mystery book store with online shop
Multilevel marketing	Leverage friends, family, and other personal networks to recommend products and act as a sales force. Works best for products needing recommendation to facilitate purchase.	Avon, Mary Kay, Amway

Type of Model	Description	Example Companies and Products
Franchise	Sell the right to use the business model in exchange for a percentage of revenues.	McDonald's, Holiday Inn, NFL
Anticipated upsell	High percentage of buyers ultimately purchase more than they expected. For instance, most new home buyers end up spending 1.2 times the base price of the home after extras. Builders bet on this upsell.	Homebuilders, car dealerships, steel fabricators
Loss leader	This model offers velocity items for a very low margin in anticipation of additional sales at a higher margin.	Gas stations, $1 menus
Subscription model	One of the more popular models because of recurring revenue. Typically involves creating a significant asset and renting a piece of it.	Health clubs, software as a service
Collective	Similar to a franchise. Involves many businesses coming together for purchasing, marketing, or operational purposes but with looser ties than a franchise. Typically, collectives aggregate buying power and don't pay ongoing royalties like a franchise.	Ace Hardware, CarQuest
Productization of services	Standardizing a predetermined bundle of services typically bought together and selling for a fixed price similar to a product. Many times it includes an element of flat-fee pricing as well.	A consultant charges $5,000 for a business plan analysis rather than charging $200 per hour, prepaid legal plans
Servitization of products	Making a product part of a larger service offering.	Rolls-Royce sells aircraft engines, not as distinct components but as complete solutions based on aviation miles. All operations and maintenance functions are included in this "Power by the Hour" plan.
Long tail	Based on Chris Anderson's famed 2004 *Wired* magazine article. Selecting a tiny niche and serving it in ways mass marketers can't. Hopefully, the tiny niche grows into a much larger one, as it did in the case of Fat Tire beer.	YouTube bands, left-handed online store, micro-breweries

(continued)

Table 3-1 *(continued)*

Type of Model	Description	Example Companies and Products
Direct sales	Bypass the traditional sales channels to target end users. Methods include door-to-door sales and company-owned stores.	Kirby Vacuums, Girl Scout cookies, outlet mall stores
Cut out the middle man	Removal of intermediaries in a supply chain. AutoZone bypasses traditional three-step distribution by skipping the warehouse distributor.	Dell Computer, farmer's markets
Freemium business model	Product is offered for free. Typically 8% of users upgrade to become paying customers of virtual goods or to get expanded access.	Angry Birds, shareware software, McAfee security
Online auctions	Create a community of buyers and sellers by using an auction-type selling process versus a set sales price.	eBay, Arriba
Hotel California model	Create a must-have product that traps customers into buying unrelated high-profit items like concessions at a baseball game.	Amusement parks, sporting events, movie theaters
Network effect	Create a product in which the value to each user becomes higher as more people use it.	Fax machines, social networks
Crowdsourcing	Leveraging users to co-create products and sell to other users.	Cafepress.com, Frito Lay new flavors, YouTube, Angie's List
Users as experts	Gives users access to technology and tools typically reserved for company employees. Users then create their own designs or versions of the product.	Cook-your-own-steak restaurants, Lego
Premium	Offer high-end products that appeal to brand-conscious consumers.	Tiffany, Rolls-Royce
Nickel and dime	Price the most cost-sensitive item as low as possible and then charge for every little extra.	Airlines
Flat fee	The opposite of nickel and dime. Most or all incidental purchases are bundled into one fee.	Sandals Resorts, Southwest Airlines

Chapter 4

Your Business Success Depends Upon Your Business Model

. . . .

In This Chapter

▶ Figuring out why it's tough to succeed without a good business model

▶ Knowing that hard work doesn't always pay

▶ Experimenting with great business models instead of waiting for divine inspiration

▶ Waiting to see whether a model will work

. . . .

Creating a great business with a lousy business model isn't possible. Plain and simple: a great business begins with a great business model. If you want to reap the maximum reward from your hard work and talent, building an outstanding business model is a prerequisite.

Plowing financial resources and energy into a business before creating an outstanding business model qualifies as putting the cart before the horse. In this chapter, you discover why great businesses are built upon great business models and why hard work can be your enemy instead of your friend.

Trying (And Failing) to Succeed without a Superior Business Model

In this section I do some side-by-side comparisons of businesses. In column 1 of Table 4-1 are some commonly sought-after business characteristics. In column 2 are the opposite traits or similar traits of a lesser degree. Pick the business you think would be more successful.

Table 4-1   Which Business Will Be More Successful?

Option 1	Option 2	Winner
Exceptional leader but lousy business model. Example: Steve Jobs excelled at Apple but failed at NeXT Computer.	Average leader but great business model. Example: I bet that every person reading this book could lead Google for a year and not mess it up.	Great business model
Great corporate culture but lousy business model. Example: IBM was the first U.S. company to offer paid holidays and is famous for many innovations in this area. But when its business model soured in the 1990s, no amount of strong culture could fix the underlying business issues.	Average culture but great business model. Example: Companies like Walmart, DISH Network, and Comcast regularly make "Worst to Work For" lists yet have highly successful businesses.	Great business model
Outstanding employees but lousy business model. Example: Kodak and Xerox recruited some of the best business and scientific minds available but still couldn't fend off massive business declines.	Average employees but great business model. Example: One of my favorite questions to ask business owners to gauge the strength of their systems is, "What if we traded your employees for McDonald's employees?" McDonald's strong business model and systemization allows for average caliber employees to function effectively. After all, it's hard to find 1.8 million great people. That's how many employees McDonald's has.	Great business model
Management excellence but lousy business model. Example: Silicon valley firms regularly swoop up entire management teams from failed companies whose business models failed.	Average management but great business model. Example: Did Facebook CEO Mark Zuckerberg or Spanx founder Sara Blakely succeed because of their management prowess? It's much more likely their superior business model was the root of the success rather than their management skill.	Great business model

You can work long and hard at perfecting your leadership and management skills only to find yourself applying those skills to a less-than-perfect business model. Without the foundation of a solid model, you're wasting these other skills.

Good news: Business models are fluid

If your focus is on leadership, management, and culture, but your business model has suffered, don't worry. Business models aren't static; they're fluid. Technology changes, buying habits change, and competitors adapt. Your business model needs to change with them. And it can.

Because business models are fluid, you have the ability to make gradual and constant changes to improve your model. Because fluidity of the market is working to erode your model, you have to constantly improve your model, or this erosion can catch up with you like it did at Blockbuster, Kodak, and BlackBerry.

Case study: Kodak versus Fujifilm

During most of the 20th century, Kodak held a dominant position in the photographic film industry. In the mid-1970s, the company held a 90-percent market share of photographic film sales and an 85-percent share of camera sales in the United States. The bulk of Kodak's profits came from sales of film and related products.

For more than 75 years, the bulk of Kodak's fortunes were built on the success of traditional film. Kodak did everything right. It recruited top talent from top universities, retained top leadership, spent significant sums on research and development, and had a winning culture.

However, none of that mattered when the quality of digital pictures approached that of traditional film. The ease, simplicity, and cost advantages of digital cameras crushed the traditional photography business.

What did Kodak do wrong? It depends how you define *wrong*. Kodak did absolutely nothing wrong in its efforts to manage and grow the traditional film business. In fact, Kodak did such a good job managing and profiting from the traditional film business, it was hard to walk away from the handsome profits despite all the signs of a dying business model. What Kodak did was underestimate the tsunami-sized force of the digital photography wave and the massive destructive effect it would have on Kodak's business model.

Despite inventing digital photography, Kodak failed to innovate its business model to account for the shift from traditional photography to digital photography. Unlike a restaurant shifting from customer preferences for hamburgers to burritos, Kodak's challenge was the shift from a consumable product, film, to a reusable product, the SD card. The digitization of film removes a significant amount of potential profit from the film industry.

Fujifilm Holdings, on the other hand, successfully navigated the shift to digital photography by leveraging the core competencies of film production to other areas. Fujifilm looked further than simply moving to digital photography.

Photographic film has 20 ultrathin layers that contain around 100 different chemical compounds. Fujifilm used its expertise in handling these chemical elements and engineering atomic-scale particles to enter new and growing areas like films used in LCD panels for computers, television sets, and other electronic devices. Fujifilm is giving cosmetics a try with its Astalift skin-care line. The cosmetic uses the same antioxidation technology that prevents photos from fading. Fujifilm fluidly moved from a film company to a high-tech chemical company by leveraging its core competences learned from film.

Equating Hard Work with Results — As Long As the Business Model is Solid

You've likely met a hard-working, well-educated, and talented business owner who never seems to find success. You've also probably met a not-so-hard-working, not-so-well-educated, and moderately talented business owner who's built a stellar business. How do you explain these differences?

It's simple. The hard-working business owner has a lousy business model and the not-so-hard-working business owner has a great business model. A great business model beats hard work every time.

It turns out all those childhood messages you got about hard work weren't entirely true. Yes, hard work is important. Yes, those who work hard do better than those who don't work hard. However, without a good business model, hard work is misdirected.

As a businessperson, you need to apply your talent and hard work to an exceptional business model. This combination yields a viable and profitable business. Figure 4-1 demonstrates how hard work on your business operations alone creates only marginal gains over time. Hard work on your business model *and* your operations yields a much better return.

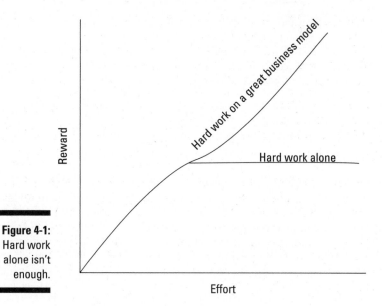

Figure 4-1:
Hard work
alone isn't
enough.

Redefining hard work

I'm going to suggest you redefine "hard work." It's not enough to work hard in your business. You can probably cite dozens of examples of hard-working businesspeople who didn't achieve the success their hard work warranted. Instead of just working hard, you first need to work hard on your business model, and then work hard on your business. This combination will result in ample rewards for your hard work. Refer to Figure 4-1 to see how hard work combined with a solid business model yields far better results than hard work alone.

Avoiding indentured servitude to a bad business model

Have you ever met business owners who say it's impossible for them to take a vacation? These business owners always seem to be going 200 miles an hour with their hair on fire. These people don't own a business — the business owns them! It's almost like an invisible gremlin called "the business" bosses them around, telling them what they can and can't do. These business owners are nothing more than indentured servants to their businesses. The inferior business model creates problem after problem, resulting in a never-ending string of low-paid work.

Be a Sally

Bob graduated with a degree in accounting. The entrepreneurial type, Bob started his own firm. Like any startup entrepreneur, Bob performed every task necessary for the firm. Bob prospected for new customers, performed the billable accounting work, and emptied the garbage. Plain and simple, Bob worked hard.

Eventually, Bob built a decent accounting practice. Bob made a better-than-average living, but he worked 60 hours a week for the next 40 years.

Sally graduated from the same school with the same accounting degree as Bob. Sally didn't want to start yet another ordinary accounting practice. Instead of just running ahead in starting a business, Sally gave some thought to her business model. Sally realized hundreds of firms in town were doing accounting work. More importantly, Sally didn't want to build a business model that leveraged only her personal relationships and skill (also known as a personal brand). Sally understood that building a practice based solely upon her personal brand could create an unleveragable business model.

After some research, Sally realized that small, independent restaurant chains were underserved in her market. These operators weren't utilizing the latest technology, which created mountains of paper that the restaurant owners typically threw in shoeboxes.

Sally built an accounting practice that helped these small restaurant operators manage their paper, added technology to their businesses, and provided niche accounting expertise. Sally's accounting practice was very different from Bob's. Sally's practice was much closer to a bookkeeping practice than an accounting practice. Because of the mountains of paper generated by her clients, she did more work to process the basic accounting than to provide pure accounting expertise. While Bob was busy doing accounting work for his clients, Sally was building a staff that could perform the more basic work, allowing her to run the firm and not just be a billable resource.

Sally's model proved superior to Bob's. Bob's accounting model was undifferentiated and unleveraged. Bob was engaged in the world's worst business model — selling your time for money. Anytime Bob took a vacation, he didn't make any money. Anytime Bob had to market for new business, he didn't make any money. Sally, on the other hand, leveraged her skills via her bookkeeping department. Sure, Sally worked very hard the first five years to build her client base. After she accomplished that, however, she made triple the income of Bob and worked about half the number of hours. The superiority of Sally's business model was at the root of her success.

Most of the time the business doesn't start off this way. When the business first starts, the business model is strong. Over time, the business model erodes. The weakened business model requires more and more hard work from the owner to simply keep pace.

You may have heard the story of the boiling frog. You can place a frog in a pot of water, and then slowly raise the temperature to a boil, but the frog won't jump out of the pot. The slow change in temperature convinces the frog that the pain of changing exceeds the pain of hotter water. Eventually the frog boils to death despite the ability to simply jump out of the pot.

Your business model has the potential to boil your frog. It can take 10 or 20 years, but all business models weaken. If business owners don't re-innovate the business model, they're in danger of becoming an indentured servant to the bad business model.

Case study: New Pig

The New Pig Corporation is a worldwide leader in industrial spill containment. If you've worked in a factory, you probably recognize the name. However, New Pig didn't always enjoy a strong business model. The company started as a sandblasting and industrial cleanup company. After years of toiling at cleaning greasy messes for their industrial customers, the owner had enough and decided there must be a better way to make a living.

During his many cleaning jobs, he noticed how inefficient cleaning oily industrial spills was. The clay used to absorb the oil stuck to everything. Through his ingenuity, he found that ground corncobs absorbed oil much better than anything in use at that time. He experimented, packing nylon stockings with ground-up husks. Customers loved his invention and ordered so many that he ditched his industrial cleanup model and switched to production of the socks. He named this invention the Pig Blanket.

Today, New Pig Corporation is a worldwide leader with more than 4,500 spill absorption, containment, and cleanup products.

Experimenting Your Way to a Great Model

Creating a great business model isn't an event — it's a process. First, you roll out the first version of your business model. Some of it will work, some won't. You augment the parts that work and fix the ones that don't. After a bunch of tweaking, you now have a great business model. You can't get around this trial and error. In the world of business models, failure is typically the precursor to success. Don't be afraid to fail. Be willing to constantly adjust and tweak your business model, and you'll be able to create a successful one.

Even venture capitalists win one-third of the time

Businesspeople are wired for success; they crave it. This desire to always win serves you well when operating a business. This desire doesn't serve you well when creating your business model. You want to put your effort into creating an incredible business model, throw it out to the world, and then watch the money come pouring in. It doesn't work that way.

Most business models start off as partial failures. After all, creating a business model is a guessing game. Sometimes you guess right, sometimes you guess wrong. Not to worry — the brightest minds in business are successful only one-third of the time.

Companies like Google, Facebook, eBay, Minute Maid, Apple, Genentech, and more all had their business models blessed by smart venture capitalists. These venture capitalists represent some of the brightest business model analysts in the world. Yet for every home-run business model, venture capitalists bless a dozen strikeouts. The point is, you can't know in advance whether a business model will be successful.

Letting the market determine how smart you are

Business models may be born in the laboratory, but they're proven in the marketplace. Many business models created by smart Harvard or Stanford MBAs have flopped. Lately, hundreds of millions of dollars from investors, venture funds, and the Chinese government have funded solar energy firms. Almost none of them are creating profits. Even the mighty Google isn't immune. Recently, Google shut down its Google Wave service. Google's theory was that e-mail was a 40-year-old concept that needed to be updated. The Wave service hosted multiple-thread email conversations to end the confusing passing and forwarding of e-mails. Sounds pretty good, right? It's from a proven winner, Google, right? It went splat. The market shouted loud and clear, "Regular, clunky, imperfect e-mail is fine."

The best business models listen to the market. It's easy to say and hard to do. Suppose you launch a new product and the market doesn't immediately accept it. Does listening to the market mean you pull back and retool the offer, or is that giving up too quickly? There's no right answer. Use your best business judgment to know when to persevere and when to retool. The factors to consider are:

- **The magnitude of the failure.** I know of an education company that did a 300,000-piece mailing to teachers with zero response. No need to persevere when it's that much of a dud.

- **Whether your changes create enough incremental improvement.** If each new version gets better results, keep with it until improvement stops. At that point, decide whether the model works or doesn't.

- **Raving fans.** A marginal model plus an ambivalent market isn't as good as a marginal model with a handful of raving fans. If you have an offering strong enough to create rabid fans, keep trying.

✔ **Sunk cost.** This is a trap. Sunk cost tends to affect decision-making far more than it should. A lousy idea you sunk $1 million into still isn't going to work. The fact that you blew a bunch of money and effort on the bad idea shouldn't play into the decision.

✔ **Difficulty of continuing.** If your business model still needs work, and it will be backbreaking to retool, it may be best to move on.

When in doubt, find a way to "try easy" and see what happens. Many times businesspeople are emotionally attached to their ideas and will try anything and everything to succeed. While this quality is admirable, sometimes 110-percent effort isn't the best option. Sometimes you can do better by using the Pareto Principle (the 80/20 rule) and skip the hard 80 percent of the work that yields only 20 percent of the results while waiting to test your latest tweak. Throw most of the idea to the market in workable but imperfect form (skipping the hard last 20 percent) and see how it goes. If the market doesn't like the 80 percent, it probably won't like the last 20 percent either.

Refusing to rely on dumb luck

Pet Rocks, George Foreman grills, and unprofitable web properties sold for billions of dollars can lead entrepreneurs to believe that dumb luck is part of the business model game. It's not. The saying "The harder I work, the luckier I get" is true. The harder you work on formulating and tweaking your business model, the luckier you'll get.

Every business will experience both good luck and bad. Plan on it. You need to persevere through some unfortunate breaks. You'll catch a lucky break every now and then, too. Don't, however, leave your business model to chance. Betting on luck is a bad bet. Bet that your business talent, research, and hard work — not luck — will result in a great business model.

Even luck isn't lucky

There's an old saying, "The grass is always greener on the other side." This saying applies to business models as well. When you look at a surprising success, like the George Foreman grill that has sold more than 100 million units, it's easy to think luck is paramount to success. Sorry to burst your bubble, but the George Foreman grill wasn't lucky.

Michael Boehm and Robert Johnson invented the grill and sold the rights to Salton Inc. The company viewed this technology as superior but couldn't find any buyers. Committed to the technology, they looked for a unique marketing partner and heard through the grapevine that George Foreman was looking for a product to pitch. Foreman tried the product at home and loved it. He agreed to put his name on the product for 40 percent of the profits. This deal netted Foreman an estimated $200 million and more than that for Salton Inc.

The George Foreman grill wasn't lucky at all. It was the combination of savvy innovation, perseverance, and marketing skill.

Case study: Toys "R" Us

Toys "R" Us is a great example of a good business model gone bad and then fixed. After World War II, Charles Lazarus founded Toys "R" Us as a baby toy store in New York. He was lucky enough to be in the right place at the right time with a good idea.

The company grew nicely and caught the eye of a large retailer, Interstate Department Stores. Under Interstate, Toys "R" Us floundered, but Interstate floundered more. The discount retailer eventually went bankrupt. This bad luck didn't last long. A handful of Toys "R" Us stores emerged as a standalone company post-bankruptcy. Unshackled from the Interstate model, Toys "R" Us created a strengthened business model focused solely on toys. The company grew to nearly 1,000 stores in 35 countries and remains one of the largest toy retailers in the world.

Toys "R" Us made the best of both good and bad luck to create one of the first superstore concepts.

Discovery-driven planning

Discovery-driven planning is an alternative planning technique introduced by Dr. Rita Gunther McGrath and Ian C. MacMillan in a 1995 Harvard Business Review article. This method states that when you're operating in arenas with significant amounts of uncertainty, you need a different approach than what's normally used in conventional planning.

In conventional planning, the objective "correctness" of a plan is generally judged by how close projections come to the outcomes. In discovery-driven planning, the assumption is that the plan may change because new information is constantly being revealed. The plan is always in motion. With conventional planning, the entire project can be funded as the expectation that a positive outcome can be predicted. In discovery-driven planning, funds are released based on the accomplishment of key milestones or checkpoints; at these points, additional funding can be made available predicated on reasonable expectations for future success.

A discovery driven plan incorporates five disciplines or plan elements:

- ✔ Definition of success for the plan or initiative, including a "reverse" income statement

- ✔ Benchmarking against market and competitive parameters

- ✔ Specification of operational requirements

- ✔ Documentation of assumptions

- ✔ Specification of key checkpoints

Part II

Creating a Winning Business Model

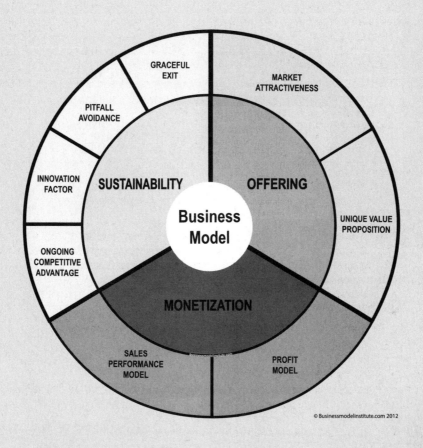

One thing to think about when creating a winning business model is your personal mix of gasoline, cigarettes, and soda. For details, head to www.dummies.com/extras/businessmodels.

In this part . . .

✔ Use a structured approach to business models instead of the back of a napkin. Stories of these seemingly quick successes tend to be greatly exaggerated.

✔ Understand the three elements to every business model: an offering, a way to monetize that offering, and a method to sustain profitability.

✔ Break down a business model into eight key components. These eight components work together to give you a practical, functional business model.

✔ Discover the Business Model Wheel as a framework to analyze your business model. See examples, figure out how to give your business model a score, and determine whether your business model would benefit from additional professional expertise.

Chapter 5

Using Tools to Design Your Business Model

In This Chapter

▶ Figuring out that designing business models the old-fashioned way doesn't work

▶ Using a structured approach for your business model

▶ Weighting the most important aspects of your business model

▶ Evaluating business model templates

A business model is more than simply a good idea. Sure, plenty of great businesses have been sketched on the backs of napkins, but such a primitive approach is like traveling by horse and buggy when you can get there a lot faster — and much more comfortably — in an automobile. However, advances in the study of business models have led to a more formalized and scientific process to create and analyze them.

In order to create the best business model possible, you should consider a structured approach. In this chapter, I show you a structured, modular approach to designing a business model, showing the components of the model, and I demonstrate why some aspects of your business model are much more important than others.

Examining Traditional Business Model Design Methods

The concept of a business model may be new, but the underlying business dynamics aren't. The East India Trading Company and Henry Ford had good business models, whether they were called business models or not. For many years, businesspeople have asked themselves two key questions:

  ✔ Is this a unique concept?

  ✔ Can I make money selling it?

If the answer was yes to both questions, they moved ahead.

Back of the napkin

Countless stories exist of great business models conceived over cocktails and jotted down on the back of a napkin. The problem with all these back-of-the-napkin stories is that they make it seem like creating a great business model is as simple as a quick doodle. The businesspeople who created the strong models in their heads and jotted down the gists on a napkin were managing hundreds of business variables in their heads. These folks were savvy enough, or lucky enough, to sift through all of them and come up with a gem of an idea.

The problem with the back-of-the-napkin method is that it usually gets over-simplified to mean, "Can I make money with this unique concept?" That's a great start for a business model, but it's not a *complete* business model.

The most famous back-of-the-napkin story is Southwest Airlines. As the story goes, Herb Kelleher and one of his law clients, Rollin King, jotted down the concept that became Southwest Airlines on a cocktail napkin in a San Antonio restaurant. Figure 5-1 shows you what this famed napkin may have looked like.

Imitation

Imitation may be the sincerest form of flattery, but it's also a common source of business models. Many business models are simply a facsimile of another known model. This imitation comes in two flavors: literally copying the model and copying the model but moving it to a different industry.

  ✔ **Literally copying:** Joe works for a successful plumbing company. Joe has always wanted to start his own plumbing business, and after 15 years at his current job, he has learned a great deal about his employer's business model. When Joe breaks away and starts his own plumbing company, guess what his most likely business model is? The same business model as his old employer. Perhaps Joe makes a change or two, but it's highly likely that the central tenants of Joe's business model are exactly the same as his old employer's.

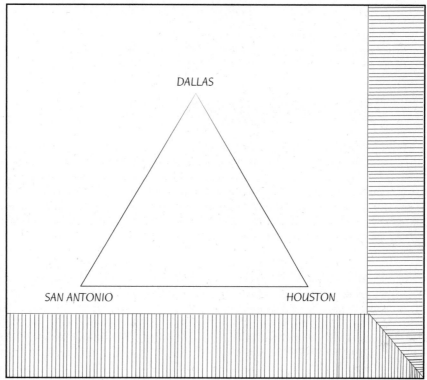

Figure 5-1:
Southwest
Airline's
back-of-
the-napkin
model.

✔ **Moving to a different industry:** In the second situation, the strong business model of a company is emulated and moved into a different market. For instance, many businesses saw the success of Henry Ford's assembly line and took portions of his business model and incorporated them in a new industry. Isn't McDonald's just an assembly line for hamburgers?

Falling into the model

Sometimes businesspeople just fall into a model. Either they don't give the business model any thought and just proceed to open the business, or one thing leads to another, and before you know it you have a business model. It's always easy to assume that planned activities are more successful than unplanned activities, but you never know. Many great inventions were discovered as a failed experiment in search of something else. I don't recommend falling into your business model, but it certainly counts as one of the options.

A few prominent high-tech companies like Twitter are proactively delaying some business-model decisions and falling into their business model. Twitter has found great success attracting users but hasn't yet figured out how to turn the popular brand into a profitable business model.

Discovering Problems with Traditional Methods

Creating a business model can be simple. You simply come up with a great idea to create a product and sell it easily and profitably. Problem solved, right? If you're lucky enough to create a great product, then yes, you may not need much more of a process. However, most businesspeople need more than just a great idea to become successful.

Too many things to remember

When creating a business model, even the brightest business minds can't possibly consider the hundreds of factors involved. Sure, the obvious factors come immediately to mind, like:

- Products that sell themselves
- Superior margin
- Little or no competition
- Competitive advantage or barriers against competition
- Sustainability
- Powerful branding

But what about the many finer points?

- Excessive investment in fixed assets causing intensive rivalries in the industry
- Upcoming technological developments that could potentially cut into margins or radically disrupt the industry (think smartphones, the Internet, or radio frequency identification)
- Disruption of the industry value chain that could severely cut sales or margins (for example, the Internet's affect on travel agents)
- Proprietary learning curves
- Higher buyer loyalty than anticipated
- Lower buyer loyalty than anticipated

✔ Unanticipated substitute products (for example, Internet TV)

✔ Governmental action or inaction

✔ Interruption of supply (for example, an oil embargo)

✔ Threat of forward or backward integration of competitors or customers

✔ Reversal of trends

✔ And many more

No human being can factor all the variables in his or her head. Business models simply have too many facets to do the math in your head. Just like a calculator is needed to solve complex math, a structured process is needed to solve complex business models.

Complex interplay

Aside from the hundreds of factors to consider in your business model, you'll need to evaluate the interplay between the variables as well. What happens to your high-margin product (variable #1) when competitors knock it off and release their own version (variable #2)? Add a recession into the mix (variable #3) and your supplier vertically integrating into one-half of your expected market (variable #4), and the math can no longer be done in your head.

REMEMBER

It takes more than just a great idea for a great business model

Crocs sandals burst onto the market a decade ago and soared to worldwide prominence. Thanks to ingenious sandal design and a proprietary closed-cell resin, Croslite™, Crocs sold millions of pairs of cheap-to-manufacture shoes for $20 to $50 retail. The company was extraordinarily profitable and the stock soared to $80/share.

The Crocs business model looks terrific if you look at marketability and monetization. The shoes enjoy a large market, loyal customers, and a good niche. The shoes are sold at high margin and many customers buy many pairs of Crocs. However, what about sustainability? It may be difficult to maintain the competitive advantage of the Croslite material as several companies have knocked off the lightweight composite. Can Crocs continue to create unique and innovative offerings equal to the original Crocs? Were Crocs just a trend that will die, or will customers continue to purchase Crocs for decades?

When you examine the sustainability aspects of the Crocs business model, it weakens. The stock market may be sensing the same thing, because Crocs stock is currently $20/share, well off the $80 top. If you examine only the marketing and monetization aspects of the Crocs model, you don't get a full picture. The Pet Rock was a highly profitable business model — for one year. The Crocs business model probably lands somewhere between the Pet Rock and Coca-Cola in regards to its sustainability.

Savvy businesspeople are subconsciously processing this interplay in the backs of their minds. Ideally, a business model evaluation process should bring the interplay to the forefront of analysis rather than rely on subconscious analysis.

Not all factors carry equal weight

In case your head isn't spinning from the hundreds of variables and their complex interplay, don't forget that some variables matter more than others. An easy-to-sell product with a good niche matters much more than the threat of governmental action. A product with great margin matters more than the ease of selling it. Just like currency, different denominations carry different weights. To carry on the analogy, if you're trying to create a $100 business model, it's going to take way too many nickels to get to $100. You need some $5 bills and $20 bills. The same is true with a business model. The top factors (marketability and margin) are the $20 bills, while other factors are the quarters and nickels.

A business model analysis that weights all factors equally fails to duly emphasize the importance of the marketing and margin aspects. Figure 5-2 shows such a model.

Unweighted Analysis

Market Attractiveness	13%
Unique Value Proposition	13%
Profit Model	13%
Sales Performance Model	13%
Competitve Advantage	13%
Innovation Factor	13%
Avoidance of Pitfalls	13%
Graceful Exit	13%

Figure 5-2:
Unweighted business model factors.

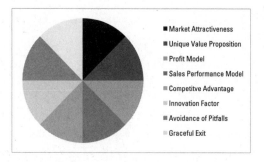

- Market Attractiveness
- Unique Value Proposition
- Profit Model
- Sales Performance Model
- Competitve Advantage
- Innovation Factor
- Avoidance of Pitfalls
- Graceful Exit

By weighing components, you can perform a more accurate analysis on the business model. Figure 5-3 shows you a weighted business model.

Weighted Analysis

Market Attractiveness	26%
Unique Value Proposition	23%
Profit Model	18%
Sales Performance Model	12%
Competitve Advantage	9%
Innovation Factor	6%
Avoidance of Pitfalls	3%
Graceful Exit	3%

Figure 5-3: Weighted business model factors.

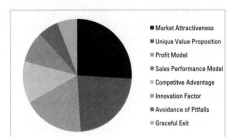

Designing a Business Model by Using a Structured Process

Until recently, no formal business model design tools existed. Entrepreneurs had no choice but to use their experience and wits to create business models. Sometimes this unstructured approach worked, and sometimes it didn't.

The founders of Southwest Airlines may have been successful doodling their business model on the back of a cocktail napkin, but you'll be better served with a more structured approach. In the following sections, I discuss three available templates to aid you in the creation of your business model.

Business Model Canvas

Authors Alexander Osterwalder and Yves Pigneur delineate a framework for a business model in their popular book *Business Model Generation* (Wiley). Osterwalder and Pigneur's Business Model Canvas can be used to brainstorm business model concepts as well as see their interactivity. The canvas is particularly useful in group sessions where brainstorming can be harnessed.

The business model designer writes key ideas or principles in the appropriate boxes on the canvas. From there, the most powerful concepts and inter-relationships can be uncovered and developed. See Figure 5-4 for a peek at the Business Model Canvas.

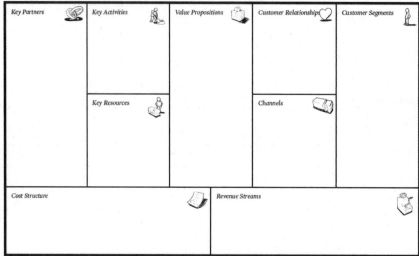

Figure 5-4: The Business Model Canvas.

This material is reproduced with permission of John Wiley & Sons, Inc.

Four-box business model

Author Mark W. Johnson proposes a four-box business model in his book *Seizing the White Space* (Harvard Business Press). Johnson's primary focus is to help companies innovate their business model into "white spaces" that are highly profitable and less competitive. Creating a new business venture is akin to ongoing business model innovation, so Johnson's format can be a good tool to assist in structuring a business model.

You may prefer the four-box model, shown in Figure 5-5, because it's a bit broader than Osterwalder and Pigneur's nine-category model and highlights the interplay between factors more prominently. The four-box model focuses on the interplay between customer value proposition, profit formula, key resources, and key processes to decipher a business model.

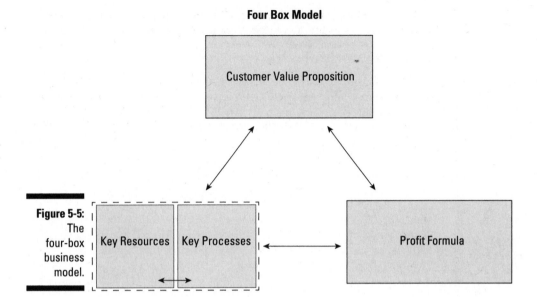

Four Box Model

Figure 5-5: The four-box business model.

Business model wheel

The Business Model Institute (BMI) has created an eight-part wheel-shaped framework to create and analyze a business model. Unlike the other templates, this version is less theoretical and more practical. The BMI framework starts with the premise that all great business models have: an outstanding offer, the ability to monetize the offer, and the ability to sustain it. Each business model is then dissected into eight key areas. I use the BMI wheel framework as the basis of discussion throughout this book. Without going into detail here, the eight areas in decreasing order of importance in the Business Model Institute wheel framework are:

- ✔ **Market attractiveness:** Selling your product to the right combination of market, niche, and customer can have a big effect on your profitability (see Chapter 6 for details).

- ✔ **Unique value proposition:** Does your product solve a compelling need that the customer can't fill elsewhere? Does the offering provide far more value to the customer than it costs? Does the offering tap an unserved or underserved market? Were you first to market with this proposition? Are similar offerings available? These factors and more comprise your unique value proposition (see Chapter 7).

✔ **Profit model:** How much profit can you make selling the product? How does the interplay among different products sold affect profitability? Do you have a cost advantage? Will your revenue be recurring or a one-time hit? Factors like these make up the profit model (check out Chapter 8).

✔ **Sales performance model:** Will you be able to sell the product for as much as you think? Can you attract customers via marketing, or will you need a heavy sales effort to push the product to the market? Can you create a proven and repeatable sales process? The sales performance model brings factors such as these into the overall business model (Chapter 9 offers more information).

✔ **Ongoing competitive advantage:** Do you possess any of the classic competitive advantages, such as cost advantage, differentiation, or access to resources? Will your model allow you to maintain and grow this advantage? Are large competitors entering your market? Is the bargaining power of buyers increasing or decreasing? These factors and more comprise your business model's ongoing competitive advantage (I tell you more in Chapter 10).

✔ **Innovation factor:** Every business needs to innovate, but how much? A parking lot maintenance company needs to innovate to stay competitive, but not as much as Intel needs to innovate. Your innovation factor is the proper balance between your need to innovate and your ability to innovate (see Chapter 11).

✔ **Avoidance of pitfalls:** Unfortunately, you can have a great product sold for high profits to a great customer niche and still have issues with your business model. Governmental regulation (or the removal of it — as was the case with airlines and telecom), severe location handicap, over-reliance on trends/fads, or legal issues can damage an otherwise good model (flip to Chapter 11 for details).

✔ **Graceful exit:** Most businesses are mid-sized and small businesses. These businesses don't have public stock to make the owner's stake liquid. Smaller businesses need to allow the owner(s) to turn their years of hard work into cash or a stream of income — also known as a graceful exit. A business model can be outstanding in all other regards but still not provide a graceful exit to the owners (see Chapter 12).

These areas cover every aspect of a business model. Check out Figure 5-6 to see the logic flow to create a business model.

By addressing all eight areas of a business model and weighing them appropriately, you can perform a complete analysis of your model. The graphical representation of this framework is in Figure 5-7.

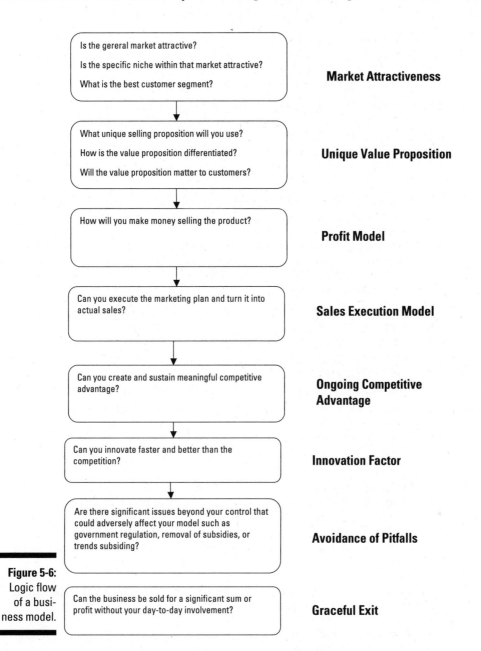

Is the gereral market attractive?

Is the specific niche within that market attractive?

What is the best customer segment?

Market Attractiveness

What unique selling proposition will you use?

How is the value proposition differentiated?

Will the value proposition matter to customers?

Unique Value Proposition

How will you make money selling the product?

Profit Model

Can you execute the marketing plan and turn it into actual sales?

Sales Execution Model

Can you create and sustain meaningful competitive advantage?

Ongoing Competitive Advantage

Can you innovate faster and better than the competition?

Innovation Factor

Are there significant issues beyond your control that could adversely affect your model such as government regulation, removal of subsidies, or trends subsiding?

Avoidance of Pitfalls

Can the business be sold for a significant sum or profit without your day-to-day involvement?

Graceful Exit

Figure 5-6:
Logic flow
of a busi-
ness model.

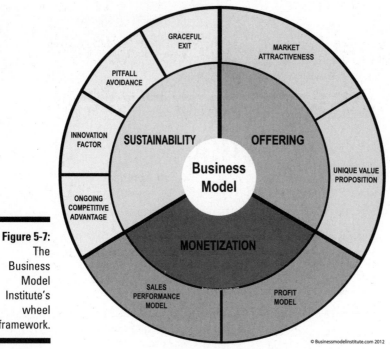

Figure 5-7:
The
Business
Model
Institute's
wheel
framework.

Figure used with permission from businessmodelinstitute.com

Chapter 6

Finding the Most Attractive Markets to Create a Powerful Offering

*T*he most important step toward creating a great business model is creating a product that customers want and will buy. This is called a *powerful offering*. The first step in creating a powerful offering is selecting the right market. Picking the combination of industry attractiveness, niche attractiveness, and customer attractiveness creates the best market for your product.

By combining industry attractiveness, niche attractiveness, and customer attractiveness, you can understand the overall market potential. I refer to this combination as the *market attractiveness* from this point forward. Market attractiveness is one of the most important aspects of your business model. It's difficult to imagine a strong business model that sells to lousy customers in a bad industry and small niche market.

Gauging the Target Market

To create the best business model, you should find a profitable and sufficiently large market segment. However, in order to have a successful and durable business model, you need to find a large market that's unserved or underserved. Finding this underserved market is paramount.

Anyone can find huge markets to attack. Hey, let's sell coffee! The market is large and growing, right? However, several large and successful companies already own pieces of this market. In general, it's unwise to attack an established competitor in the exact same market segment. Traditionally, the first mover or incumbent wins.

If you want to go after the coffee market, you need to find a viable market segment that's unserved or underserved by Starbucks and similar companies. I break down the target market into four pieces to make things easier:

- ✔ **How attractive is the industry itself?** For instance, software companies tend to be more profitable than construction companies. Professor Scott A. Shane conducted research for his book, *The Illusions of Entrepreneurship: The Costly Myths That Entrepreneurs, Investors, and Policy Makers Live By* (Yale University Press). That research offers significant data that some industries are more viable and profitable than others. Of course, the other areas of the business model have great effect upon the overall profitability; however, if you're looking for the best model, software development is a better choice than an airline (see the later section "Case study: Software versus airlines").

- ✔ **How attractive is the niche within the industry?** Typically, packaged software developers are more profitable than custom software developers. You want to pick a niche that offers the best potential profitability.

- ✔ **How attractive is the customer segment?** The high-end customer targeted by Starbucks is more profitable than the customer targeted by McDonald's. An attractive customer doesn't have to be a wealthy customer. An attractive customer is the one who can make your business model work best. For instance, many profitable business models are being created for the unbanked (people without checking accounts).

- ✔ **Is it big enough to provide a good opportunity for you to enter it and sell enough product or services, at a price point that will allow you to create a viable business?** Prosthetic limbs for pet dogs may seem like a great idea, but can you sell enough of them at a high enough price to be able to make any money doing it?

Determining Industry Attractiveness

An *industry* is the broadest category or definition of the business you'll be in. Examples of industry include the following:

- Automotive aftermarket manufacturing
- Business consulting
- General contracting
- Home remodeling
- Lawn and garden distribution
- Legal services
- Medical
- Pet care
- Residential landscaping
- Software development

Within a broad industry are often-defined industry segments that further refine the offering. Here are some examples:

- The vehicle manufacturing industry has segments for heavy-duty trucks, electric automobiles, recreational vehicles, and more.
- The restaurant industry has segments for fast food, fine dining, casual dining, and so on.
- Clothing manufacturers have segments for athletic wear, men's suits, lingerie, women's business attire, and bridal gowns, among others.
- The medical doctor industry has segmentation for general practitioners, surgeons, podiatrists, holistic, ophthalmologists, and hundreds more.
- The HVAC (heating, ventilation, and air conditioning) industry has segments for light-duty, boilers, and heavy-duty systems.

You're much more likely to be successful in a "good" industry than a "bad" one. In a good industry, most companies are successful; examples include software development, mineral extraction, and insurance. In a bad industry, margins are historically low and/or competition is overly intense; examples include airlines and construction. However, you can find numerous examples of companies that entered unattractive industries and were successful because their business model was strong in other areas. Examples include Waste Management (garbage), Apple (computer hardware), Nike (shoes), and Vistaprint (commercial printing).

What's the difference between a market and an industry?

Many businesspeople use the term *market* as a catch-all for the combination of *industry, segment, niche,* and *customer* (in other words, who will pay you for your product). Although simply referring to *the market* is easier, I try to break things down into more discreet pieces so you can gain additional insight into your model. These concepts, however, bleed into one another. If your industry niche is electric cars,

your customer segment is probably dictated by the fact that you make electric cars. The two complement and bleed into each other.

I use the term *market* when *industry, segment, niche,* or *customer segment* simply doesn't fully cover all the bases. When I use the term *industry,* I'm referring to the industry and the industry segment.

You have a much greater chance of success if you pick an attractive industry. Consider these factors:

- ✔ Is this industry, as a whole, growing or shrinking?
- ✔ Will this industry be strong in ten years?
- ✔ How many incumbents are in this industry, and how strong are they?
- ✔ Do you see an opportunity for this industry to overlap into a different existing market (convergence)?
- ✔ Could the industry provide powerful synergies with an existing part of your business?

After you identify an attractive industry, identify the best subset of that market, or niche, and then identify the best customers to serve within that niche. Working in an attractive industry is helpful, but it isn't a prerequisite. Many great business models have been created in bad industries by carving out attractive customer segments, niches, or both.

Vistaprint created an excellent business model serving customers no one wanted (microbusinesses) in an industry no one wanted to be in (printing). Vistaprint succeeded by leveraging a highly differentiated sales, distribution, and cost model.

There's an old saying, "Everyone thinks they know how to run a restaurant because they know how to eat." Every industry and business can be learned. However, if you're unfamiliar with an industry, count on some hard work to get up to speed.

Changing industries may grow your market

For 30 years, commercial alarm companies enjoyed sole reign over protecting premises via wired motion detection, sensors, and video. As wireless technology developed, sensors and video cameras migrated to wireless versions, and computer wiring companies who were much more familiar with wireless technology began to infiltrate alarm companies' markets.

Many alarm companies found themselves bidding against nontraditional competitors from the computer or wireless businesses. IT companies won many of these bids due to their perceived superiority in wireless technology. The convergence of alarms and wireless technology reduced the market size for the alarm companies but increased it for IT companies. Cable and mobile phone companies are now entering this space, too, so IT companies are now under attack in these markets.

As you choose your industry, keep in mind that the business landscape is always changing. Gas stations used to fix cars; now they sell donuts and sandwiches. If you look into the future, it can help you determine whether your chosen industry has peripheral growth opportunities or potential threats. (See the nearby sidebar, "Changing industries may grow your market" for an example.)

Finding the best industry

Picking an attractive industry for your business model may seem simple. The key lies in research. Gather as much independent information as possible regarding current and future trends. By doing so, you're able to make the best choice of industry for your model. Places to find industry data and trends are:

- ✔ Paid services such as Gartner (www.gartner.com) and Forrester Research (www.forrester.com)
- ✔ General business publications like *Business Week* (www.businessweek.com), *Inc.* (www.inc.com), *Barron's* (barrons.com), and *Money* (cnnmoney.com)
- ✔ Books
- ✔ Futurists such as Faith Popcorn, author of many books on business trends, including *Clicking: 17 Trends That Drive Your Business — And Your Life* (HarperBusiness)
- ✔ Industry trade publications

Watch out for bias when using trade publications as a resource. Such publications put the most positive spin on the industry. For instance, I bet that travel industry trade publications were still positive on the industry in 2000 even though Internet sites like `Priceline.com` and `Expedia.com` were beginning to destroy portions of the business.

✔ Industry associations

✔ Personal experience

✔ IRS or state government (Look for the number of businesses in an industry starting or filing bankruptcy.)

Without proprietary information, you're picking your industry with the same data as your competition. Entrepreneurs are guilty of over-researching industries, trying to mitigate risk. Business is inherently risky. No amount of research is a substitute for time in the marketplace. At some point, you will have done your homework, taken your best guess, and will need to take the leap.

Working in unserved or underserved markets

Unserved or underserved markets offer significantly better opportunities than most. Underserved markets have growth potential and less competition. Position yourself in an underserved market and your business model will be much stronger. Markets are underserved because

✔ The market is growing and too few vendors serve the market. Most new businesses chase this classic market. Markets like Android application development, social media platforms, 3D printing, and passenger space travel are examples of markets expected to have explosive growth.

✔ The market is stagnant or shrinking and vendors flee. An overcorrection by competition can create opportunities.

✔ The market is considered unattractive due to

- Perceived profitability. Rent-a-Center profits in a market others consider too dicey.

- Perceived size. Walmart found a market serving towns under 20,000 in population while competitors focused on large cities.

- Being unsexy. Markets like portable toilets, paper manufacturing, and salt mining have far less sex appeal than iPhone application development and can offer opportunities because of this lack of appeal.

Some markets are underserved for a reason. Carefully examine the market opportunity, take off the rose-colored glasses, and be brutally honest with yourself — and then pick based on all the criteria.

Case study: Software versus airlines

It's quite difficult to make money in some industries. Case in point is the airline industry. All major U.S. carriers except Southwest Airlines have filed for bankruptcy protection. Yes, all of them. Southwest is not only the top performing airline, but also well respected globally as an outstanding company.

Southwest is an exceptionally well-run company; Southwest is the top performer in its industry by light years; and Southwest earns net profit around 2 percent of sales. So the best performer in the industry can look forward to a dismal 2 percent net profit and a 1.8 percent return on assets? Wait, that doesn't sound too bad with sales in the billions. What does it take to get into the airline business? First, go hire tens of thousands of employees (46,128 to be exact): flight attendants, pilots, mechanics, ground crews, and so on. Then go purchase a few billion dollars' worth of airplanes, and you're set.

Contrast the airline industry to the software industry. Unlike an airline, the software industry doesn't require massive capital investment, nor does it require tens of thousands of employees. Typically, the software industry offers better margins, higher net profits, fewer employee issues, and higher returns on assets.

Intuit, the maker of Quicken software, is a high-performing company but isn't the top performing company in the software industry. How does it compare to Southwest Airlines? Intuit was able to generate profits of $634 million in 2011 with only 8,500 employees versus Southwest's net profit of $178 million the same year. Intuit earned net profit of 18.48 percent versus Southwest's 1.98 percent.

Nothing against Intuit, but Southwest is the better-run company. Southwest is the best in its industry, by far. Southwest is a revered company. What is Southwest's reward for outstanding performance in the airline industry? Well, the reward stinks! Because Southwest is in a lousy industry, Southwest can perform only to a certain level.

Heed the lessons in this example: If you pick the right industry, your business model will be much better than if you pick poorly. In other words, please don't start an airline!

Looking for Niche Attractiveness

After you pick an attractive industry for your business model (see the previous section), it's time to find an attractive niche. Your niche market is a subset of the overall market you participate in. Discovery Networks International participates in the broadcast television industry, but its niche is infotainment. Shows like *MythBusters, Dirty Jobs,* and *Deadliest Catch* entertain with an educational bent. The shows on Discovery Networks' channels attract a certain type of audience. This niche has proven to be a good one. Discovery Networks has grown steadily to reach more than 300 million international subscribers.

The power of a good niche

Picking the right niche may be more important than picking the right industry. Vistaprint was founded in 1995 when the traditional printing business was getting crushed. Thousands of printers went out of business during the 1990s and early 2000s. During that time, Vistaprint grew into a billion-dollar business. How could Vistaprint grow when other printers were dramatically shrinking? Vistaprint targeted micro and small businesses considered too small for traditional printers. Combined with ingenious leverage of technology, Vistaprint turned unprofitable small customers into one of the most profitable printing operations in the world.

Unlimited niches exist

Good news! You can find unlimited niches within any market. At the core of many successful companies' strategies was the creation or refinement of a new niche. Here are some examples:

- **Panera Bread:** Healthier, higher-quality sandwiches aimed at the fast food industry.

- **Häagen-Dazs:** High-end ice cream at triple the price versus other ice creams in the frozen desert industry.

- **Starbucks:** Not just a cup of joe — an experience. You could argue that Starbucks is in the restaurant industry, and it is. However, Starbucks also competes against convenience stores for coffee sales. The niche in either case is the customer who wants the full Starbucks coffee experience.

✔ **McDonald's:** Fast, consistent quality food. This niche in the restaurant business is mature and crowded today, but when McDonald's started, it was a new and untapped market. By catering to customers who wanted consistency in fast food, McDonald's dominated this niche.

✔ **Coach:** Everyday luxury. Coach bags are more stylish than a department store brand but priced much more reasonably than high-fashion brands. This half high-fashion, half department-store niche has worked well for Coach and other everyday luxury brands.

✔ **iPad:** An e-mail and Internet toy. Apple found a great niche between a laptop, Gameboy, and smartphone.

How many different niches can the hamburger business support? A lot more than anyone expected. The hamburger was invented around 1890, and the first hamburger restaurants began appearing in the 1920s. Since then, dozens of spins on making a hamburger have appeared. Here's a partial list of hamburger chains and their niches.

Chain	*Niche*
McDonald's	The kids' burger chain
Wendy's	The adults' burger chain
Red Robin	Gourmet burgers
White Castle	Craveable sliders
Rally's	Drive-through only
Steak 'n Shake	Sit-down burgers with a diner feel
Five Guys	Simple, fresher burgers and fries

Markets have a habit of splitting

As markets mature, they tend to split into more and more niches. Niches that used to comprise a small portion of the market can become huge. Fifty years ago, abrasive cleaners such as Comet dominated the household cleaner market. In 1977, the Clorox Company introduced the niche cleaner Soft Scrub. The product had a limited market for those looking for an occasional alternative to hard abrasives. Over time, cream cleaners became the largest segment of the household cleaner market. Now you can find niche cream products such as CeramaBryte Stovetop cleaner for specialty uses.

If you think of the overall market as a bell curve in which the largest market exists in the fat portion of the bell curve, the best niches exist on the fringes of the market. Think of the left fringe as low-cost options and the right edge as high-cost options. Figure 6-1 shows bell curves for the household cleaner market.

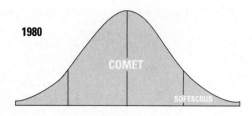

1980

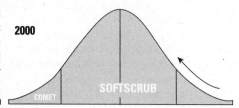

Figure 6-1:
Bell curves
for the
household
cleaner
market.

2000

At one time, dry cleaners like Comet held the bulk of the market. Softscrub entered the market as a liquid specialty cleaner on the right fringe of the market. Softscrub garnered customers who didn't want the harsh abrasive in a dry cleaner. Over time, the appeal of liquid cleaners versus dry cleaners grew, and Softscrub replaced Comet as the main portion of the market (the fat part of the bell curve). Comet was relegated to the least attractive portion of the market (the left fringe), appealing to cost-sensitive customers willing to use old-fashioned cleaners.

Both edges of the bell curve offer a variety of niches. Walmart found a niche on the left fringe by providing buyers in small towns a low-cost department store. Today, Walmart represents the fat part of the bell curve, and dollar stores have carved out a niche on the left fringe.

Generally, your business model should *not* attempt to enter a market in the fat portion of the bell curve. These established markets have strong, established players that are typically tough to beat at their own game. Instead, find a fringe to attack (as I show you in Figure 6-2). Most likely, the established players won't want to leave their large markets to mess with your little niche . . . yet.

Figure 6-2:
Entering the
market on
the fringes.

ENTER THE MARKET HERE

Niche markets aren't always logical

Creating a niche may be easier than you think. Take the iPad for example. The iPad should *not* have worked for lots of reasons:

✔ Tablet computers had been tried by dozens of companies, including Apple, without success

✔ Smartphones do more than an iPad

✔ An iPad isn't quite a laptop and doesn't allow easy typing

✔ You can't use an iPad as a phone even though you have to pay for phone service

✔ Smartphones are portable; an iPad is much less portable

✔ Isn't an iPad just a giant iPod?

One hundred million iPads later, all these reasons don't matter. Apple's secret with the iPad was niching the product differently than all the previously failed tablet computers. Previous tablets tried to be computers in tablet form. The iPad is *not* a computer — it's a giant iPod. The iPad does many things well, but being a computer isn't one of them. Apple was smart enough to see the unmet demand for unserved customers looking for fast-boot Internet, easy e-mail access, a screen big enough to read, enough portability to be acceptable, and a cool factor to create a brand-new niche.

In Jack Trout's classic marketing book, *The 22 Immutable Laws of Marketing* (HarperBusiness), he says that your goal as a marketer is to create a Kleenex or Jell-O type brand. Kleenex is a tissue. Jell-O is gelatin. Xerox is a photocopier. These brands created new niches and dominated the niche to such an extent that the market renamed the category after the brand. This is the gold standard of niche creation.

Find unserved or underserved markets

The best way to create a good niche is to find an unserved or underserved market. All blockbuster products do this. To paraphrase Strategyn founder Tony Ulwick, "We don't buy products for their features and benefits; we buy them to help do specific jobs." No one bought a cellphone for what it was; they bought it for what it *did* — made them safer and more productive while driving. The underserved market for cellphones wasn't one for better phones; it was for the ability to communicate in situations where it was previously impossible.

What does *underserved* mean? If the market was obviously underserved, an existing player in the market would fill the void. Some guesswork is involved in predicting what underserved means. You have to use your business judgment, and then guess. Only the market knows what's needed, and the only way to find out is to take it to the market.

Sometimes it's easy to identify an underserved market. A fast-growing suburb needs gas stations, restaurants, and services in prime retail locations. Exponential growth in use of smartphones creates users faster than the applications needed to serve them.

If you choose a niche in an easy-to-identify growth area, keep in mind that competitors can easily find this niche too. Count on lots of competition.

Instead of going for the obvious niche, be willing to take some chances and pick a less obvious niche. If everyone is chasing mobile phone growth by writing iPhone and Android apps, take a chance on Microsoft apps. For smaller companies, having a less competitive niche can be far more advantageous than being a very small fish in the big pond.

How can you find these elusive unserved or underserved markets?

- **Personal experience:** Many great products and companies have been created by an entrepreneur's discontent with the status quo. Fred Smith wondered why letters couldn't be delivered overnight when he conceived FedEx. While traveling in Italy, Howard Schultz wondered why European-style cafes wouldn't work in America.

- **Friends and relatives:** If you aren't the cutting-edge type, look to friends who are. What products and services are they buying and why? What problems do they wish they could solve?

- **Research trends:** You don't need to catch a trend to find a great niche; however, catching a trend can make your niche much better because the growth is built-in.

- **Hired experts:** Professional business plan writers, business model consultants, futurists, or other gurus can help you find a niche.

- **Luck:** Popular website Angie's List was founded in 1995 when the Internet didn't exist for very many people. Angie's List was simply a monthly booklet sent to members with reviews of home contractors. Its popularity was concentrated in historic neighborhoods where repairs were frequent and expensive. Angie's List was a nice little business that never envisioned the tidal wave that would carry it to become the leader in its niche. When the Internet turned the Angie's List business model upside down, it also made it better. Instead of a localized printer of recommendation booklets, Angie's List became a social media powerhouse.

Checking Out Customer Attractiveness

You can create an attractive market niche (see the previous section), but have it destroyed by bad customers. *Attractive customers* have a strong need for your offering, value the solution to their problem more than your product costs (that's a *strong value proposition*), have disposable income to spend on your offering, pay their bills on time, and exist in sufficient numbers to make your venture profitable. (If you think I'm kidding about paying their bills on time, consider that many big-box retailers are notorious for stringing out vendors 120 days or more and severely hamstringing cash flow.)

Most business models have customers that are neither exceptionally attractive nor exceptionally unattractive. Most business models don't need to focus on customer attractiveness for long because the old mantra "all customers are good customers" is true most the time. However, you do have to study customer attractiveness.

The most prominent example of gaining the most attractive customer is the retail mantra "location, location, location." What does an outstanding retail location get you? Outstanding customers, that's what. A high-end retail mall has the same industry attractiveness and niche attractiveness regardless of where it's located. Whether the mall is located in the hottest new suburb or the middle of farmland, the industry and niche attractiveness remain the same. However, the high-income customers available in the hot new suburb are typically viewed as more attractive than those in rural locations.

Rent-A-Center is in the same industry as Best Buy. The two companies have some niche overlap, but they serve significantly different customers. Best Buy serves customers who can afford to purchase a television in full. These customers have either cash or pre-arranged financing like a credit card. Rent-A-Center caters to customers with lesser credit availability. Rent-A-Center extends credit to buyers deemed undesirable by traditional retailers like Best Buy. Rent-A-Center accepts monthly or weekly payments from customers until the item is paid in full. Due to the differences in the customer segments they serve, Rent-A-Center's business model is significantly different from Best Buy's:

> ✔ Best Buy serves a larger number of buyers who are more financially stable and makes money with a traditional retail business model — buying and selling merchandise.

✔ Rent-A-Center is closer to a specialty finance company that happens to sell appliances. Because Rent-A-Center doesn't collect payment in full upfront, the company has many profit areas that Best Buy doesn't have. Finance fees, high interest rates on loans, repossession fees, and more account for the bulk of Rent-A-Center's profit.

Many businesses would consider the customers of Rent-A-Center less than desirable. However, Rent-A-Center has created a profitable business model selling to these supposedly less-than-desirable customers. Because the Rent-A-Center model accounts for sporadic and occasional nonpayment, it's a workable business model.

More affluent customers don't make a market segment more attractive. Typically, more affluent customers can afford to pay a higher price for goods and services. High margin typically follows these higher prices, but may well be set off by higher overheads and lower volumes owing to a higher degree of exclusivity. Simply chasing affluent customers isn't always the best strategy. Remember the old adage, "Sell to the masses, live with the classes. Sell to the classes, live with the masses."

If you meet ten business owners in the construction industry, you'll probably meet someone whose business was destroyed by a slow-paying or nonpaying customer. A workable business model can be destroyed by the wrong customers.

As a businessperson, you must eliminate or account for bad customers in your business model.

Interestingly, you can have a customer niche within your customer niche. Your products are marketed to target a certain segment or niche. However, customers within any niche, no matter how tight, are widely varied. Coach bags fill a niche between the everyday bags you can find at JCPenney's and the high-end bags you can find in Paris. Within this niche you can find Louis Vuitton customers slumming it a bit and middle-class folks looking for a bit of everyday luxury.

The question you need to answer is which of the sub-segments the marketing is directed to. In the case of Coach bags, the marketing is clearly directed at the middle-class buyer looking for everyday luxury.

Starbucks attracts the most affluent and desired customers in the coffee industry. However, within Starbucks's niche are buyers who stretch themselves financially to buy a $5 latte and buyers who spend hundreds of dollars every month at Starbucks. The niche Starbucks markets to is customers who want Starbucks as a lifestyle choice rather than just a cup of coffee.

Mortgage brokers

Many mortgage brokers had outstanding business models during the early 2000s. Their business models were highly leverageable and profitable. For many years these business models worked well. However, as lending standards allowed more and more questionable buyers, the business model began to deteriorate. You probably know how the story ends. A significant percentage of mortgage brokers went out of business due solely to the poor quality of customers.

Finding Your Place on the Industry Value Chain

To create the best business model possible, find the best place on the industry value chain. Every firm involved in getting a product from initial creation to purchase and consumption by the end consumer adds value in the form of activities, incurs costs, and has a resulting margin. Some positions in this value chain offer a greater opportunity than others.

Different industries value the places on this value chain differently. For instance, clothing retailers enjoy a more profitable position on their value chain than the clothing manufacturers. In automobiles, retailers tend to make less than the manufacturers. In some industries, no desirable places on the value chain are available, making the overall market less attractive for your business.

Consider a cup of coffee. Several operators add value to your daily cup of joe. However, the market rewards some activities much more richly than others. If your business model is to be the most successful, you want to assume a position on the value chain that offers the best potential profits. Table 6-1 shows the value chain for coffee.

Table 6-1	Value Chain for Coffee	
Firm	*Value Added*	*Key Activities*
Coffee bean grower	Operations	Farming
Shipper	Logistics	Transportation and logistics

(continued)

Table 6-1 *(continued)*

Firm	Value Added	Key Activities
Coffee roaster	Operations	Converting beans into drinkable coffee
Marketers (Folgers, Starbucks)	Sales	Branding, sales, customer service
Retailer	Sales	Merchandising

Whole green Columbian coffee beans sell for $1.97 a pound. Assume the farmer has cost equal to about half that. The farmer's margin is 98.5 cents per pound of coffee. The roaster buys the coffee from the farmer for $1.97 a pound and transports it, roasts it, and grinds it. The cost of logistics and transportation is around 2 cents per pound. The roaster then sells it to a coffee service, consumer products company, or retail outlet. Unbranded wholesale coffee sells for around $5 per pound. If the coffee roaster's cost of operations is about half the $3.03 per pound value added, then the coffee roaster makes a margin of around $1.51. If the coffee is branded (Starbucks, Folgers, Seattle's Best), add a dollar or two to the value added. Note that almost all the value added by branding drops to profit/margin. Finally, a company like Starbucks, Folgers, Kroger, or a coffee service delivers the coffee to the consumer. Folgers coffee sells for a $9.99 a pound (Starbucks $13.95 per pound). Therefore, the retail seller of Folgers has added about $4 of value (mostly margin). This comprises the entire value chain for a one-pound bag of coffee.

Table 6-2 shows the value added by each function and the approximate margin. Note that the marketing and sales related functions are much more handsomely rewarded than the functions that make the product.

Table 6-2 — Value Added for Coffee

Firm	Cost Added per Pound	Margin Earned per Pound	Total Value Added
Coffee bean grower	$0.985	$0.985	$1.97
Shipper	$0.015	$0.005	$.02
Coffee roaster	$1.52	$1.51	$3.03
Marketers (Folgers, Starbucks)	$0	$2	$2
Retailer	$2	$2	$4

Some places on the coffee value chain are much more profitable than others. To maximize the effectiveness of your business model, find the most profitable portion of the value chain. Usually, the closer you are to the end user or consumer, the greater the opportunity for margin. Don't misconstrue this statement. I'm not suggesting that the best business models are retail models. What I'm suggesting is that as manufacturing has shifted to low-wage countries, the value add for manufacturing and related activities has gone down dramatically. As the ability to add value for manufacturing has decreased, the ability to add value through sales, distribution, and branding has increased. This shift has provided opportunities for savvy entrepreneurs.

Savvy entrepreneurs have also created new positions on the value chain to carve value away from existing players. For example, in the field of law, several new players have emerged to carve out a portion of the value chain traditionally owned by lawyers. Law firms in India specialize in large-scale complex research only. Some firms audit bills from law firms in an attempt to save their clients money. Both of these industries used to be part of the law firm value chain.

Ironically, there seems to be very little correlation between the amount of work or the difficulty of work and the amount of value added in the value chain. As you can see from the coffee example, the hardest work is done by the farmer. The farmer takes the risk of bad weather, has the highest number of employees, and puts in the most hours proportionately. However, the farmer makes the least amount of money on the value chain.

Certain portions of the value chain tend to add more value than others. Note that value added is the difference between sales price and cost. An item may have a large percentage of the total sales price to the end consumer, but add little value on the chain.

Many businesspeople pick an industry because they're familiar with it. If you're an HVAC technician, you tend to create a business model in the HVAC industry. It makes sense. However, your HVAC skills can be applied to many industries, some of which may be more attractive than HVAC.

Big changes in the travel industry

For decades, travel agents performed a variety of functions on the traveler's value chain. Travel agents performed logistics to make the trip go smoothly; they shared a valuable knowledge base about the best hotels, tours, and airlines; and they provided access to the computer booking system, which was unavailable to everyday consumers.

Today, the travel value chain is vastly different. Consumers have access to the same booking data, online reviews have taken the place

(continued)

(continued)

of referrals, and consumers self-serve the logistical aspects. To say that travel agents were replaced by the Internet would be overly simplistic. Travel agents were displaced by a shift in the value chain. Their exclusive access to booking data was removed. Their hard-to-get individual knowledge of hotels and destinations was crowdsourced to the entire Internet. After those two key portions of the value they provided were removed, it made sense for consumers to self-serve the logistical aspects. The value chain didn't change — just the providers. The following list shows you the shift.

Value Added by Travel Agents	Now Provided By
Flight pricing, schedules	Airline websites, Expedia, Priceline
Ability to book flights	Various websites
Knowledge of best hotels, tours, and so on	Crowdsourced via public ranking, voting, and commenting
Suggestions for travel destinations	Google searches, blogs, travel TV shows, and so on
Logistical support	Largely self service, credit card company add-on service such as American Express

Chapter 7

Completing Your Offering with a Unique Value Proposition

In This Chapter

▶ Making your value proposition unique

▶ Considering your unique selling proposition

▶ Getting the most from your product

▶ Using your UVP to become more marketable

▶ Creating a powerful brand

After you know the most attractive market for your business (see Chapter 6 for details on determining market attractiveness), you want to create a differentiated offer by defining your unique selling proposition, price point(s), unique value proposition, and brand. The combination of your strong offer and excellent market niche comprises the most important aspect of your business model.

Building a Unique Value Proposition

You don't need a unique offering in order to have a business model. If, however, you want to have the most successful model possible, you want to offer customers something they can't get somewhere else. This uniqueness may be only one thing, such as the sole gas station on a particular corner, or it may be a combination of product and service features, such as those in a Lexus automobile. All the differences of your offer versus your competitors' equate to your unique value proposition.

Nearly every market is crowded with an abundance of offerings and competition, yet many of these same markets have one company that dominates. How do these companies rise above so much competition and do it profitably? These stellar companies — like Apple, Virgin Airways, Amazon, Discovery Networks, and Priceline — have captured large market shares by offering customers something they simply can't buy somewhere else.

Traditionally, customers not only choose these differentiated offerings over those of competitors, but also pay a premium price for them.

Examples of differentiated offerings include the following:

- **Morton salt** is differentiated by tradition, reputation, and brand. Morton was the first company to offer salt in convenient cylindrical containers as well as the first to add iodine to salt. This addition may not seem like a big deal, but it solved a national health crisis. Thyroid-related growths called *goiters* were common, and small amounts of iodine in the diet prevented them. Morton established a dominant market share in the 1920s and still maintains it. More importantly, this market-leading brand sells for two to three times more than generic salt, which is virtually identical.

- **Sony televisions** sell for nearly double the cheapest brands in the market. Sony's reputation for quality and cutting-edge features allows the company to command a large market share and premium pricing.

- **Disney theme parks** are 95 percent the same as hundreds of other theme parks. All theme parks have carnival rides, mascot-type characters, shows, lousy food, and prime rides/attractions. Yet Disneyland can command 25 percent more for admission than Six Flags Magic Mountain, which is right down the road. Disneyland drew 16.14 million patrons in 2011 versus Magic Mountain's 2.7 million. That last 5 percent difference — memorable movie characters, magical atmosphere, clean parks, impeccable service levels, and a corporate culture built upon memorable customer experiences — *matters*!

- **Toyota Prius** wasn't the first hybrid car. Believe it or not, hybrid vehicles pre-date most combustion vehicles and were available as early as 1870. The Prius wasn't the first hybrid available in the U.S. (although it was the first hybrid available in Japan). In the U.S., the Honda Insight was released a year earlier than the Prius and got 10 mpg better mileage. The Prius, however, was more like a "real car" and not like an electric car trying to be a real car. Because buyers could be environmentally conscious *and* have a vehicle that functioned like every other car they had owned, it was a huge hit.

- `Priceline.com`'s name-your-own-price system is so unique it's patented. Other travel sites simply aggregate hotel and airline offers and display the results to customers. Priceline effectively flipped the role of buyer and seller. When customers are on other sites, their option is "here's the price; take it or leave it." Priceline offers buyers the opportunity to name the price they're willing to pay, and the hotel or airline has the right to take it or leave it. This approach can result in a win-win, in which the buyer gets a great deal and the hotel or airline gets at least some money for an otherwise empty seat or hotel room.

Different is almost always better than better.

Differentiation comes from unique product attributes. Good news! Just about anything can be unique. Examples of uniqueness include these factors:

- ✔ **Convenience:** Think corner location, ingress/egress, online
- ✔ **Emotions the product invokes:** AT&T's call-home campaign or Newman's Own donating profits to charity
- ✔ **Expertise:** This factor is particularly important for doctors and lawyers
- ✔ **Higher quality:** Toyota and Panera Bread offer higher quality than their competitors
- ✔ **Longer-lasting:** Maytag washer and Steinway piano differentiate themselves this way
- ✔ **One-stop-shop/integration:** Meijer and Amazon led the way in this category
- ✔ **Physical location:** Corner lots are so important to Walgreen's business model that the company even made it part of the slogan
- ✔ **Pricing:** Dollar stores and Big Lots offer low prices
- ✔ **Product attribute:** Toothpaste with baking soda is one example
- ✔ **Scale:** Not many companies can build skyscrapers or space shuttles
- ✔ **Service:** Nordstrom's offers exceptional service, and Ed Debevic's offers unique service (see the nearby sidebar for details)
- ✔ **Speed:** Domino's and Jimmy John's deliver quickly

You gonna order or what?

Legendary burger joint Ed Debevic's has differentiated itself on its service, or more accurately, lack of service. You can find the same burgers and fries at Ed Debevic's as you can at thousands of roadside diners. What you get at Ed Debevic's is service with an attitude.

The first time my family dined there, our waitress said, "So, are you gonna order or what? It's not that complicated." Last summer, our waiter wadded up our bill and threw it at us. You don't eat there for the food; you eat there for the entertaining wait staff. If you have a thick skin, they're hilarious.

Evidently, lots of people find this anti-service strategy entertaining. The restaurant is a must-see tourist attraction in Chicago.

Comparing a Unique Selling Proposition to a Unique Value Proposition

The goal of any great business model is to have a high-profit product that customers want to buy. A highly marketable product is traditionally described as having a unique selling proposition. Whole Foods offers only healthy choices in its stores. Domino's Pizza grew rapidly because of its super-fast delivery. UGG boots are not only fashionable but also allow you to walk comfortably without socks. These are all unique selling propositions.

Your product also needs a unique value proposition. *Value* is what the product does for customers that they're prepared to pay you for — not its features. A product can have unique features, but do they benefit the customer, and is the customer prepared to pay for them? Recently, minivan manufacturers decided that more cup holders are better. Some minivans offer a dozen or more cup holders. This feature is unique and offers a unique selling proposition. However, if the customer doesn't value the cup holders, the value proposition is weak. In order to create the best possible business model, you must create the right combination of features and value.

Defining unique selling proposition

Rosser Reeves was the author of the phrase *unique selling proposition,* or USP, which is a unique message about your business versus the competition. The USP is a marketing concept that was first proposed as a theory to understand a pattern in successful advertising campaigns in the early 1940s. The theory states that campaigns made unique propositions to the customer, and this unique proposition convinced them to switch brands. Put another way, a USP is why a customer should care about your brand.

What's tricky about a USP is that being unique is easy. Simply pick something obscure like raw octopus ice cream and, boom, you're unique. However, you must be unique *and* attract a large number of profitable customers. UGG boots started as a small, unique market for sheepskin boots. This unique niche caught fire and UGG now sells millions each year.

The Dave Matthews Band started off small, playing bars, fraternity parties, and small venues for years. The band's music was somewhat unique, but not enough to be considered a USP. The Dave Matthews Band did, however, allow and encourage recording at their events. Generally, taping live events was discouraged or illegal during this time period. Not only did DMB allow taping, they encouraged it. Fans were allowed to plug directly into the sound mixing system for high quality recordings, which they enthusiastically traded. Matthews believes these recordings were instrumental to the band's success.

Typically, market winners start off with a few loyal customers that love the value proposition. Eventually the value proposition, which was targeted to the loyal few, grows beyond expectations and becomes a market winner. The trick is to find the loyal and fanatical first customers. You can't be all things to all people, so don't try. If your product doesn't create rabid fans, you probably don't have a strong USP.

Defining your USP means examining your business in detail; hence, you may start with a freeform brainstorming session, and go over these main content areas:

- **Audience:** Who is your ideal customer? Be as specific as possible, and don't be afraid to exclude people. (You may even think about who *isn't* in your audience.)

- **Problem:** What problem do you solve for your ideal customer? Ideally, your product solves a specific problem that other products can't solve. What pain are you eliminating? How is your customer better off after working with you or buying your product versus the alternatives?

- **Uniqueness:** What sets you apart from others? Better yet, what *meaningfully* sets you apart? A USP of yoga shoes for women meaningfully sets you apart from other athletic shoes. A USP of athletic shoes for teenage women/girls probably doesn't. You can differentiate yourself in thousands of ways: service, range, experience, technique, guarantee, features, and so on (see the earlier section "Building a Unique Value Proposition" for details). Focus on a handful of things that really make you one-of-a-kind — things that make a tangible difference to your audience.

A great USP comes from a deep understanding of who your customers are, what they want, what they value, and what motivates them. It should also cause your prospects to crave your product or service. It should cause them to see almost instantly that they'd be foolish not to investigate your company and your product. You'll likely have a different USP for each product or service you offer.

Why is the USP so important? Think about it this way: If you can't differentiate yourself from the hundreds or thousands of other choices out there, how do you expect your customer to do it?

The following list shows you some good examples of products with a clear USP and tagline:

- **BMW:** The Ultimate Driving Machine

- **Dawn Dishwashing Liquid:** Gets grease out of your way

- **Domino's Pizza:** You get fresh, hot pizza delivered to your door in 30 minutes or less — or it's free

  ✔ **FedEx:** When it absolutely, positively has to get there overnight

  ✔ **MetLife:** Get Met. It Pays.

  ✔ **M&M's:** Melts in your mouth, not in your hand

  ✔ **Target:** Expect more. Pay less.

  ✔ **Walmart:** Everyday low prices

When you're creating your USP, don't forget the old saying, "Price, quality, service: Pick any two." You can't be all things to all people. Starbucks can't deliver the highest quality coffee with expert baristas at the same price as McDonald's coffee. By the same token, you won't get the same shopping experience at Walmart that you get at Nordstrom's. You're far better off to excel at something than be acceptable at everything. USPs are about being exceptional at something — anything.

Defining unique value proposition

The *unique value proposition* (UVP) extends the concept of the unique selling proposition (USP; see the previous section) to include the benefits derived by the customer. Customers ask themselves, "Are the unique features of this product worth the price?" Customers engage in this features–value weighing for all purchases. Augmenting your USP with a strong value proposition creates customers' desires to trade their hard-earned dollars for your product.

One model, the Value Proposition Builder, creates six stages for value proposition analysis:

  ✔ For what market is the value proposition being created?

  ✔ What does the market value the most — the value experience or the customer experience?

  ✔ What products are being offered?

  ✔ What benefits will the customer derive from the product?

  ✔ What alternative options exist?

  ✔ What evidence substantiates your value proposition?

Famed business author Neil Rackham believes a value proposition consists of four main parts: capability, impact, proof, and cost.

Being average is underrated

Former Cap Gemini Ernst & Young consultants Fred Crawford and Ryan Mathews wrote a terrific book, *The Myth of Excellence: Why Great Companies Never Try to Be the Best at Everything* (Crown Business). The authors identify five key areas of the commercial transaction: price, product, access, experience, and service. They found that dominating one element, differentiating on a second, and being at industry par (in other words, average) on the rest was the secret of the top performers.

It's surprising but true. You need to be only average on three of the five aspects if — repeat *if* — you're world-class on some aspect that matters to the customer.

Making the comparison

You could have a strong selling proposition, but a weak value proposition. A Rolls-Royce automobile has a unique selling proposition as the most luxurious, hand-crafted automobile in the world. But for many buyers, the UVP of Rolls-Royce is weak. Is a $262,000 Rolls-Royce Phantom a better value to the high-end car buyer than a top-of-the-line $137,000 BMW 7 Series or a $213,000 Mercedes CL65 AMG? All these cars have a USP that doesn't factor cost or perceived customer value. In order to get the full picture, also consider the customer's weighing of the unique value provided by the product and the financial or opportunity cost to purchase.

The unique selling proposition combined with the unique value proposition shows how marketable the product can be. It isn't enough to be unique; you must be unique in a way that creates the perception of good value to the customer.

> USP + UVP = Marketable Product

Business models with a strong USP and UVP have an excellent foundation. Here are some examples of companies or products in which both USP and UVP are strong:

- ✔ **Cheesecake Factory:** Freshly-cooked, creative meals in ample portions, served in an inviting atmosphere, for a reasonable price.
- ✔ **Hyundai:** Lots of options for not a lot of money.
- ✔ **Target:** Save money but still get cool stuff.

✔ **Whole Foods:** The groceries may cost a lot, but the value of being healthy outweighs the cost.

✔ **Zappos:** The world's largest shoe store delivered to your door with free shipping both ways.

Some of these companies offer higher-priced products than their competitors. However, when customers weigh the benefits versus the value provided, they choose to spend more because the additional perceived value exceeds the additional cost.

Maximizing Product Potential

After you create a strong USP and UVP (see the previous section "Comparing a Unique Selling Proposition to a Unique Value Proposition" for details), you can assess the market potential of your product or service. Will you be filling an important unmet need in a multibillion dollar industry or simply babysitting for friends in your neighborhood? Both of these examples are perfectly valid markets. However, creating the next iPad will create a much larger market than babysitting for your neighbors. Answer the following important questions:

✔ **Do you fill a compelling unserved or underserved market?** You can create a strong value proposition for a market that's too small, too crowded, or too risky. The new Newton by Apple was a sophisticated product with a strong selling proposition and value proposition — on paper, that is. Despite all the signs of success, the Newton wasn't a commercial success. What Apple deemed to be an unserved market was in fact a market that wasn't ready to be served. Another example is a much-needed product for an extremely small niche. Dozens of products would probably fill the needs of sword fishing enthusiasts, but the market is very small.

✔ **How valuable is this USP?** Being the only whitening toothpaste is much more valuable than being the most experienced plumber in a town of 1,000 people. Balance a strong and focused USP with a market worth chasing. When Apple succeeded in creating a market for tablet computers, the market was worth billions.

✔ **Do you have a blue ocean strategy?** In their groundbreaking book, *Blue Ocean Strategy* (Harvard Business Review Press), W. Chan Kim and Renée Mauborgne suggest that powerful new markets can be created by challenging the existing paradigm of competing better in existing markets, which they call red water. They suggest that these overfished, bloody waters are no place to build a long-lasting business. Instead, the authors suggest finding deep blue water to fish by challenging conventional wisdom. After you find the blue water, you can fish prosperously for a long time. For more information on the blue ocean strategy, see the nearby sidebar.

Delving into Blue Ocean Strategy

In their book *Blue Ocean Strategy* (Harvard Business Review Press), W. Chan Kim and Renée Mauborgne create a roadmap to find large, untapped markets. Products like the iPod, the Model T, Cirque Du Soleil, Nintendo Wii, Southwest Airlines, and Yellow Tail wine have all found blue oceans. The following list shows the difference between the traditional competitive strategies in red oceans versus the more profitable blue oceans.

Red Ocean Strategy	**Blue Ocean Strategy**
Compete in the existing market	Create an uncontested market
Beat the competition	Make the competition irrelevant
Exploit existing demand	Create and capture new demand
Make the value–cost trade-off	Break the value–cost trade-off
Align the whole system of a firm's activities with its strategic choice of differentiation or low cost	Align the whole system of a firm's activities in pursuit of differentiation and low cost

Building Marketability

The best products are highly marketable. Everyone knows the story of the better mousetrap. The new mousetrap may be vastly superior to any other mousetrap on the market; however, no one buys it. Customers don't want or need a new mousetrap. They're satisfied with the old one. The new mousetrap isn't marketable. Make sure you don't fall into the better mousetrap trap!

Summing up your unique value proposition in one sentence

Can you clearly and effectively explain your unique value proposition in one sentence? It's not always easy, but it's absolutely necessary. If it takes a paragraph to explain why people should buy your product, a) they'll tune you out after ten words and miss the important stuff, and b) your value proposition won't be finely tuned enough to stand out in a crowded marketplace.

Your UVP should be:

✔ **Specific:** "I'm a dentist" is too vague and short to be unique. What type of dentist? What special client needs do you meet? A stronger UVP may be, "I'm a dentist who has sensitive teeth, so I built my practice to make dental visits painless."

✔ **Succinct:** Some value propositions sound like, "Our software company works with manufactures, distributors, retailers, and other companies to increase efficiencies by leveraging synergies with their existing human capital infrastructure and cutting-edge technological solutions."

Huh? This UVP is too long, serves too many customers, and doesn't offer a specific solution the buyer can envision. Something better may be, "Our software leverages valuable internal human and intellectual capital, resulting in lower turnover and training costs."

✔ **Meaningful:** Your UVP is always interesting to you; it's your company after all. Unfortunately, your customers are overwhelmed with other offerings and advertising overload. A UVP like, "We are the most respected men's clothier in town," may sound great internally. However, to the customer it sounds like, "We think we're pretty awesome . . . blah blah . . . something about clothes." This clothier may do better with something like, "The most expensive suit in town, for a reason," or "For more than 100 years, men have trusted their most important dates to us."

Being first to market

One of the best ways to have a highly marketable product is to be first in the market. There are several ways to define *first to market*. Crest toothpaste has been the most successful toothpaste brand in history. Crest wasn't, however, the first toothpaste; Colgate was. Crest was the first fluoride toothpaste. Being the first to market with the significant feature of cavity protection catapulted Crest to the number one position for decades. Many times, being first with a significant feature or differentiation has the same benefit as being the first to offer the product at all.

Focus on creating a niche where you can be first. Being first in a niche makes you the only option for the customer and effectively leaves you with no competition. My recommendation is to be first to claim a USP rather than be first to market with an entirely new product category. The financial and human resources needed to be first to market are simply too expensive for most mid-sized and small businesses.

Creating a new USP when yours gets crowded

Pay attention to how many of your competitors have a similar USP. When Crest toothpaste first entered the market as the only cavity protection option, the USP was extremely powerful. Many competitors adopt what markets refer to as the "me too" strategy. They put little time, money, or effort into identifying or developing niche markets. But they do make it their business to be extremely quick and very good at ripping off successful entrants into lucrative niche markets with very similar or even flat-out generic offerings. As other "me too" toothpastes entered the market, Crest's value proposition was weakened simply by the sheer number of participants claiming a similar USP. The value of your USP fluctuates with not only its uniqueness, but also the number of competitors claiming similar USPs.

From 1901–1950, the only three brands of toothpaste were Arm & Hammer, Colgate, and Ipana. Today you can find 34 brands of toothpaste and dozens of sub-brands (such as Crest with Scope or Colgate Total). The toothpaste category provides an outstanding lesson in how selling propositions can be carved ever smaller. In the early days, competitors simply focused on being a quality toothpaste that didn't taste horrible. Then fluoride came onto the market and created two categories, fluoride and non-fluoride toothpaste. Next came toothpaste aimed at children. Whitening toothpaste came to market next. Today, all-in-one toothpastes that do everything — whiten, control gum disease, taste good, and vacuum your floor — seem to be the rage.

Making your value proposition matter to customers

Your customers determine what your unique selling proposition is. Other companies may be fighting for a similar USP with the same customer. Many companies are battling for similar USPs in the toothpaste market. You may be a Colgate user and view that toothpaste's value proposition as the best one for you. Your next-door neighbor may be a Crest user and feel the value proposition for Crest is better. Effectively, the USPs for Colgate and Crest are nearly identical. However, in the mind of the customer, the USPs are very different. What the customer believes the USP is matters — what you believe it is doesn't matter. What a product represents to an individual is called branding or, more specifically, brand loyalty.

Ask yourself whether most prospects or customers would agree that you *own* your USP. Many businesses claim that they're the most reliable plumber in town or the best product to meet some specific client need. Would your customers agree with your claims? Ideally, there should be no doubt in the customers' minds that your product has the best value proposition for their needs. If you can clearly communicate a differentiated strategy in one sentence or less, you have a much better chance of successfully owning this USP with your customers. (If you can't communicate your differentiated strategy in one sentence, see the earlier section "Summing up your unique value proposition in one sentence" for help.) If it takes a paragraph or a long-winded soliloquy to communicate your value to customers, your odds of owning the USP in the customers' minds are slim. The best value propositions are usually the simplest ones because they're the easiest ones on which to build a strong brand.

Can customers clearly differentiate your product? This is the "me too" test (see the previous section, "Creating a new USP when yours gets crowded" for more on the "me too" test). Your value proposition is highly differentiated and incredibly valuable — *to you.* Let's face it, this is your baby and it's beautiful. Every other business owner feels the same way about his or her business.

Unfortunately, sometimes customers don't see things the same way you do. They may not view your differentiators as all that differentiated. It's frustrating, but take a pragmatic and customer-centered view of your differentiators. Do customers see you as just another plumber, dentist, or product? A simple way to tell whether your product may be undifferentiated or commoditized in the eyes of the customer is excessive price competition. If the customer is obsessed with low price and discards or undervalues your features and differentiation, the message from the customer may be, "We don't view your product as differentiated," so the only thing left to discuss is the price.

Creating strong value proposition isn't easy. What's meaningful to you may not be meaningful to the customer. These phrases are usually a signal that your value proposition needs some work:

- ✔ **Best:** Okay, you say you're the best. Doesn't the customer get to decide who's best?

- ✔ **Fast:** Does this mean fast by your definition or mine? What does fast service mean? To me, fast means "right now," but I bet the service guy doesn't show up right now.

- ✔ **Quality:** Does quality mean it never breaks or doesn't break very often? The customer's expectations define what quality means, and it typically can be defined as something less ambiguous. "Never needs repairs," "always starts on the first pull," "perfect fits and finishes," and "the last one you will ever buy" are much more meaningful ways to say "high quality."

- ✔ **Customer service:** Every company views its customer service as exceptional. I'm sure the credit card companies even have stats to show the excellence of their customer service. That doesn't mean the customer thinks their service is good. Better value propositions include: all calls answered on the first ring, all calls answered by a human, or all calls resolved on the first call.

Does your product solve a problem customers *want* to be fixed, rather than need to be fixed? "Need" can be a dirty word. Many times businesspeople say, "People really need this," and try to sell something customers need but don't want. The market for health clubs should be significantly larger than it is. As society gets less and less active, the need for health clubs continues to grow. However, only those who *want* to exercise join a health club — not all those who need to exercise.

Create a product the client wants to buy, not one the customer needs to be convinced to buy.

Sensing a change in consumer preferences, McDonald's introduced the Arch Deluxe in 1991 with a $150 million advertising campaign. Boasting less calories and fat, the Arch Deluxe seemed to be a perfect fit for the growing health-conscious demographic. Companies like Whole Foods were growing rapidly by catering to this market. However, the Arch Deluxe failed miserably and McDonald's removed it from its menu in 1996. The lesson of the Arch Deluxe is that people buy what they want — not what they need. McDonald's learned the hard way that all the research in the world can tell you what
the customer *should* want, but only customers can tell you what they *do* want.

Creating a Powerful Brand

It's possible to create a strong selling proposition and value proposition but not create a powerful brand. The Newton by Apple had both a strong USP and UVP but failed to create a good brand for Apple. Part of your goal in creating a great business model should be to create a powerful brand.

All companies and products have a brand. Branding isn't exclusively for consumer products. Service companies, manufacturers, distributors, and all other types of businesses have brands. Your brand is simply the emotional linkage that your customer has to your product. The more unique and useful your brand is to the customer, the more valuable it is to you.

Your brand in the eyes of your customer

It doesn't matter what you think your brand is; only the customer's perception of your brand matters. To you, Starbucks coffee may mean a delicious pick-me-up on the way to work. To your neighbor, Starbucks coffee may mean a brief indulgence during a tough day.

Laying down the law

One of the best books on branding and marketing is *The 22 Immutable Laws of Marketing* by Al Ries and Jack Trout (HarperBusiness). The book offers extensive advice on how to best market your product and create a powerful brand. Here are some of my favorites of the 22 laws:

- The Law of Leadership
- The Law of the Category
- The Law of Perception
- The Law of the Ladder
- The Law of the Opposite
- The Law of Sacrifice
- The Law of Candor

One of the interesting points in the book is that some categories of products are more important in the minds of your customers than others. If I asked you to name ten brands of cars, you could do so quickly. If I asked you to name ten brands of foot powder, you could name only a few. The same holds true for your brand. If you're a wholesale supplier of nuts and bolts, this brand may be an occasional afterthought to your clients until they run out of bolts. You can't do much about the mindset of your prospect. Like it or not, the sports scores will always be more important than nuts and bolts. The best you can do is to highly differentiate your nuts and bolts with a great brand and value proposition.

What does your brand mean to your customer? Is your brand meaningful in the eyes of the customer? In order to be meaningful to your customers, your brand should solve an important problem for them. Meaningful brands can be difficult to create for some business models. A distributor of wholesale plumbing supplies is the important vendor to its customers, but it may be difficult to turn into a meaningful brand simply because of the business type. This is the curse of non-consumer businesses. It's much easier to create a powerful brand for a consumer-based business than for a business that sells to other businesses.

Don't use this difficulty as an excuse not to develop your brand. Many business-to-business companies have created powerful brands despite this handicap. Some examples include:

- BASF ("We don't make the things you buy, we make the things you buy better")
- Boeing
- FedEx
- Intel Inside
- Snap-On Tools

Augmenting your USP and value proposition with a strong brand gives your business model a solid foundation. You can have a solid business model without a strong brand; however, competitors will have the opportunity to steal market share if they can create a good brand.

Other brand considerations

As you build your brand, you may want to consider these factors too:

- **Do you have a compelling price/value combination?** Tide is a great detergent, but it's also competitively priced. It's almost certain that sales of Tide would drop dramatically if the price of Tide were doubled. The market will bear a premium price for a high-quality brand like Tide. However, there's a limit to the price the market will bear. Having a strong price-and-value combination will only strengthen your brand.

- **What is your current market share?** Great brands have great market share. The trick is how you define market share. Starbucks has a 29-percent share of the coffee shop/convenience store market. However, Starbucks' internal data shows it has only a one-percent share of the global coffee market. If Starbucks expanded the analysis to include all dining establishments, this share would be even less. Starbucks' share of total beverages consumed — both in the home and at restaurants (and including soda, water, juice, and so on) — becomes minuscule compared to its significant market share in coffee shops. Most often, you want to use the narrowest definition of market share. Twenty-five-percent market share for plumbers in the North suburbs of Atlanta is more relevant than the market share for all of Atlanta or all of Georgia.

- **Can you pass the Warren Buffett test?** Buffett has stated that if you don't have the power to raise pricing, you're in the wrong business. If you were forced to raise prices five percent immediately, how much business would you lose? If you'd lose a lot of business, you don't have the pricing power Buffett desires. Buffett's investments in companies like Coca-Cola have proven his theory correct. In 1945, a bottle of Coke cost a nickel. Today, the same amount of Coke costs 14 times more.

- **Is the overall market expected to grow/shrink?** Blockbuster Video enjoyed a 40 percent market share of all U.S. video rentals. The company enjoyed an impeccable brand and profits to match. You know the rest of the story. With the availability of easy-to-mail DVDs, Netflix entered the market and took a sizeable foothold in Blockbuster's market. The next blow to Blockbuster came with the introduction of streaming technology. Now customers can instantly download and view videos without having to go to the store. Eventually, the once great Blockbuster brand succumbed to the shrinking market.

Brand loyalty is very fickle in commoditized niches. Consumer product marketers for products that don't have a highly differentiated USP (think toothpaste) know that if they can get a consumer to try their product, they'll likely switch to the alternative brand. This is why you see coupon and sample wars for toothpaste all the time. This is all low-margin, high-promotion costs terrain that you'd do well to stay out of unless you know exactly what you're doing and have the budget and the skills to fight the promotion wars.

Chapter 8

Making Money with Your Business Model

*A*fter you identify an attractive market for your product and have a plan to market it, you're ready to figure out how to make money with it. Even with an outstanding market niche and a stellar marketing process, you have to sell your product for a handsome profit in order to have a great business model. Let's face it: Selling something for little or no profit is easy to do, but trading dollars doesn't make for a great model. In this chapter, I tell you how to maximize the profitability of your business model.

Building a Profitable Revenue Model

At the core of a great business model is the ability to generate superior profits. In order to generate the superior profits, you need to create a profitable revenue model. A profitable revenue model has two components:

✔ Your revenue model should generate high gross margins.

✔ The total gross margin generated needs to exceed your operational or overhead cost.

Ideally, your revenue model should include products with margins superior to competitors' margins. BMW makes significantly more profit per car than General Motors or Ford. Starbucks makes much more profit per cup of coffee than Dunkin Donuts.

Your revenue model should ideally include proprietary revenue streams, margin, as well as avoid common pitfalls, such as technological obsolescence or an overcrowded marketplace.

Generating exceptional margin

There's no such thing as a great business model with poor margins. Superior margins versus the competition are in large part what will make your business model great.

The standard for exceptional margin is determined by comparison to others in the industry rather than a generic profit percentage. If the average shoe manufacturer generates a 25-percent margin and you generate 35 percent, you have generated superior margin.

Exceptional margins do more for your business than generate a good bottom line. If your margins are superior to the competition you can

✔ Hire better people because you can afford to.

✔ Provide a higher level of customer service.

✔ Have more room for sales negotiations.

✔ Keep your bank and investors happy.

✔ Engage in research and development.

Creating a product with superior margin

The most profitable industrial product of all time is the Xerox copier. During the 1960s and 1970s, margins on the product were obscene. The copiers were so profitable that Xerox quickly determined that selling the copiers was a bad business model, because the entire cost of the copier could be paid off in a few months of rent. Xerox had no competition, huge demand, and a proprietary product. The product created so much cash flow that Xerox struggled to invest the money into the business. With a small portion of the profits, Xerox created the famed PARC research facility. As a result of Xerox's research efforts, consumers now enjoy the mouse, laser printer, Ethernet, PCs, graphical user interface (GUI), object-oriented programs, and amorphous silicon applications created by PARC.

Unfortunately, you can't generate superior margin by simply asking your customers to pay more. You have to earn it. Ask yourself, "Why does a customer pay more for an item than it costs to make it?" Here are some answers:

✔ **Access:** You can't buy gasoline at the refinery or lumber at the sawmill.

✔ **Branding:** Take a $29 pair of eyeglasses and slap Jennifer Lopez's name on the side and they transform into $129 glasses.

✔ **Convenience:** You can drive to Alabama and buy shrimp off the boat, but it's a long drive from New York.

✔ **Desire:** You don't need a vacation, but when you want one badly enough, you'll pay a premium.

✔ **Feelings:** That cup of Starbucks coffee should cost only $0.50, but it makes you feel *so* good that you pay much more.

✔ **Problem-solving:** That bandage may cost only a few pennies, but it's worth thousands of dollars if you're bleeding badly.

✔ **Proprietary features/patents:** The patent on the original Xerox 914 copier gave the company a 15-year stranglehold on the photocopier market. The iPhone leapfrogged other smartphones in feature set; it captured a large market share and sold for a significant price premium. Rolls-Royce aircraft engines have a turbine blade made from a secret super-strong material made by Rolls-Royce for their engines. Coca-Cola's secret formula assures that no other soft drink can taste like Coke.

✔ **Status:** The only difference between the top-of-the-line Camry and the cheapest Lexus is the L on the front — and $2,500.

✔ **Value chain:** Walmart manages portions of the value chain such as logistics more efficiently than the competition and enjoys better margin as a result. For instance, Walmart discourages the use of sales representative agencies as an added cost that must be passed to consumers. Walmart also manages inbound and outbound logistics with Swiss-like precision to avoid adding unnecessary distribution cost.

How effectively you employ these factors determines your margin. Of course, you aren't operating in a vacuum. These factors are relative to the competition. Your competitors are busy trying to accomplish the exact same thing — better margins. As they improve their business model, it becomes harder to improve yours. This never-ending treadmill can be frustrating. You need to outsmart and out-innovate your competition in order to consistently generate superior margin.

If you're looking for the gold standard of margin innovation, look no further than the Minnesota Mining and Manufacturing Company (3M). Growing from a humble sandpaper manufacturer, 3M is now a Fortune 100 global powerhouse with 84,000 employees in 65 countries. 3M's growth is a result of relentless innovation. The company historically encouraged its 10,000 researchers to spend 15 percent of their workday on a hobby or pet project. Even though this practice has waned at 3M, the result of this decades-long commitment to innovation is that 3M holds more than 20,000 patents and gets 25 percent of its revenue from products that are less than five years old. These new, innovative products carry a healthy margin too. Some of 3M's product innovations/inventions include:

✔ Masking tape

✔ Post-it Notes

- Reflective road signs
- Scotchgard fabric protector
- Scotch Tape (the first cellophane tape)
- Waterproof sandpaper

3M's innovations also include items not quite so familiar. Vikuiti is a multi-layer reflective polarizer film used in the LCD display market. It was the first prismatic brightness enhancement film (Vikuiti BEF) and multilayer based reflective polarizer film (Vikuiti DBEF). What that garbledegook means is that this product allows backlight to be used more effectively which, in turn, allows for longer life of cellphone and laptop batteries. 3M recently introduced the first electronic stethoscope with Bluetooth technology.

Dozens of factors, including the following, can increase your margin:

- **Access to resources:** Why are many high-tech companies located in Silicon Valley? They have access to employees, venture capital, and other much-needed resources there. Eastern Washington has aluminum smelting operations located there because of the abundance of cheap hydro-electric power.

- **Better clients:** Company A's clients don't pay their bills, are fussy, and never reorder without significant involvement from the sales force. Company B, in the same business, has clients who always pay their bills, aren't demanding, and typically reorder with no questions asked. Does Company B enjoy better margins than Company A? You bet. Check out Chapter 6 for details on customer attractiveness.

- **Control of the distribution channel:** It's rumored that Apple intentionally purchases a multiyear supply of the key components for their products to lock up 100 percent of the supply of the vendor. If competitors want to knock off an iPhone or iPad, they're forced to do so without being able to purchase components from the same suppliers. Apple's tactic not only slows down competitor innovation, but also forces the competition to source from second-best vendors.

- **First mover:** Being a first mover can help you create a category of one. No one knows whether the iPad will continue to sell well ten years from now. However, it's a fairly safe bet that Apple had an easier time selling iPads at a greater margin when they had the market all to themselves.

- **Focus:** Taiwan Semiconductor doesn't design or market computer chips. Taiwan Semi focuses solely on manufacturing chips. This extreme focus has resulted in Taiwan Semi being able to produce chips for less than nearly all its competitors.

✔ **Guts:** Mid-sized and small companies generally fear raising prices. Sometimes the easiest way to increase margins is to simply ask customers to pay more.

✔ **Innovation:** A company that can out-innovate its competitors always has an advantage and can typically make other higher-margin products. Part IV is full of in-depth information on innovation.

✔ **Location:** Customers pay a premium to buy the right item at the right place.

✔ **Lower cost structure:** Rather than build the same cookie-cutter store, Dollar General tries to locate in inexpensive locations. For instance, as CVS has moved many of its locations from strip malls to larger corner lots, Dollar General has moved into these old CVS locations cheaply.

✔ **Move up the value chain:** In most markets, some vendors create more value than others. Sometimes it's hard to understand why the market values some activities more than others, but it does. In many situations, the vendor closest to the end purchaser makes better margins. The Gap makes $5 selling a $10 t-shirt. The manufacturer of the t-shirt makes only $1. The company removing crude oil from the earth (Chevron, Exxon) and the company supplying oil field equipment/services (Oceaneering, Halliburton) tend to make better margins than the gasoline retailer or refiner. If you're stuck in the lower value added portion of the chain, moving to a more lucrative portion can be beneficial. For instance, IBM realized that selling software and services to customers is more profitable than selling hardware and shifted its focus to these better margin items.

✔ **Product mix:** When McDonald's first came out with its dollar menu, some franchisees refused to offer many of the items for $1. It's tough to run a business by selling a double cheeseburger that costs $0.65 for a buck. However, these franchisees eventually discovered that the cheap cheeseburgers got customers to buy high-margin French fries and sodas. Getting your customers to buy more of your high-margin items can make a big difference in total margin generated. See the later section, "Creating the right product mix: Gasoline, cigarettes, and soda," for more info.

✔ **Proprietary feature:** Something proprietary about your offering puts you in a category of one. Some portion of the market will always pay a premium for this feature. Chapter 2 tells you more about proprietary business models.

✔ **Strategic vendor:** Have you ever had a vendor you wanted to keep secret? Sometimes, having access to the right vendor can create a strategic advantage resulting in greater margin. Coca-Cola bottlers enjoy a strategic and protected relationship with Coca-Cola that allows them access to the syrup.

✔ **Strong brand:** Companies like Coach, BMW, Starbucks, Cisco, and Disney command strong premiums for their products versus the competition. See Chapter 7 for more on the benefits of a strong brand.

✔ **Vertical integration:** In many cases, vertical integration increases the total margin generated from a single sale. Integration could include expanding forward into your customer's markets to gain control of distribution channels or backward into your supply chain to reduce the power suppliers have over your company. An example of backward integration is a clothing manufacturer buying or starting a fabric company.

A company that has successfully integrated forward, and — more importantly — maintained vastly superior margins, is the sunglasses company Luxottica. Sunglass Hut was a strategic acquisition because it not only generated 80 percent of Luxottica's sales, but also accounted for 21 percent of the sales of a competitor, Oakley. The ensuing spat hurt Oakley's sales badly. Because Luxottica had already acquired brands like Armani and companies like LensCrafters and Ray-Ban, it was no surprise when Oakley was acquired by Luxottica. As long as the integration is strategic, it typically works.

Not all businesses have 90-percent margins. Your margin is based upon your competitors or industry. You can have a terrific business model with only a 10-percent margin, as long as your competitors have a 5-percent margin.

Gaining staying power from proprietary margin

Proprietary margin is the ability of your business model to make more money from the same customer than a competitor. You can accomplish this by

✔ **Getting the customer to pay more for a similar product of similar cost.** A cup of Starbucks coffee doesn't cost more than other coffees; it's branded and marketed better to command better margin per sale.

✔ **Capitalizing on revenue streams your competitors can't.** In the early 2000s, Best Buy made 60 percent of its profit by selling extended warranties. The massive volume of warranty-friendly products Best Buy sold led to a significant revenue stream.

✔ **Being creative.** Everyone wants a good deal when purchasing a car. This psychological need for a good deal drives where you shop and how much you'll pay.

When a car dealer sells you a car for "invoice," the dealer still makes money. The automotive companies and car dealers have many alternative revenue sources — like extended warranties, loan rate markups, volume bonuses, dealer incentives, floor plan allowances, and dealer fees. The dealer PACK is an ingenious invention that auto dealers use to boost their margins. The dealer adds up the total cost of running the business — utilities, rent, advertising, secretaries, interest expense, sweeping the parking lot, prepping cars for sale — you name it. The dealer calls this the PACK cost. When I went to accounting school, we called this overhead. They divide this "cost" figure by the number of total cars they expect to sell that year and maybe add a little to it for "cushion." The result, or the PACK, is the profit the dealer pays itself before determining sales commission (about $1,200–$1,600 per car). Hey, give them credit. PACK is an ingenious way to boost margins.

✔ **Having a leading brand *and* large volume.** Tide is the #1 selling laundry detergent by sales dollars and gallons sold. Guess what the least expensive detergent to produce is? Yep, it's Tide. Having an industry-leading brand and economies of scale in production leads to proprietary margin.

✔ **Using proprietary supplemental products.** The connectors, iPhones, and iPads are unique to those products. Apple creates proprietary margin when users need to replace chargers and cables.

Don't be discouraged if your business model doesn't have proprietary revenue. The business models of Anheuser-Busch InBev (makers of Budweiser) and Miller Coors (makers of Coors and Miller Lite) are nearly identical. Neither of these brewers has proprietary revenue streams, but that didn't stop InBev from earning profits of $7.96 billion in 2011 and Miller Coors from earning $4.9 billion the same year.

Making the most of each sale

In another life, I owned several Meineke Discount Muffler shops. Many times you would see two shops in the same town with very different average tickets (the amount spent per customer). One shop would have a $300 average ticket and another down the road would have only a $125 ticket. This metric was the best indicator of profitability in that industry and was directly indicative of the shops' overall profits. After a car is fixed, it's fixed for a long time. The customer is gone. You'd think that by being part of the same franchise, their business models would have been the same. But if you look at the monetization component, you see that store #1 generated more than double the profit from every sale than store #2. The ability to create significantly more revenue from the same potential customer was proprietary to store #1's business model.

Winning big by creating proprietary revenue streams

A *proprietary revenue stream* is a revenue source unique to your business model. By creating a proprietary revenue stream, you've figured out how to monetize something that your competitors haven't. As you can imagine, this isn't easy to do. However, if you can find one, a proprietary revenue stream is usually a big winner. Here are some examples:

- **Dallas Cowboys** owner Jerry Jones revolutionized the way the NFL made money. Jones added revenue streams like $30 million for Pepsi to become the official soft drink sponsor, Victoria's Secret stores in the stadium, sponsored club levels, 100,000-seat stadiums, and selling admission to watch a giant TV outside the stadium. Ironically, Jones missed the chance to sell the rights to the demolition of Texas Stadium. The city of Irving got Kraft Macaroni and Cheese to pay $150,000 for the privilege.

- **General Motor's OnStar** system not only helps sell GM cars, but also creates a proprietary recurring revenue stream as long as the car is in use. OnStar's premium plan costs $299 per year. General Motors may make more profit on a ten-year OnStar subscriber than on the sale of the car.

- **Greenlight,** the collectible car maker, spent years creating a loyal following. It turned this following into a collectors' club whose 5,000 members were willing to pay for special access, higher-end products, and events.

- **Hospital newborn wards** charge extra for live video feeds of the newborn to faraway relatives and offer high-end photography of your newborn in case you still have money left after paying the hospital bill.

- **iTunes** isn't a big moneymaker for Apple, but the portal has created a unique revenue stream.

- **JP Morgan Chase** holds billions of dollars in customer deposits. Rather than make money the old-fashioned (and risky) way by lending these deposits to consumers and businesses, JP Morgan Chase uses the money in complex trading operations. Despite a recent trading loss of 7.5 billion, Chase has outperformed most other banks' return on assets.

- **Movie studios** have been highly creative at creating proprietary revenue streams. Revenues from theater ticket sales continue to rise, but Hollywood hasn't stopped there. Movie properties are leveraged in dozens of ways, including DVD sales, character licensing, product placements in the movie, sequels, television rights, on-demand rights, hotel movies, digital streaming, toys, clothing, and more. Movies like Star Wars and Transformers bring in hundreds of millions of dollars from ticket and DVD sales and even more from toy and clothing licensing.

✔ **TiVo** sells digital video recorders and subscription services. While TiVo is helping you decide what show to record, it's also tracking what you watch. This data is collected and analyzed. When TiVo knows your preferences and viewing patterns, it sells targeted advertising on your TiVo to advertisers. You may have noticed this advertising when you hit the pause button.

Watching out for potential drags on margin

As you design your business model, focus on your product's positioning, marketing, and sales process without worrying excessively about competition. You don't win the race by looking backward. By the same token, completely ignoring the competitive landscape can adversely affect your model. Here are some factors that can drag down your margin:

✔ **Attractive market:** High potential markets attract competitors. Competition drives down margins. In the late 1990s, dozens of large companies rushed to the phone and data transport business, creating a world-wide glut of capacity. Many of these companies, such as Global Crossing and WorldCom, went bust. Today you see a piranha-like frenzy to create iPhone and Android apps. Plenty of companies, such as Zynga, are doing well, but it remains to be seen how many of these companies will have staying power.

✔ **Fast-changing technology:** Disruptive technology can be dramatically less expensive and can wreak havoc on margins. Blockbuster, BlackBerry, and the U.S. Postal Service have all had to deal with this issue.

✔ **Inconvenience:** Inconvenience could mean anything from a physical location off the beaten path to the inability of the customer to buy everything needed from you. Small vendors are experiencing this issue with large companies that refuse to buy from vendors with only one item they need. In fact, some vendors have been forced by companies like Walmart to sell to another of their vendors simply to streamline Walmart's buying process. One of my clients had a margin of 75 percent selling directly to Walmart, and its margin dropped to 35 percent after being forced to sell to the larger vendor.

✔ **Lack of integration:** In some instances, vertical integration by competitors can be a cost advantage for them and force your margins down. For example, Starbucks' Keurig-style coffee maker doesn't need to sell for a profit. The Verismo machine's purpose isn't to generate profits from its sale. The machine was designed to sell Starbucks coffee for home use. The Amazon Kindle tablet computer is reportedly sold for $5 less than it costs to make. Why? Because the Kindle is a portable store to purchase Amazon books and products.

✔ **Me-too product:** Products with no must-have features sell for much less.

✔ **Operational inefficiency:** If your operations are less efficient than your competition, you may need to lower margins to compensate.

✔ **Poor salesmanship:** Many a great business model calls for a sales price of $X but the under-skilled sales force sells it for $½X. Every dollar the salesperson discounts comes straight out of your margin.

✔ **Shrinking market demand:** Similar to excessive competition, a declining overall market lowers the tide for all boats. The next step is for one of your competitors to get desperate and lower pricing.

✔ **Superior buying power of competitors:** Generating superior margins is difficult if you buy a pallet of material at a time and your competitor buys a truckload.

✔ **Too many competitors:** There are only so many buyers. If too many competitors are chasing too few deals, prices tend to fall. Airlines, auto manufacturers, and granite countertop installers are all examples of markets with limited buyers.

Assessing Your Competition

Any competition drags down margins. Fighting for customers always leads to price/margin cutting. The only way to maintain high margins is to preemptively move to new and better markets before the competition gets intense.

The following sections tell you about three types of competitors: good, bad, and indirect.

Good competitors

Most competitors are good competitors. They act ethically, focus on marketing their own products without destroying yours, and act with long-term focus to maintain a healthy market for you both. You can build a good business in the face of good competition and even maintain a good relationship with your competitors.

Bad competitors

Bad competitors can make your life miserable and ruin your business model. Building a great business in the face of bad competition is difficult or impossible. Bad competitors fall into two categories: unethical and dumb.

Unethical competitors

- ✔ Engage in unfair business practices.
- ✔ Engage in predatory pricing practices.
- ✔ Sell items below cost for extended time periods.
- ✔ Attempt to unduly influence government officials.
- ✔ Exhibit monopolistic behavior.
- ✔ Engage in illegal practices, such as operating in violation of health and safety codes, hiring undocumented workers, toxic waste dumping, or paying less than minimum wage.
- ✔ Engage in pay-per-click fraud or post negative information on public sites like Wikipedia.

Dumb competitors

- ✔ Lower prices below sustainable levels to gain volume.
- ✔ Bad-mouth competition, hoping to gain business.
- ✔ Sell excess inventory to distributors to boost short-term sales (channel inventory).
- ✔ Sell against the competition instead of standing on their own product's merits (think politicians).
- ✔ Continue to pour organizational time and effort into overcrowded markets.
- ✔ Continue fighting even after the battle is lost.
- ✔ Employ poor sales techniques, like simply lowering prices, rather than looking for ways to add value.
- ✔ Are bad at accounting. You've met these types before. It takes X amount of business to reinvest in equipment, R&D, training, and overhead. Yet these types ignore the reality of accounting for all overheads, or set aside provisions to cover the long-term cost of being in business and wind up selling products barely above marginal cost. Yes, they'll go out of business eventually, but when and at what cost to you? It's best to help these competitors go out of business faster or to run from them.

Stay away from markets with bad competition. Dumb competitors rarely turn smart. If you started in a market with good competition but find the market now has bad competition, find a way to exit the market. Bad competition only leads to a war of attrition that no one wins and after the market has been damaged, it's a very hard place to come back from and make money.

Indirect competitors

Everyone has competition. You may be lucky enough to have no *direct* competitors in your niche, but everyone has indirect competition. Examples of indirect competition include the following:

- Gas stations compete with other gas stations but also with natural gas or electric vehicles.

- Gas stations also compete with alternative modes of transport, such as walking or bicycling.

- Gas stations also compete with non-consumption — simply not driving at all.

Generating Enough Total Margin Dollars

Generally, companies with better business models have superior margin versus their competition. Table 8-1 shows the profit per vehicle for several automakers in 2010. Which business model do you think is superior?

Table 8-1	Automakers' Profit Per Vehicle				
Automaker	Profit Per Vehicle	Vehicles Sold	Profit (Millions)	Profit Per Vehicle Rank	Total Profit Rank
Daimler	$3,316	1,170,000	3,880	1	4
BMW	$3,000	1,224,280	3,673	2	5
Renault	$1,741	1,668,615	2,905	3	6
Nissan	$1,500	3,088,298	4,632	4	3
Ford	$1,320	4,320,792	5,703	5	1
VW	$1,288	4,407,062	5,676	6	1
Honda	$833	3,152,197	2,626	7	7
Hyundai	$810	2,931,325	2,374	8	8
GM	$553	2,202,927	1,218	9	10
Tata	$400	803,322	321	10	12
Toyota	$349	5,496,346	1,918	11	9
Fiat	$292	1,853,282	541	12	11
Mazda	$154	1,307,540	201	13	13
Chrysler	($438)	1,085,211	(475)	14	14

Not all manufacturers listed.

From this data, it seems that BMW and Daimler (Mercedes-Benz) have the best business models. These models generate exceptional overall profits as well as industry-leading profit per vehicle.

Turning margin into profits

While the design of business models tends to focus on the gross margin generated, you must balance the total margin generated with your overhead expenses. It's possible to have outstanding margins and still have a poor business model. For example, suppose you create a $100 piece of software that you sell on the Internet that costs nearly nothing to manufacture/ distribute. So far, your business model is great; you have a 100-percent margin. What if you work full-time for your fledgling software company and sell only ten copies per year? You're working for $0.50 per hour. Ouch! Your business model needs excellent margin percentage plus enough total dollars of margin to be successful.

Solazyme has an interesting business model. The company makes synthetic oil from algae. Its proprietary process can produce products ranging from diesel fuel to $1,000/gallon cosmetic oil. The company's average gross margin is 92.2 percent. Sounds pretty good so far, right? However, because the company is in perpetual R&D mode, the cost of all those smart scientists is outpacing the margin generated. For now, Solazyme has a business model issue. As you can see from the stock market chart in Figure 8-1, the market agrees. The market was excited about the business model when the company went public, but has cooled off as the company has failed to turn a profit.

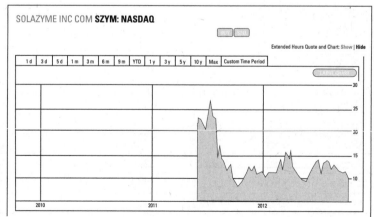

Figure 8-1:
Solazyme
stock price.

Creating the right product mix: Gasoline, cigarettes, and soda

Having the right product mix can be an important component of your business model. Most businesses have several product or service offerings. Some of these offerings have low gross margin, some have high gross margin. A business model that can successfully sell more of the high-margin items is significantly better than a business model that sells only the low-margin items.

I like to call this phenomenon *gasoline, cigarettes, and soda.* The typical corner gas station costs approximately $4 million in land, building, and equipment to build. This same gas station sells 1 to 2 million gallons of gasoline per year at a gross profit around $0.25 per gallon. If you run the math, that's $250,000 to $500,000 of gross margin before paying any expenses — such as rent, interest, utilities, employees, regulatory fees, and more. If you're thinking what I'm thinking, you're thinking that this is a lousy business model. However, gas stations also sell cigarettes, soda, chips, coffee, bottled water, candy, car washes, and so on.

Gas stations lose money pumping gas. Gas stations make excellent margins on everything but gas. Here are the margins on some of their best-sellers:

- ✔ **Bottled water:** 60-percent margin
- ✔ **Soda:** 80-percent margin
- ✔ **Candy:** 50+-percent margin
- ✔ **Cigarettes:** Best of all, a $0.75-per-pack profit on fast-moving cigarettes. A typical gas station turns the entire inventory of cigarettes in two days.

The key is for gas stations to maintain the right mix of gasoline, cigarettes, and soda. If the gas station fails to attract customers with its unprofitable gas, sales of profitable soda and cigarettes will suffer. If the gas station sells only gas, it generates insufficient gross margin to support the enterprise. The same holds true for your business. To maximize profitability, minimize sales of your lowest-margin items while maximizing sales of your highest-margin items.

Sounds simple right? It isn't! In many business models, the low-margin gasoline is the customer acquisition item. If the gas station prices gasoline $0.10 more per gallon than the station across the street, it fails to sell not only gas but also cigarettes and soda. Design your business model to ensure you sell more than just the low-margin gasoline.

Cutting through the razor and blade model

You may have heard of the razor and blade business model. Pioneered by King Gillette and his innovative safety razor, the model is still in use today by cable companies, cellphone carriers, inkjet printer manufacturers, and many more. When Gillette invented the safety razor, most men were shaving with a straight edge razor and hoping not to slice themselves open. The safety razor was a huge improvement over the straight edge. Gillette knew if he could get men to use safety razors, they would purchase replacement blades forever. The replacement blades had staggeringly high margins. Unable to sell his razors, Gillette found creative ways to get them into the hands of potential users for free.

Today, Gillette still uses the razor and blade model. Many 16-year-old boys find free Gillette razors in their mailbox. It's rumored that Gillette loses money on the sale of the razors, even when sold at retail. However, a Mach3 blade sells for $2 and costs $0.09 to manufacture.

Creating a Meaningful Cost Advantage

If you've ever had to compete with a company that can deliver the same thing as you for less, you've experienced the power of a meaningful cost advantage. When a company has a meaningful cost advantage, it has contrived a business model that's more efficient than the competition. This cost efficiency can be leveraged in the form of lower prices to the consumer in order to gain market share, to build a war chest to ward off competitive attacks, or in the form of higher margins.

Even more powerful is a business model combining a well marketed product delivered by a true low-cost provider. A true cost advantage is difficult to overcome, especially in a price-sensitive market. A company that can create a meaningful cost advantage is playing with a stacked deck. Some examples include:

- ✔ The most difficult offshore oil drilling costs as much as $50/barrel to produce versus Saudi Arabian oil costs at only $2/barrel to produce.

- ✔ Producers of plastics and fertilizer near cheap U.S. natural gas sources are currently enjoying prices three times lower than in China or Europe.

- ✔ Walmart's obsession with keeping operating costs low has resulted in the most efficient distribution system in the industry. Walmart can always sell a product for less than competitors, because it costs them less to purchase (volume) and distribute.

- Toyota created significant savings by adopting lean manufacturing principles before its competitors were forced to follow its lead.

- A software developer created a system to divide development into manageable pieces, allowing unpaid college interns to develop a new version of the product for free.

- Company stores or outlets that sell goods without distributors can shift margin from one division to another, creating margin subsidies.

You can create a cost advantage in many ways. Three of the most common methods are economies of scale, smart use of technology, and leveraging the value chain. (I cover each of these methods in the upcoming sections.) You can also create meaningful cost advantage by

- Developing superior purchasing power or ability. Companies like Walmart have a reputation for beating the lowest prices out of vendors.

- Selecting better vendors. Sometimes you can find an alternative vendor whose products are significantly cheaper than the industry norm.

- Hiring less expensive employees. This isn't a commentary on the benefits or detriments of low-wage employees. However, some companies have found operational methodologies that utilize lower-paid employees with equal effectiveness as their competitors' higher-paid employees.

   A software developer hires most of its staff directly out of college. Most competitors have no interest in recent grads because of the need to train and the time needed to get them up to full speed. This software company has created a training and selection process that allows it to effectively hire these lower-paid grads.

- Cultivating virtual work environments. Citibank used to rent large office buildings and fill them with thousands of customer service reps. Now Citibank leverages voiceover Internet technology to allow workers around the globe the ability to handle calls from their living room.

- Creating a superior process. McDonald's has consistently improved its operational processes in order to be more efficient than its competitors.

- Creating a culture of cost containment like Walmart.

- Working harder than your competitors. Creating a hard-working business culture can translate into a lower cost of operation.

- Controlling trade secrets, intellectual property, or patents. A manufacturer created a custom piece of testing equipment that increased throughput five times. Use of this machine lowered the cost of production $0.20 per unit. Because none of the competitors had the machine, they all had a higher cost of production.

Economies of scale

The most time-tested method of creating cost advantage is to create economies of scale. The great companies from the industrial revolution — railroads, steel, oil, banking, and automotive manufacturing — all utilized economies of scale. After a certain level of production, or scale, was achieved, significant cost savings or additional profits were achieved. These economies of scale acted as a barrier of entry for competition or as a profit buffer.

A small pharmaceutical company creates an innovative prenatal vitamin. Because the company is small, it can purchase only tiny quantities of the chemicals needed to produce the vitamins. At its current low volume, each bottle of vitamins costs the company $10 to produce. To be in line with the going market price, the company must sell the vitamins for $20 a bottle. With only a 50-percent gross margin, the small pharmaceutical company has little money to hire talented scientists and engage in additional research. The volume squeeze puts it at a competitive disadvantage. If the company can double sales volume, it can justify purchasing truckloads of chemicals instead of small pallets, reducing the cost per bottle of vitamins to $7 each, and greatly increasing the competitive position of the company.

Economies of scale can affect all aspects of a business, not just purchasing power. McDonald's 14,098 locations dwarf the next closest hamburger chain Wendy's 5,876 locations. Assuming each chain spends the same amount per location on advertising, McDonald's spends triple the amount Wendy's does promoting its burgers. This marketing economy of scale serves McDonald's in several ways. First, the average person sees a McDonald's ad three times more often than a Wendy's ad, which should lead to greater sales. Second, McDonald's has more locations at which to purchase hamburgers, so the advertising has a greater chance of pulling a consumer into a McDonald's. Third, the large marketing expenditure created by combining 14,000 locations creates a massive moat protecting McDonald's from competition.

The industrial revolution is over, and gone with it is some of the power of economies of scale. Today, businesses of all sizes can compete with large multinational corporations, particularly on the Internet. The Internet acts as a great equalizer, allowing small companies access to business resources previously reserved for large companies. The Internet allows businesses to

- ✔ Reach customers all around the world without the expense of a physical outlet.
- ✔ Market products very inexpensively.
- ✔ Attack previously unprofitable, tiny niche markets.

✔ Access vendors and talent from around the world.

✔ Operate virtual offices, eliminating the need for expensive overhead.

✔ Teleconference and videoconference for little or no money, eliminating the need for expensive travel.

By leveraging the Internet, companies of all sizes can remove the barriers of economies of scale.

When Amazon.com was launched, Jeff Bezos was operating out of his garage. Today Amazon boasts sales in excess of $50 million annually. Google was a school project of Serge Brin and Larry Page. Mark Zuckerberg was horsing around when he created Facebook in his dorm room. Some of today's largest and most profitable businesses started as tiny ventures that leveraged the Internet.

Smart use of technology

The use of technology can create cost savings and competitive advantage. Most business technology is simply codifying work being performed in an inexpensive fashion and moving the operations to a less expensive option. The Gutenberg press revolutionized books because it allowed for mass production of pages rather than hand copying. Computerized accounting software took the place of hand written ledgers and adding machines. Robotic welders at automotive plants work 24 hours a day and perform a perfect weld every time.

Good business models find a way to leverage technology to their competitive advantage. Consider these examples:

✔ Skype took a free ride on the Internet highway and created a premium soft phone product. The company was eventually sold to Microsoft for $8.5 billion.

✔ Although the urban legend that eBay was created to help the founder's fiancé sell her Pez candy dispensers isn't true, eBay did leverage emerging Internet technology to become the world's largest garage sale, and more.

✔ When the Procter & Gamble truck loaded with Pampers unloads at the Walmart warehouse, the diapers never touch a shelf. Walmart has created an elaborate system of conveyors that allow the Pampers to move from the supply truck directly to a truck headed to a Walmart store that needs the product.

✔ Companies who were early adopters of BlackBerry e-mail devices eliminated unnecessary delays, communication issues, and snafus. The improved communication and speed translated to competitive advantage for the users of the BlackBerry.

✔ Singer Esmée Denters started her career covering songs on YouTube. Her talent attracted the attention of Justin Timberlake, who asked Denters to open for him in London and subsequently signed her to his record label.

✔ Attorneys leveraged expensive cellphone technologies in the 1980s to turn drive time into billable hours.

Better value chain management

The value chain describes how firms strategically add activities and costs, making a product more valuable to the consumer. The more strategically and efficiently a firm can manage the value chain, the lower its costs and the greater its competitive cost advantage.

Professor Michael Porter, the inventor of value chain analysis, says that primary activities tend to drive the bulk of the value created for the customer. He describes primary activities as:

✔ Inbound logistics

✔ Operations

✔ Outbound logistics

✔ Marketing and sales

✔ Service

Support activities can drive value but tend to more often be cost centers. Support activities are:

✔ Firm infrastructure

✔ Human resource management

✔ Technology development

✔ Procurement

The interplay of these components drives customer value and cost, generating the firm's margin.

Porter identified ten cost drivers related to value chain activities:

- **Economies of scale:** The overhead costs of a business go up only slightly as volume increases. This reduces the overhead cost per item and creates economies of scale.

- **Timing of market entry:** Early entrants in markets are sometimes plagued by lack of resources and vendor quality. This handicap translates to a less efficient value chain and higher costs. Late entries to a market may find themselves competing with companies with well-established and more efficient value chains. This puts the late entry at a cost disadvantage.

- **Degree of vertical integration:** A firm that's vertically integrated has the ability to insource activities on the value chain rather than purchase them from a vendor. Because vendors typically charge a markup, the vertically integrated firm can avoid this markup and improve its value chain.

- **Ability to learn:** Learning can affect the value chain in several ways. Some companies learn faster than others. A speedy learning curve translates into a cost advantage. Some companies learn slowly. Japanese manufacturers benefitted greatly from adopting W. Edwards Deming's quality control techniques. Despite their obvious benefits, U.S. auto manufacturers took decades to adopt them.

- **Capability utilization:** A firm that fully utilizes all the capabilities it has paid to develop has a stronger value chain.

- **Interrelationships among business units:** In the 1970s, Greyhound Dial Corporation had business units producing soap and running a bus line. The large disparity in these business units hurt the company's value chain. Procter & Gamble (makers of Pampers, Dawn, Cascade, Swiffer, and Mr. Clean) is an $82 billion conglomerate with a tight relationship among the units. All P&G's products are sold to consumers in the categories of food, beverage, cleaning agents, and personal care.

- **Linkages among activities:** Purchasing new robotics can lower direct labor costs but increase technology costs. Advantages can be derived for linkages between activities within cascading value chains within the overall supply chain. For example, by integrating information systems between suppliers and customers, inventories can be leaned out without causing disruptions while releasing working capital. The driver for demand within the broader supply chain can be changed from a push system based on forecasts to a pull system based on actual demand.

- **Firm's policy of costs or differentiation:** Retailer Nordstrom has a reputation for providing a higher level of customer service than competitors. This policy adds costs and activities to Nordstrom's value chain.

✔ **Geographic location:** Glass manufacturer PPG tries to locate its factories within a few miles of its automotive customers' assembly plants. Because glass is bulky and expensive to transport, close proximity to customers makes PPG's value chain more efficient.

✔ **Institutional factors such as regulation, taxes, union activity, and so on:** Many companies located manufacturing facilities in Sun Belt states because of favorable business climates, lower taxes, and fewer unions.

If you can better manage your value chain, you can create competitive cost advantage. Many times, firms drive costs out of the value chain in creative ways instead of beating up vendors, employees, and everyone else for lower costs. For instance, you can remove costs from the value chain and improve competitive position by allowing customers to self-service issues on the Internet with FAQs or web-based access to parts/order databases, using video-based selling instead of salespeople, or delivering invoices via e-mail or not at all. Sometimes it's tough to translate a theory like the value chain to the real world. The following list shows some common methodologies used by businesses to accomplish these theoretical goals:

✔ **Eliminate costs:** Aldi has customers provide their own bags and return their shopping carts. This practice not only cuts cost but also completely eliminates functions. The best way to cut costs can be to simply eliminate them.

✔ **Outsource:** Outsourcing portions of the value chain can lower overall costs. IBM outsources parts distribution to FedEx. IBM has found that FedEx can perform the function with greater efficiency than it can. Entire industries have been created from the need for temporary staffing, professional employer organizations (PEOs, also known as employee leasing), personnel recruiters, payroll processing firms, logistics companies, IT service firms, and many more.

✔ **Insource:** Insourcing a previously outsourced function can improve the value chain on occasion. This dynamic typically occurs when a firm reaches economies of scale. The prior volume level made performing the function in-house inefficient, so it was outsourced. Now, volume allows the function to be performed by the company rather than a vendor, and significant savings can be achieved.

✔ **Customer self-service:** This is such a powerful dynamic it deserves a category to itself. Self-service gets a bad rap. When you think of self-service, you imagine yourself wandering around a store with no insight to help you. That's an example of customer self-service gone bad. However, customers benefit from self-service in many ways while it lowers your cost. ATM machines allow customers the benefit of 24/7 access to a virtual teller. The banks benefit because ATMs are less expensive to operate than a live teller. Many consumers prefer filling their own soda cup to waiting in line for an employee to fill it for them. The customer benefits with ease and convenience of self-service and the restaurant with labor and operational cost savings.

✔ **Transparency:** Adding transparency can lower costs. The entire travel industry was decimated by transparency. Up until the 1990s, consumers had to use travel agents to find flight schedules and costs. The Internet provided access to this information to all consumers. By allowing consumers transparency into the formerly proprietary system, the travel value chain was permanently altered.

✔ **Consolidation of vendors:** Many large corporations have reduced the total number of suppliers from thousands to hundreds. These companies found the value created from so many additional vendors was less than the cost of managing them.

✔ **Collapsing the value chain:** Political reporter Brian Howie was a long-time beat reporter for a major newspaper. The value chain to get Howie's writing to consumers included a massive newspaper staff, printing presses, newspaper delivery, and more. Now Howie writes a subscription blog and eliminates much of the old value chain.

Cost reduction does not equal strategic cost advantage. Example: You find a way to trim five percent from your freight costs. How long before your competitors discover the same trick? Temporary cost reduction does *not* lead to strategic cost advantage. Use your creative talents to reconfigure the value chain rather than focus only on cost reduction.

Corporate culture is part of your value chain

Ross Perot successfully built Electronic Data Systems into one of the world's largest IT firms. Perot sold EDS to General Motors in 1984 for $2.5 billion. As a member of the General Motors board, Perot clashed with the existing General Motors culture. Perot was a get-it-done kind of guy, and General Motors was a huge bureaucracy. After Perot's buyout, he was quoted as saying:

"The General Motors system is like a blanket of fog that keeps these people from doing what they know needs to be done. I come from an environment where, if you see a snake, you kill it. At GM,

if you see a snake, the first thing you do is go hire a consultant on snakes. Then you get a committee on snakes, and then you discuss it for a couple of years. The most likely course of action is — nothing. You figure, the snake hasn't bitten anybody yet, so you just let him crawl around on the factory floor. We need to build an environment where the first guy who sees the snake kills it."

Can you image the unnecessary layers of cost present at General Motors at that time? Creating a *get-it-done* culture can translate into a better value chain.

Creating Valuable Recurring Revenue Streams

All revenue isn't equal. During my lifetime I've bought 300 quarter pounders, ten cars, two houses, and one engagement ring. All the companies who sold me these items put considerable effort into selling me the first one. From a repeating revenue perspective, McDonald's is doing much better than the company that sold me the engagement ring. When my 1995 Ford Taurus lease was up, I simply went and bought a 1998 Taurus — the world's easiest sale. Your business model should try to leverage easy sales too.

Business models with built-in repeating revenue have an advantage over models in which you must fight for one sale, and then you never see the customer again. A customer of mine sells replacement windows. When a house is old enough to need new windows and good replacements are installed, no one ever buys again. On the flip side, I started using Crest toothpaste when I was three years old, and I still use it. The sale to that three-year-old yielded hundreds of recurring purchases. Examples of businesses with strong repeating revenue include the following:

- ✔ **Accounting firms:** After a business teaches its accountants the business's ins and outs, the inconvenience of changing firms tends to exceed any small price increases. Many clients stay with the same firm for decades.

- ✔ **Cellphones, cable, and utilities:** It's tough to shut off your cable or phone, so customers tend to stay for very long tenures.

- ✔ **Health clubs:** They enjoy strong ongoing revenue after the initial sale.

- ✔ **Sales rep firms:** Many sales reps get five percent of the sales to the accounts they land. Usually, much work is required to generate the initial sale. However, nowhere near as much work is needed to retain the customer, yet they still continue to get five percent of the sales.

- ✔ **Software-as-a-Service providers:** SaaS providers like `Salesforce.com` are heavily integrated into the customer's operation, so the revenue tends to continue for long periods.

Try to emulate the successful practices of these industries in your business model.

Repeating revenue lowers sales cost

There's a fine line between repeating revenue and recurring revenue. My repeat purchases of Crest toothpaste are repetitive but not recurring. Because I'm not contractually bound to purchase Crest, the revenue is repeating. For purposes of the business model, you should look at the *likelihood* the customer will repurchase and not worry as much about the contract. Contracts can be broken; my bond with Crest is less likely to break.

The reason repeating revenue is so desirable is the *market once, sell many* aspect. This dynamic lowers the overall cost of sales and makes the business model more attractive. An accounting firm may spend $5,000 marketing for a new $20,000/year client. This is a hefty marketing cost if the client stays only one year, but if the client stays 20 years, the marketing cost drops from 25 percent of sales to 1.25 percent.

When evaluating your business model, look at the lifetime margin generated from the customer versus the marketing and sales cost.

$5,000/year sales × 50% margin = $2,500 margin per year

5-year average client tenure × $2,500/year = $12,500 lifetime margin

$1,000 marketing and sales expense to acquire client ÷ $12,500 lifetime margin = 8% marketing cost

Traditionally, repeating revenue businesses have lower cost of marketing than one-time-sale businesses.

When recurring revenue really isn't

Many businesspeople think of recurring revenue as perpetual revenue; it's not. The business model community places a premium on recurring, contractual revenue because it feels like a warm, safe blanket. The fact is recurring revenue is almost always finite in term. Consider the following:

- ✔ Eventually I will get old and quit my health club. The club may get 35 years out of me, but not 150 years. The membership dues are finite.

- ✔ Plenty of companies go bankrupt. Someone signed a long-term contract with Enron in July 2001 and watched the once-valuable contract turn worthless as Enron filed bankruptcy that fall.

- ✔ Big companies can, and do, break contracts they don't like, especially those with small companies. What are you going to do, sue them? Don't bother; the only winner in these cases is the lawyers.

- ✔ New technology comes along and obsoletes you or changes customer preferences. For examples, consider BlackBerry, landlines, video rental, 1960s milkmen, and blacksmiths, just to name a few.

One-time sale leads to recurring revenue

Wheelabrator is a leader in the metal parts cleaning industry. A Wheelabrator is bigger than your car and costs more than $100,000. The machine automates the cleaning of metal parts by spraying them with tiny BB-like metal called shot. Critical to the operation is a giant rubberized or metal belt with holes that allows the shot to fall into a collector and be recycled to the fan blade. You can probably imagine the beating this belt takes getting pounded by metal BBs all day. Guess where you have to purchase this several-thousand-dollar belt? Correct. Wheelabrator.

The machine itself is an unattractive one-time sale, but the recurring and captive purchases of the belts are highly profitable and very low cost of sales.

Don't assume your repeating revenue will last forever; be pragmatic. Guess a finite term your customers will buy, and don't presuppose that they'll stay forever. That's a bad bet.

Sometimes businesspeople assume a recurring revenue sale automatically has better collectability. Just because you booked ten years of revenue doesn't mean you'll collect it. Unfortunately, lots can go wrong — adverse shifts in your customer's market resulting in difficulties or even bankruptcy, legal shenanigans, or a botched delivery. The same rules apply to recurring revenue as all other sales — your receivables are only as good as the customer's willingness and ability to pay.

Avoiding Pitfalls

In order to maximize the benefit and staying power of your business model, ensure that your revenue model or cost advantage will work for the long haul. Avoiding a few subtle pitfalls can be the difference between success and failure.

Making sure you own the customer

You may be asking, "How can I own my customer?" Make sure the customer's primary allegiance is to you. The firm in control of the customer relationship dictates the terms and makes the bulk of the profit in the value chain.

Many firms contribute to the manufacturing and marketing of automobiles: component manufacturers, automotive assemblers like Toyota, Madison Avenue ad agencies, and car dealers. But who owns or controls the bulk of the buyer's loyalty? In the case of an automobile, several companies influence the buyer's loyalty. Many component manufacturers have strong brands that influence buyers — like Michelin tires, Bose sound systems, Eddie Bauer trim packages, or Cummins turbo diesel engines. Car manufacturers like Chevrolet, Ford, Toyota, Honda, and Dodge have strong brand loyalty as well. Local dealerships finalize the sale and have customers loyal to them too.

Examine the purchase of a pickup truck. If I prefer Toyota trucks, Cummins diesel engines, and my best friend sells Chevys, which car do I buy? Said another way, which one of these companies controls the relationship with me the most and can turn that influence into a purchase of its product versus the others? Cummins engines aren't available in Toyota vehicles. If this is my primary loyalty, Cummins wins, Toyota loses. If my loyalty is to my friend, I buy a Chevy even though I can't get my Cummins engine or my Toyota model. Everyone makes these choices every day. Consider these examples:

- ✔ Who owns the gasoline customer: Shell, Exxon, the oil company brand, or the convenient gas station with reasonably priced gas? I bet you're like me. Convenient station wins.

- ✔ If you prefer Intel chips in your laptop, would you buy a brand you like with an AMD chip? Some people won't. In this case, Intel controls the client, not the laptop company. This is an important distinction because Intel doesn't make the final sale. You don't need to deal directly with the customer to be the one in control.

- ✔ I bet I'm not the only one who has chosen not to eat lunch at a fast food restaurant because it has Pepsi instead of Coke. Yes, Coca-Cola occasionally controls where I eat food.

The company that controls the customer has the ability to dictate terms to others in the channel and, more importantly, grab the big piece of the margin pie. If you find yourself on the wrong end of this dynamic, you'll find the *true* owner of the customer continues to demand better and better terms from you. Walmart is infamous for squeezing vendors for better and better terms. Walmart can get away with it because vendors know Walmart controls the customer, and without Walmart, a large portion of their volume disappears.

Several years ago, Walmart and Procter & Gamble found themselves in a mini war over this issue. Walmart nicely rejected a P&G price increase. Even though Walmart represented 20 percent of P&G's sales, P&G took exception. P&G brands comprise around five percent of Walmart sales, but more importantly, have huge brand loyalty. Imagine shopping at Walmart only to find the store didn't carry Scope, Crest, Tide, Pampers, Swiffer, Gillette, Ivory, Olay, and Mr. Clean. Walmart realized P&G had just as much control of the customer as it did and capitulated.

Getting creative with accounting

Accounting may seem like a science, but you have plenty of room for creativity. When designing a business model, decide how to account for costs that determine margin. Decisions such as what costs are variable, fixed, or even exist affect how you think about your model. How you think about your model affects how aggressively you market and price your offering. These decisions, in turn, affect the performance of your model.

Take the business model of a ladder manufacturer. Twenty years ago a decent seven-step ladder cost $20. That same ladder sells for $80 today. Granted, aluminum is more expensive, but what's really gone up is the cost of lawsuits. When the ladder manufacturer conceived its business model many years ago, it probably set the cost of legal protection at 0.5 percent of sales — or just ignored it. A few big lawsuits later, the manufacturer realized the business model was flawed and adjusted the sales price upward to properly account for lawsuits.

Your business model can appear significantly better or worse depending on how you choose to categorize expenses and revenues. Over-conservatism and pushing every conceivable cost against direct margin makes the model look less profitable than it probably is. Under-conservatism — like not budgeting capital equipment replacement or research/innovation — artificially inflates the prospects of the model. Accounting may seem like a science, but decisions like these are subjective rather than objective. How you choose to account for the ongoing costs of the business can impact your business model. The following list shows some specific ways your accounting practices can affect the way you think about your business model and run your business:

- Do the ladder manufacturer's legal costs count as overhead or direct cost of goods? Accounting for the legal costs in direct margin affects the business model more than accounting for them in overhead. That's not to say the affect is good or bad, it just has a bigger impact.

- Consider the price of a postage stamp. As the postal service grapples with previously ignored pension liabilities, the price of a stamp has skyrocketed.

- How should an airline account for the massive cost of engines and airframes? Should it add $25/ticket to cover the cost or add a cost per mile? This decision affects pricing, margin, and competitive position.

- How should obsolescence be accounted for? For instance, software products need to work on new platforms (iPad, Windows 8). What funds the development cost? If you account for the cost of development as a direct cost of goods — in other words, $10 per unit sold — you'd think your cost per unit is higher. If you treat the development as an overhead cost, you may be lulled to sleep by your overstated margin.

- How should you account for sunk costs like unused capacity? Do you treat it like it's free, because it's already paid for? This approach can create a financial free-rider problem. Do you allocate this cost the same way as other products? This approach can overly allocate cost and make the model look less profitable than it actually is.

✔ Artificial subsidies come in dozens of forms and can be accounted for in many ways.

- What makes the profit on a value meal? Is it the French fries, the soda, or the hamburger?

- Sally moonlights as an electrician. She makes $50/hour, which is more than her day job pays. Sally debates quitting her day job and opening her own electrical contracting business. However, Sally needs to account for all the free-riding. She currently has no rent, because she works from home, and her day job takes care of her expenses. After these subsidies are removed, much more pressure will be placed on the business model.

- Sears is spinning off its Hometown Stores as a separate entity. This unit has been one of the few profitable ones for Sears. How much of the profitability was due to piggybacking on Sears' buying power, operational infrastructure, and advertising? As a pure standalone entity, will it remain profitable?

Believe it or not, it's possible to make money in the airline business. Fuel costs only amount to 40 percent of the fare paid. Add another 25 percent cost of goods for all employees, including pilots, and the formula looks good. But wait; don't forget the cost of all those airplanes and the retirees. In 2010, U.S. Air's pilot cost per active seat mile was a reasonable $0.61, but the cost per active seat mile for ex-pilots was $1.40 (2.3 times more). How airlines account for pension costs affects their pricing. If they account for these costs conservatively, pricing is uncompetitive. Seats are unfilled and heavy equipment investments are underutilized, creating losses. The decision on how to account for pension costs can greatly affect the airline's business model.

Technology: Killing margins fast

Just like a strategic investment in technology helped Walmart leapfrog competitors, technological change can wreak havoc on your margins. This disruption could appear in several forms:

✔ **Superior technology:** Superior technology adopted by your competitors that improves their existing processes. Examples include customer relationship software, mobile asset management, and RFID.

✔ **New technology:** New technology that replaces or radically changes business processes. Travel agencies still exist, but Internet self-booking sites like Expedia and Priceline have eliminated most of the profit agencies used to make on airline tickets and hotel nights. Kodak continued to make money for 20 years after digital cameras were introduced, but the margin generated from film sales disintegrated over time.

✔ **Freemiums:** Using technology for a freemium model. Technology can drive out so much of the traditional cost of an item that a savvy competitor may convert an item the industry has typically charged to a free giveaway to entice other paid sales (freemium). This dynamic has happened in the following industries:

- **Printing:** Vistaprint gives away free business cards as a freemium in order to gain more profitable orders for other print products.

- **Newspapers:** With tons of free content available on the Internet, traditional newspaper publishers have struggled to maintain margins. Major large-city publications are giving away Sunday editions of the paper, which they used to charge for.

- **Advertising:** Today's younger generations spend nearly as much time watching videos on YouTube as on TV. The problem advertising companies face is 25 percent of television viewing time is spent watching ads. On the Internet, only 3 percent of the user's time is spent looking at ads.

- **Software:** Tired of paying $100 for the latest copy of Windows? Switch to Linux, it's free. Don't feel like upgrading Quicken? Try mint.com. Free alternative software programs exist, and more are developed every day.

✔ **Transparency:** Transparency kills margins. Transparency isn't reserved for the Internet, but the Internet makes transparency easy and cheap. Thanks to this dynamic, you now have

- Vendors holding online eBay-style auctions for the privilege of becoming a vendor. May the lowest bid win!

- Easy public access to bid documents so all competitors can see everyone else's computations.

- Websites like Nextag that provide quick price comparisons for dozens of vendors.

- Showrooming. Mobile applications like Amazon's Price Check allow consumers to scan product barcodes in stores and instantly compare the price to offers on Amazon — and then they can push a button to buy it on Amazon while standing in front of the same item in the store. This practice has become so prevalent that many retailers, including Target and Best Buy, have had to cut margins and offer Internet price-matching promises.

High volume sellers on Amazon pay tens of thousands of dollars per month for sophisticated software to insure their products are $0.01 lower than the rest. Some items, like DVDs, are very price sensitive and the lowest price ensures significantly more sales — and lousy margins.

Chapter 9

Monetization through Sales Performance

. . . .

In This Chapter

▶ Identifying and working on common sales problems

▶ Knowing the value of marketing in relation to sales

▶ Creating a proven process to turn a prospect into a paying customer — again and again

. . . .

*O*ccasionally, a potentially great business model falls prey to a poor sales system. Every product needs to be sold. That doesn't mean sold by a person — just sold. In order for your business model to be successful, you need to create a sales system to finalize the marketing process that turns customer needs into cash in your pocket.

This chapter discusses how to create a proven and repeatable sales process to ensure that your marketing concepts turn into sufficient quantities of actual sales.

It's difficult to imagine a world without the light bulb. Imagine living in the 1880s, before buildings and homes were safely and easily lit. Back then, people used candles and gas lamps to illuminate buildings. It would seem that the easiest sale ever was to sell a cheaper, easier, and better way to illuminate. It wasn't. No one would install Thomas Edison's light bulbs because they were afraid light bulbs would burn down the building. Ironic, isn't it? In order to get people to try light bulbs, Edison had to install lighting in a New York office building for free. The point: Nothing sells itself, not even the greatest invention of the century.

Closing the Deal

You can create an excellent product, pick the right market niche, and have an excellent marketing program, but none of it matters if you can't sell it. Every product needs to be sold. Even the best-conceived products can fall victim to a sales execution issue. Most sales conversion issues fall into three categories: excessive sales cost to acquire a new customer, significantly underestimating the difficulty of the sales process, and difficulty making repeat sales.

Obtaining customers for an unreasonable cost

To have a strong business model, the cost of sales versus the margin generated must be reasonable. For example, a computer router manufacturer sees the growth of the home wireless networks as attractive and sells a product to a big box retailer like Best Buy. The retailer promises big sales, so the router manufacturer cuts margins significantly to only $20 per router. However, the router manufacturer underestimates the support needs of technically challenged customers. The customer support per router amounts to $7 of the $20 margin per router. At only $13 per router margin, the organization can't sustain this sales channel.

Groupon has built a multibillion-dollar business helping retailers find new (or hopefully new) customers. For instance, Groupon asks a restaurant to offer a 50-percent discount on a meal. The restaurant wins because hundreds of new buyers are exposed to the restaurant and become repeat customers. The businesses using Groupon to acquire new customers, however, have been offering significant pushback. Here's why:

- ✔ After the 50-percent discount, the retailer splits the sale with Groupon. If a restaurant offers a $20 meal for a $10 Groupon, the restaurant receives only $5 for what used to be a $20 meal. Of course, the cost of the meal stays the same for the restaurant and may create an unprofitable transaction.

- ✔ Many of the Groupon purchasers may be existing customers. Now the restaurant has cannibalized a $20 meal into a $5 meal.

- ✔ Many of the new customers are ultra price sensitive and not particularly loyal. They're willing to try new places for half price, but they won't return for full price later. They'll just buy a Groupon for a different restaurant.

Underestimating sales difficulty

Sometimes, business model architects underestimate the difficulty of the sales process. When you spend so much time and effort conceiving your offering, planning the marketing, and designing all the operational details, it's easy to fall in love with your baby, and it becomes difficult to see things objectively. This difficulty can translate into overestimating the ease of the sales process. When this happens, the company can end up with a high cost of customer acquisition or find that the product is far too difficult to sell to have a viable business model.

MULEKICK

The Groupon test

Many businesses have had a positive experience on Groupon. Many have not. If your product is high margin and you'll expose your offer to lots of new customers, Groupon is great. If you operate a lower margin business, such as a restaurant, you may be better off looking at the underlying reason you need Groupon.

I call this the Groupon test. Many businesses using Groupon are desperate enough to take the deal even though getting 25 percent of the regular sales price makes little economic sense. Why are these businesses so desperate? They can't acquire enough customers through their own marketing and need Groupon to help. Instead of selling their soul, these businesses should tune up their marketing. When was the last time you saw a Starbucks Groupon? Well-marketed businesses don't need Groupon.

When Walmart expanded into Germany, it figured its finely tuned U.S. business model would easily conquer competitors. Walmart's analysis showed that it could save customers money with its low-cost model. Despite lower pricing, Walmart failed miserably in Germany. Pundits enumerate dozens of theories why: Germany was too "green" for Walmart, Germany has a pro–labor union culture, Germany is anti-American when it comes to name-brand retailers, or German consumers prefer small neighborhood stores.

Whether you're Walmart or Bob's Mart, underestimating the difficulty of selling your product can radically disrupt your business model.

Assuming repeat sales will come easily

When most people are designing a business model, they assume that repeat customer sales are easy. Most of the time, they are. But take an objective look at the difficulty of resale when designing your business model. Don't just assume the customer will re-purchase with little or no effort. The consequence of overestimating the ease of resale is over-inflation of your anticipated margin. In this scenario, you'll believe that you're making much more margin than you actually are. This problem cascades into other aspects of your business model, as follows:

- ✔ You could overspend on fixed assets/costs because you believe the additional margin exists.

- ✔ You could decide to spend on additional direct costs because you have the margin available. For instance, buying better coffee beans to improve the quality of the product.

✔ You could under-invest in your sales force.

✔ You could lose sales volume to a competitor who better assesses the resale process.

I'll bet the people at Comcast are frustrated with this dynamic. For 20 years, when someone switched their service to Comcast, the company enjoyed a long uninterrupted tenure. As competition with Dish TV and DirecTV intensified, Comcast has been forced to offer incentives like lower pricing and free hardware to existing customers to entice them to stay.

Take a hard, objective look at your resale process. Very few products have a no-cost, automatic resale. A little effort and money allotted toward reselling can go a long way. Better to overestimate the difficulty of resale than underestimate it.

Marketing Beats Sales

There's nothing wrong with an old-fashioned sales process. However, from a business model perspective, products that can be sold primarily through marketing are preferred over products that require a blood-and-guts sales process. Procter & Gamble convinced me to buy Crest through marketing 40 years ago, and it's never had to sell me since.

For many years, Kirby sold its vacuum cleaners via a massive door-to-door sales force. The vacuum cleaners were expensive, so margins were good. However, the turnover and perpetual training of new salespeople had to weigh on margin significantly. Dyson, on the other hand, relied on a few highly differentiated features of the product and good marketing. In only ten years, Dyson captured 23 percent of the U.S. vacuum cleaner market with a product costing double that of previous industry leader Hoover.

Forget which brand of vacuum cleaner you like for a moment and ask yourself, "Which business model is better: Dyson's or Kirby's?" Before you answer, don't let the difficult nature of the door-to-door Kirby model dissuade you. If the thought of door-to-door selling turns your stomach, that isn't relevant. What's relevant is the strength of the business model and its ability to make money. That said, the Dyson model is better. The Dyson model is better because marketing usually beats sales.

Marketing is far more controllable than sales. Marketing is far more predictable than sales. Marketing is more scalable than sales. Marketing has more variable cost and less fixed cost than sales. As you design your business model, lean toward marketing and not sales.

Creating a Proven and Repeatable Sales Process

Your product must have a proven and repeatable sales process. This fact may seem obvious, but you must be able to clearly communicate the road-map of how you'll turn a prospect into a paying customer.

The most common trap that business model designers fall into when they're trying to create a proven sales process is having a non-duplicable sales process. A common example of a non-duplicable process occurs in the consulting world. Sally leaves the corporate world to become a consultant. Because Sally is a gifted businesswoman, many of her friends and colleagues value her services. She immediately signs several of these people as clients and builds a healthy practice. Sally works for several years serving these clients, and then the projects end. All her previous customers were people Sally spent years developing relationships with. Now Sally is out of folks who know, like, and trust her, and she's stuck selling to the rest of the world. Sally has no process to sell people who haven't seen the quality of her work. Until Sally finds a way to sell her services to complete strangers, she doesn't have a proven and repeatable sales process.

Many mid-sized businesses have a proven sales process, but only the owner or the select sales superstar can execute it. This is non-duplicable as well. Bob creates a better mousetrap. The product fills a much-needed niche and has many advantages over the competition. Unfortunately, the market doesn't seem to care. Out of Bob's ten-person sales force, only the two highest skilled salespeople can sell a reasonable amount of product. Bob's solution to this problem is to build a sales force of ten superstars instead of only two. Bob is wasting his time. This is the *selling ice to Eskimos* issue. Bob is effectively saying, "If I had nothing but salespeople who were capable of selling ice to Eskimos, we wouldn't have a problem." Of course, Bob is forgetting that highly talented salespeople who can sell anything to anyone are highly compensated. Bob hasn't budgeted that high cost into his business model. On top of that, there aren't enough highly talented salespeople in the market to enable Bob to successfully hire ten of them. The problem isn't the talent of Bob's sales staff, it's the marketability of Bob's product. When Bob addresses this core business model issue, he won't have a problem with the sales staff. In order to qualify as a proven and repeatable sales process, an average salesperson can sell an acceptable volume of product.

EMC Corporation is a worldwide leader in enterprise storage solutions. Founded in 1979 during the peak of IBM's Big Blue days, EMC faced a serious uphill battle convincing buyers to switch from IBM. After all, no one ever got fired for buying IBM. The company knew it would be a very difficult sale, but also understood that it couldn't afford to pay a squadron of superstars. The company adopted an innovative strategy to deal with the significant uphill battle of fighting the Goliath, IBM. Based in the Boston area, the company hired recent college graduates who were also ex-athletes. The logic was that these ex-athletes were used to fighting difficult battles and wouldn't shy away from a fight with IBM. In addition, the company specifically picked salespeople not yet familiar with the "no one ever got fired buying IBM" dynamic. The company trained the staff on the benefits of EMC storage versus IBM's older technology and convinced/brainwashed them that there was absolutely no reason anyone would buy the older IBM technology over EMC's superior solution. This crazy plan worked and EMC is a $20 billion business today.

Chapter 10

Making Your Business Model Last

*U*p to this point, you have found a great market for your product, created a niche, picked quality customers, and found a way to sell your product for a profit. Great job! Now it's time to find a way to make it last.

Business would be much easier without those pesky competitors. You come up with a great business model, and they steal all your great ideas. Unfortunately, competitors emulating your best practices won't go away, but you can mitigate the adverse effects of competition by creating sustainable competitive advantages. It also helps to out-innovate the competition and to avoid pitfalls. (I cover these topics in Chapter 11.) Business models that leverage these factors have more success than those that don't.

In this chapter I show you how to protect your business model from competitors and keep it humming for a long time. By fully understanding and then fine-tuning your competitive advantage, you can complete the building of a strong business model.

Creating Meaningful Competitive Advantage

Competitive advantage is a complex and far-reaching concept. In the interests of keeping it simple, *competitive advantage* is what keeps your business model strong and your competitors at bay. In order to have a solid and durable business model, you *must* always work on having some form of meaningful competitive advantage. Without it, your business doesn't have long-term staying power.

I discuss many of the classic aspects of competitive advantage in Chapters 6, 7, and 8. I'll spare you the duplication. Your competitive advantage is the sum of all the aspects of your business model (core competencies and culture) that your competitors *wish* they could copy, *but can't.* Your advantage can be as simple as

- ✔ Doing business in a better or different way that customers appreciate — like Southwest Airlines' fun-loving staff.
- ✔ Having a great location on a busy suburban corner or on Wall Street.
- ✔ Finding a better way to make your widget, which makes it unique or saves cost.
- ✔ Keeping your website's homepage clean and simple, like Google's.
- ✔ Keeping it simple like 37 Signals, who insists its software products be so simple to use, they don't require a manual.
- ✔ Owning the formula or key process, like Coca-Cola.
- ✔ Having exclusive distribution rights in a protected area.
- ✔ Know-how. If you're the only mechanic in town who can fix a Model A Ford, you have a competitive advantage.
- ✔ Leveraging key relationships. The senator in charge of approving your project is your former college roommate, huh?
- ✔ Being first to a market and grabbing (and defending) a large share, like Apple's iPad or Dippin Dots.
- ✔ Brand loyalty. Loyalty to your product can go a long way toward creating competitive advantage. Think Google among search engines, Tide among detergents, and Listerine among mouthwashes.

Often, your competitive advantage will arise from a combination of factors, which brought together, enable you to outwit the competition. Of course these factors, or at least the way in which you combine them, must be unique to you, and many may have relevance to your cost structure or how strongly you compete within your industry. The real issue is whether you have enough factors that truly matter to the customer and motivate them to want to do business with you consistently rather than with a competitor.

If you're first to market (competitive advantage #1) with an exclusively distributed product (competitive advantage #2) that uses a proprietary manufacturing process (competitive advantage #3), but the product features are unimportant to the customer, none of the advantages matter. Sometimes popular U.S. brands taken overseas flop despite their competitive advantage at home. Best Buy and Disney failed in Europe while Coca-Cola and McDonald's succeeded.

Leveraging intellectual property

If you buy into the premise that competitive advantage is created by out-smarting the competition, then *smarts* are the key component to creating and maintaining your competitive advantage. Another word for business smarts is *intellectual property* (IP). Intellectual property isn't just patents and trademarks; it's every aspect of your business that you've applied your smarts to. It could be something as simple as a unique training method or a great marketing idea.

Everyone is in the intellectual property business

You may not consider yourself a student of business theory, but here's one of those highfalutin theories that's important: Everyone is in the intellectual property business. Every business has core competencies, secrets, pro-cesses, brainpower, talent, organizational wisdom, and tricks of the trade that equate to IP. Your intellectual property may include

✔ Patents, trademarks, and copyrights.

✔ Unpatented ideas or processes.

   Colonel Sanders' secret 11 herbs and spices formula isn't patented. Instead, Yum Brands uses an ingenious system to protect the formula. Ingredients are shipped to Yum-controlled facilities marked "Secret Ingredient #1," "Secret Ingredient #2," and so on. They are then mixed in the correct proportions and placed in a bag marked "11 Herbs and Spices" before being shipped to restaurants.

✔ An in-house sales training program that consistently turns raw young recruits into productive salespeople.

✔ Personal or organizational connections.

✔ Organizational wisdom. In the late 1990s, large corporations spent bil-lions on knowledge management systems designed to hold and save organizational knowledge. Imagine how much IP is lost when a research scientist retires. These systems were designed to mitigate that loss.

✔ Better ways of doing business, including superior processes, use of human resources, or technological improvement — like Southwest Airlines' point-to-point system, team trucking, or custom software.

✔ Marketing prowess. Steve Jobs had a knack for creating winning products. This significant IP will be difficult to replace at Apple.

✔ Your brand. A strong brand is a significant intangible asset of your business.

✔ Being the first to use and leverage emerging technology. The technology doesn't need to be ultrahigh tech. Ray Kroc saw the potential of the milkshake machine early; use of this technology was key at McDonald's.

After you realize your *real* business is building and growing your intellectual property, you can focus on what *really* makes you money — your ever-growing IP. The faster and better you can grow your organizational IP, the stronger your competitive advantage.

As the developed world moves from an industrial-based economy to a knowledge-based economy, the importance of quality intellectual property will only intensify.

Protect your intellectual property

Intellectual property tends to leak. Apple created a tremendous amount of IP involving the iPhone. Over time, innovation diffuses, IP slowly leaks, and competitors take away the advantage. Here are some ways IP leaks:

- **Employees:** Yahoo! hired Marissa Mayer away from Google. She brought with her tremendous knowledge learned at Google and started using it against her former employer. Yahoo! has already made significant gains under Mayer's leadership.

- **Web:** Many companies are too transparent on the web. "Hey, thanks for putting your entire sales team and their contact information on the web. I was looking for a good salesperson. No need to recruit my own; I'll just steal yours."

- **Vendors:** Your rivet supplier helps you create a more efficient process. Then the vendor immediately shares the IP with your competitor in hopes of getting a sale from them.

- **Sales process:** In an attempt to create more revenue, salespeople sometimes go too far and reveal intellectual property.

Those three little tricks

A businessman I respect greatly owns a commercial lighting business. His company installs, services, and repairs outdoor lighting. Like most construction-related businesses, it's tough to make a buck. Despite an industry loaded with "one guy and a truck" competitors and tight-fisted property managers, he has built a very profitable business.

I asked him how he made excellent profits while everyone else in his industry was fighting to break even. What he said applies to every business, "Over the last 20 years, I've learned three tricks that account for every single dollar of my profit. If I hadn't learned these tricks, I'd be breaking even like the rest of them."

These three tricks amount to intellectual property controlled by my friend and unknown to his competitors. This highly-leveraged intellectual property creates competitive advantage and profits.

If you buy the premise that your IP is your company's most valuable asset, you should protect it. The following sections tell you how.

Legal protection

One option for protecting your IP is through the traditional legal system, with patents, trademarks, and copyrights. Copyrights and trademarks are very inexpensive. If in doubt, trademark or copyright your IP. It's too inexpensive not to.

Patents can cost as little as $5,000 or up to hundreds of thousands, even millions, of dollars. That's just to file the patent. Your patent may be denied. If it is granted, failing to spend thousands of dollars to defend it could effectively make the patent worthless. If you really think patent protection is necessary, be prepared to spend lots of money to defend it. Apple and Samsung have been doing exactly this all over the globe hoping to gain competitive advantage by defending their respective tablet computer IP.

Many businesspeople have filed a patent thinking it was the holy grail of intellectual property protection only to be disappointed in the result. The bottom line is, if the idea you're protecting isn't worth a million dollars or more, it may not be worth the bother to patent it.

Physical protection

The second way to protect your IP is to simply treat your intellectual property like any other valued asset. You closely guard your customer list because it's valuable. Your customer list is IP. What about your little secrets in hiring and training? That IP needs to be protected as well.

Most mid-sized and small businesses should *not* bother to patent their IP. You have to give away your secrets when you patent them, and most of these companies won't spend the funds needed for legal fees to enforce the patent. Be pragmatic and ask yourself:

- ✔ **What is the IP really worth?** If it's millions or billions, by all means, patent it. If not, the legal cost may exceed the benefits.

- ✔ **Can you do an un-patent like Coca-Cola?** The formula for Coke is a closely guarded trade secret, not a patent. Sometimes a well-protected trade secret is better than a patent. You'll have to create a clever protection scheme like Colonel Sanders or Coke. Only two people know the formula for Coke.

- ✔ **What are the odds your patent will be granted?** Approximately 54 percent of all patent applications are approved. Thirty percent of patent applications make duplicate claims (something an existing patent does) and patents functionally redundant. No statistics are available to tell how many patents never make it off patent attorney's desks to the patent office. Many of these would-be patents are nixed by an attorney's research into existing patents only to find an existing patent filed. Other patents die on attorney's desks when the legal bill rises to a level that calling off the patent application is more palatable than more legal bills.

✔ **What are the odds your competitors can change some small aspect of your patent to get around it?** This is a big disappointment for many. They file a patent to protect their IP only to help their competitors reverse engineer it.

Products, ideas, software code, or business processes that have substantial value *should* be patented. If they have substantial value and unique IP, by all means, patent them. I've seen many companies become disappointed when their patent was denied or diluted beyond usefulness. I encourage you to strongly consider the un-patent option before diving into expensive legal protections.

Establishing a financial advantage

Some financial aspects of your business model translate into the amount of margin you can generate. Other financial aspects can provide competitive advantage and keep competitors at bay. Economies of scale, the size of your war chest, corporate culture, and flexibility can equate to a financial competitive advantage.

Many times, a financial advantage can become the ultimate competitive advantage — one that simply can't be overcome. To compensate for the financial advantage and overtake you, a competitor would have to sell for a reduced margin, make huge investments *hoping* to catch you, or both. This strong economic moat can last for decades.

Invention of the laser

It isn't clear whether Gordon Gould invented the laser. He did file for a patent for it in April 1959. The U.S. Patent Office denied his application and a year later awarded a patent to Bell Labs instead. That provoked a 28-year lawsuit that cost Gould millions. Gould eventually won the patent battle and the prestige and royalties that came with it. Gould signed away 80 percent of the proceeds in order to finance his court costs but still made millions.

Economies of scale

Many financial advantages fall under the broad heading "economies of scale." These advantages aren't just the minimum economy of scale needed to effectively get in the game, but an economy of scale your competitors can't match. Ideally, you'd be the only company to reach an economy of scale. That would serve as a strong competitive advantage.

An economy of scale doesn't have to be a giant steel mill or a thousand computer programmers. You can obtain economies of scale for processes or any other facet of your business. The advantage comes from having enough volume/repetition of the item to create scale when others don't have it. Companies that currently have such economies of scale include the following:

- Starbucks has 29 percent of the U.S. coffee shop market. It leveraged this scale to introduce a Keurig-style home coffee maker, the Verismo.

- Amazon's large distribution network allows the company to add product after product at a lower cost than any other web provider.

- The largest electrician in town buys enough wire to hedge bets with commodity trades. When copper prices spike, this contractor is protected from the increase and wins a large construction project because of the cost advantage.

- Big 4 accounting firms hire enough new employees every year to make recruiting from top business schools economically viable. This gives the Big 4 the opportunity to pluck the most talented new accountants every year. Competitors are forced to hire second-tier graduates or older employees who are more expensive.

- Building a golf driving range in a rapidly growing suburb combines first-mover advantage and economies of scale. The large land acquisition cost required for a driving range precludes a second entry.

- An automotive remanufacturer saw unusually high volume of one alternator part number. After researching it, he found the volume was abnormally high due to a design flaw from the OEM. Realizing he had a future hot seller, he created a unique marketing approach outside the normal sales channel. This additional volume allowed him to run a separate production line for this one part number. The tailored production line was significantly more efficient, allowing the manufacturer to undercut the completion, further increasing volume. This was a small company relative to the competition. This company didn't have economies of scale on all alternators, just this one part number.

- Tesla produces fewer than 20,000 automobiles per year. However, because Tesla manufactures only high-performance all-electric vehicles, Tesla achieves economies of scale within this tight scope.

Flexible financial structure

A flexible cost structure can also provide a competitive cost advantage. A flexible cost structure allows costs to move as closely as possible with sales. Usually, costs that move in conjunction with sales are called variable costs. Fixed costs don't vary with sales. If sales go down, your cost of goods goes down with it, but your rent doesn't.

Flexible financial structures allow you to flex when sales go up without financial distribution as well as when sales go down. Generally, you want to minimize fixed costs and maximize variable costs by

- ✔ **Having the ability to significantly increase production without increasing costs.** Staffing is generally one of the largest cost elements in any business, so how you structure your labor can be a deal breaker. If I have to pay overtime in order to complete a job and you don't, you have a more flexible model. Completing the job without paying overtime could be accomplished via creative staffing, use of contractors versus employees, or by a variety of other means.

- ✔ **Having the ability to absorb seasonal or unexpectedly slow periods without overhead killing profits.** Fixed expenses like administrative staff, buildings, and equipment weigh heavily on profits when sales slump.

- ✔ **Staying nimble.** Fixed-base roofing companies (in other words, they work in only one location) have a hard time finding quality roofers when a storm hits. Specialty roofing companies that move from town to town after storms have a more flexible model and move the business to where the profitable work is.

- ✔ **Planning for contingencies.** Any business working with China has learned the perils of Chinese New Year supply disruptions. A union strike at a vendor shouldn't kill your profitability. U.S. drywall vendors couldn't meet demand in the mid-2000s. Builders didn't have alternative vendors and purchased defective Chinese drywall that contained contaminants. As a result, major lawsuits were filed against these builders, erasing any profits.

- ✔ **Controlling organizational inertia.** It can be hard to fight, "We can't because," or "We've always done it that way." When costs are embedded into an organization, you become less financially flexible. Fight these costs from becoming nonnegotiable.

By designing your business model using a flexible financial structure, you can achieve advantage over the competition by not only being able to manage costs better but, more importantly, being more proactive about opportunities and threats.

Fireworks: More bang for your buck

Every July, fireworks stores pop up along major roads in many cities. The margin selling fireworks is extremely attractive. So far, this looks like a good business model. It has great margins and strong demand every year. However, the seasonal nature of the business is brutal. The demand disappears on July 5th. How do you rent a building for one month? How do you staff a business for one month? Sure, you can hire temps or seasonal workers every year, but you need some continuity. Someone has to know the business. Everyone can't be new.

Fireworks providers have successfully overcome these obstacles and created very profitable business models by staying flexible. Here's how they overcome the obstacles:

- Don't worry about a consistent retail location. Rent high-traffic retail locations from desperate landlords willing to take two months' rent instead of nothing.

- Keep a skeleton staff year-round to train new employees and manage them.

- Hire college students who are always off in the summer, and pay them better than other retailers.

- If you find a highly desirable retail location for which the landlords won't accept a two-month deal, lease for six months or even a year. Sell Halloween costumes and Christmas items to cover the additional rent.

- Use logistics companies to handle incoming fireworks shipments, warehousing, and distribution to all stores. This detail may seem minor, but a good-sized fireworks company can have hundreds of locations needing inventory daily.

The ability to flex with market demand and keep operating costs low allows fireworks companies to be exceptionally profitable.

Corporate culture

Walmart is famous for holding purchasing meetings in what is effectively a huge barn in Bentonville, Arkansas. High-powered executives from companies hoping to sell Walmart sit at picnic tables to pitch their wares. Walmart even charges $0.10 for coffee. Walmart isn't messing around with vendors or crying poor. This no-frills approach to purchasing is part of a culture of thrift at Walmart.

Walmart is one of the most profitable corporations in the world. Walmart could have its headquarters in a Manhattan high-rise. Instead, Walmart keeps overhead low by staying in its original headquarters in Bentonville. Everything Walmart does focuses on keeping costs low and passing the savings on to customers. This culture creates a financial advantage for Walmart in the cost-sensitive general retailing business.

Just like Walmart, you can use your corporate culture to create competitive advantage. Walmart has chosen a culture of thrift to lower costs. You can also create a culture of innovation to lower costs. Toyota's lean manufacturing process has innovated how cars are produced and has dramatically lowered costs.

Sustaining Your Competitive Advantage

Even if you create a meaningful competitive advantage, your competitors aren't going to stand still. Their job is to remove this advantage, and fast. How will you sustain this valuable asset? Protecting your competitive advantage falls under two broad categories: offensive tactics and defensive tactics.

Defensive tactics

Use defensive tactics to slow down or stop competitive advances. When discount realtors entered the market, full-service realtors reacted swiftly with several defensive tactics, like exclusion from listing on the MLS and refusing to show houses listed by discounters. Other defensive tactics include:

- **Moats:** After you build a castle, a moat can protect you. McDonald's has created a moat by spending a hefty nine percent of revenue on advertising. The largest courier in Indiana, Now Courier, invested a whopping $30,000 per vehicle for GPS while it was still an emerging technology. Why would the company spend so much? To enhance performance and solidify its reputation as the fastest service available. Now Courier was the only courier that could afford such an investment. By acting preemptively, it created a moat.

- **Intransparency:** Plain and simple, transparency lowers margins. Employees go to salary.com and see the going rate; wages rise; margins decrease. Internet price shopping becomes simple and widespread; margins decrease. You get my point. Fighting transparency whenever possible doesn't eliminate erosion of competitive advantage, but it can slow it down. Here's a simple rule: If in doubt, don't shout it out. In other words, keep your secrets secret.

- **Updates:** Examples include updating the version of your software before it gets stale or restaurants renovating before they look tired. Wendy's recently commented that stores undergoing renovation saw a 30 percent bump in sales.

- **Guarding assets like your IP, talent, and brand:** If you agree that everyone is in the intellectual property business, treat your IP like gold.

- **Legalities:** Non-compete agreements for key employees, non-disclosure agreements for vendors and customers, accompanied by aggressive enforcement of them, can serve as a defensive move.

✔ **Falling on the price sword:** In order to maintain market share in a mature market, you'll most likely settle for decreasing margins. Insisting on maintaining your old, premature market margins probably won't work.

✔ **Being offensive:** The best defense is a strong offense. Defensive moves will only slow down the decay of your competitive advantage. Your competitors aren't sitting still, so you shouldn't be either. Constant innovation and forward thinking is the best defense. Look at Apple for great examples of this move. Apple has continued to stay one step ahead of the competition, forcing competitors to constantly play catch-up.

Offensive tactics

Defensive tactics only slow down the competition. Use offense to add competitive advantage as well as stifle the competition. When preparing your offensive tactics, consider the following:

✔ **Innovation:** Perhaps the best protection of your competitive advantage is constant innovation. Blockbuster Video was the dominant industry leader but failed to innovate. This failure allowed Netflix and Redbox to capture a significant portion of Blockbuster's market share.

✔ **Speed:** Being able to move faster than your competitors equates to a competitive advantage. Steve Jobs was famous for driving his product development teams hard. This tactic seems to have worked as Apple continually beats competitors to market.

✔ **Culture:** Southwest Airlines has a fun-loving, get-it-done culture. This culture has been ingrained in every employee for more than 30 years. Southwest can leverage this culture to sustain and grow its competitive advantage.

✔ **Talent:** A business with superior talent in key positions has the opportunity to grow competitive advantage. Intel scientist Ajay V. Bhatt helped define and develop several technologies, including USB (Universal Serial Bus), AGP (Accelerated Graphics Port), and PCI Express. He holds 31 patents. The employment of a superstar like Bhatt represented ongoing competitive advantage for Intel.

✔ **Bet on change, not lack of it:** One of the most frustrating dynamics in business is spending years striving for a goal, reaching that goal, and then realizing you don't get to relax as a reward, because another goal needs to be chased. Be assured, change is inevitable and you never really reach the destination. The journey is perpetual. Savvy businesspeople know that change is inevitable, and banking on things to stay the same is for suckers.

✔ **Rope-a-dope:** This boxing tactic made famous by Muhammad Ali allowed the competitor to feel like he was winning, only to have Ali pounce later in the bout. If you have a nagging competitor that's constantly copying your innovations, stealing your best employees, or any other competitive-advantage-draining activity, an option is to send the competitor on a wild goose chase. Here are some interesting rope-a-dope moves I've seen:

- A once-valued employee turned bad. A competitor attempted to steal him away. The company helped the competitor do so.

- A technology company suspected a competitor of stealing inside information. The company created a fake project and treated it with high priority, hoping the competitor would steal it and waste resources.

- A competitor was following a coffee service's employees on their sales route and then lowball pricing to steal them away. The company hired a temporary employee to call on fired customers and other bad prospects to throw the competitor off the scent.

Hopefully you never need to use any type of shenanigans (like the rope-a-dope tactics), but you can't always control your competitors, and it's important to be prepared with good offensive tactics.

Gauging Competitive Advantage by Using Porter's Five Forces Model

Guru Michael Porter offers insight into how to gauge the strength of your competitive advantage as well as the likelihood of sustaining it. Porter's five forces model breaks down the five most common ways competitive advantage can be challenged. Figure 10-1 shows the interplay of the five forces.

✔ **Threat of new entrants:** Congratulations, the iPad is a giant hit. Now you can expect every technology manufacturing company to be nipping at your heels. Technology businesses tend to run a high risk of new entrants chasing the next big thing. However, if you discover a great niche or product for a gravel quarry, your threat of new entrants is significantly lower.

✔ **Power of buyers:** Large automotive manufacturers enjoy significant power over their vendors. On the other hand, a client of mine manufacturers complex cabling for the Army. Some of the connectors on these cables are nearly impossible to source. Whenever my client orders any of these connectors, he basically has to mail the vendor a blank check and say "Thank you for filling my order."

✔ **Power of suppliers:** OPEC is a great example of the power of suppliers. The supply of raw crude oil is more critical than any of the products created from it, so OPEC has significant power over its customers.

✔ **Intensity of competitive rivalry:** Industries with high fixed cost of entry tend to have intensive rivalries, especially if the business is cyclical. Companies spend hundreds of millions of dollars building physical plants and then volume decreases due to a recession. Companies don't just walk away from their large investment, they fight.

✔ **Threat of substitutes:** Cable television providers have been using this dynamic for years. Cable providers used to enjoy a virtual monopoly until satellite became a viable option. Customers who may have been inclined to switch found it to be expensive and cumbersome. BlackBerry has found itself on the wrong end of this dynamic. In its early days, BlackBerry enjoyed proprietary technology, making the cost and pain of switching to another technology significant. As competitors created substitute solutions with similar functionality, the difficulty and cost of switching went down dramatically — as did BlackBerry sales.

Diagram of Porter's Five Forces

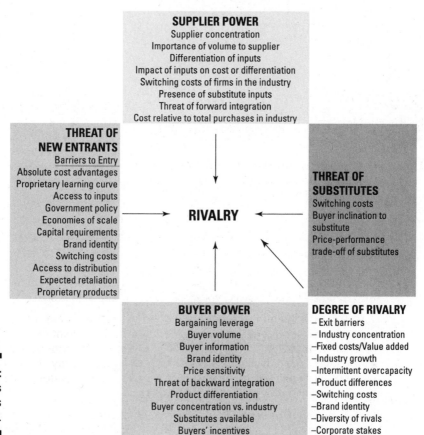

Figure 10-1:
Porter's
five forces
model.

Porter's five forces model was published in 1980. There have been challenges to the model since then, primary among them that Porter views most threats in the context of an established industry. This is a valid concern. Threats can come from inside the industry or from unrelated foes. Consider the hit casual dining restaurants took during the last recession. The problem wasn't the restaurant down the street; it was gas prices eating away the customer's disposable income.

The media has recently covered the trend of consumers having ample funds for the latest smartphone or electronic gadget but skimping on clothing, driving cars longer, and otherwise cutting elsewhere. These threats aren't covered by Porter's model but deserve some thought.

Chapter 11

Sustaining Your Business Model: Innovating and Avoiding Pitfalls

In This Chapter

▶ Leveraging innovation

▶ Knowing your innovation factor

▶ Sidestepping common pitfalls

A complete and well-rounded business model is able to continue its viability for an extended period of time. Beanie Babies were a bonanza for their maker, Ty. When the trend died down, sales suffered but the company lives on. Crocs shoes were a massive trend that put Crocs Inc. on the map. The once red-hot shoes have died off significantly, but the company has successfully moved into other areas and is a profitable public company.

The best method to continue to grow the strength of your business model is through innovation. Innovation in any and all areas will strengthen your model and your ability to compete.

Innovation can take many forms. Your model can be strengthened by changing your target market, your marketing model, what you sell and for how much, the products you sell or their mix, improving the sales model or delivery system, or innovating away a pitfall.

A pitfall is a potential glitch in your business model. Ideally, your business model can avoid pitfalls such as governmental interference, overreliance on a few customers, overreliance on key employees, location handicaps, excessive legal concerns, or other traps.

Pitfalls don't make a business model nonviable, but they do make it less attractive. Whether the model is modestly unattractive (a fashion business's constantly changing trends) or significantly unattractive (handgun ban, military spending freeze, coastal Venice real estate combined with melting polar icecaps), pitfalls should be considered as potential risks to the model.

Maintaining the Strength of Your Model with Innovation

What do Blockbuster, Yellow Pages, Borders, Circuit City, the Chicago Tribune, WGN, Musicland, and radio stations all have in common? They all had their business models destroyed by the Internet. Blacksmiths had their business model ruined by automotive technology. Railroads succumbed to the Wright Brothers' invention. Kodak fell to digital cameras, and now digital cameras are falling to cellphone cameras. Fail to innovate, and your business model is in jeopardy. If you don't innovate, someone else will.

Before you say, "Yeah but . . .," I admit that some companies need to innovate more than others. A landscape company doesn't need to innovate as much as a biotech company, but *both* need to innovate to maintain their competitive advantage. All companies have the *ability* to innovate, which they balance with their *need* to innovate. This is their *innovation factor*.

Understanding your innovation factor

The need to innovate is set by your industry. If you're in the microchip or biotech industry, your need innovate is sky high. If you fail to innovate, competitors will leapfrog you and quickly steal your market share. If you're a manufacturer, the need is probably average. If you're a commercial landscaper or a bowling alley operator, the need for innovation is relatively low. In these industries, you could build a successful business with virtually no innovation, but that's no reason to be complacent.

The need to innovate is referenced against your firm's ability to innovate. If a computer chip company has a high need to innovate but a poor ability to innovate, guess what happens — bye-bye. A company that excels at innovation in an industry requiring lots of innovation (Intel, Genentech, 3M, Amazon, and Google) not only succeeds but succeeds in a big way.

Innovative companies like Starbucks, UPS, BigBelly Solar, and the NFL have used out-innovating their competitors as competitive leverage in lower need-for-innovation industries. Figure 11-1 shows the relationship between a company's need to innovate and its ability to do so. Companies with a high need for innovation will either excel as a result of their innovation or be punished by their lack of innovation. Companies with a lower competitive need to innovate have the potential to over-innovate and devote too many resources to a marketplace that doesn't need or want excessive innovation. For instance, a local lawn mowing service should stay on top of equipment and design trends. However, if the company is constantly spending precious resources building customer equipment at the cutting edge simply to mow yards, the market may not reward this effort. If the mowing company changes its business model and begins selling the inventions, the need for innovation in the equipment manufacturing industry is much higher than it is for a lawn mowing company and the problem is fixed.

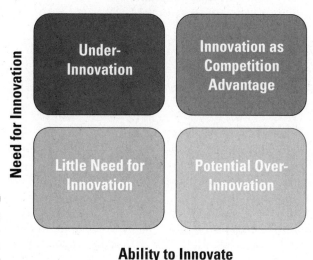

Innovation Factor

Need for Innovation

Under-Innovation

Innovation as Competition Advantage

Little Need for Innovation

Potential Over-Innovation

Ability to Innovate

Figure 11-1:
Your innovation factor.

Image courtesy of businessmodelinstitute.com

Remembering that you need to innovate

Innovation doesn't have to be the invention of a new drug or smartphone. Innovation is any improvement to the business model. This innovation could be a marketing innovation — like using Twitter to grow sales, creating a new product, or a powerful marketing campaign (Joe Isuzu, Where's the Beef, The Most Interesting Man in the World). Innovation could be a creative business process — like mobile restaurants bringing the food to people or a self-service salad bar. Innovation could be adopting the use of new equipment before the competition. Innovation isn't just for technology companies; it's for all companies.

Cyndi Lauper versus Madonna

Both Cyndi Lauper and Madonna were top-selling female recording artists during the 1980s. Lauper had several hits, including *Time After Time* and *Girls Just Want to Have Fun,* won a Grammy Award, and sold more than 40 million albums/songs. Madonna was having success during the same period with songs like *Borderline* and *Like a Virgin.*

Each woman was one of the top recording artists of the period. The difference between these two artists is that Lauper wasn't able to transition her "she's so unusual" style to the next big thing, despite her considerable talent. By 1993, Lauper's fourth album, *Hat Full of Stars/Twelve Deadly Cyns,* sold only 120,000 copies. Lauper was unable to innovate.

Madonna, on the other hand, has been masterful at innovation. She keeps changing her look and sound to reinvigorate her career. At 53 she was still one of the top performers in her field, performing at the Super Bowl.

Staying ahead in the innovation game

Innovation is for leaders, not followers. You don't need to be a brazen risk-taker to innovate. If you understand your innovation factor, you'll know how much or how little your business model needs. Simply adjust your risk-taking to meet the needs of your industry.

Putting R&D in the budget

One of the best practices you can follow is to budget for research and development (R&D). Research is where innovation comes from. Fortune 500 companies all have an R&D budget. Mid-sized and small businesses rarely budget for research or innovation. They tend to take a reactive approach. This approach often leaves smaller businesses playing catch-up. You have a chance to do it right.

Add research and development cost to your financial model. Budgeting one or two percent of revenue will keep you consistently focused on innovation and provide a much greater chance for successful innovation. Also, don't lose sight of any possibilities for local, state, or federal incentives or tax credits that help mitigate these types of expenses.

As you can see from the R&D spending chart in Table 11-1, innovation and R&D spending are inseparable. You probably recognize most or all of these companies as some of the most successful companies in the world . . . for a reason. These companies spend heavily on research. Research leads to innovation, and innovation powers your business model. You can't innovate without investing in order to accomplish it.

Table 11-1   50 Biggest R&D Spenders, 2006–2007

Rank	Company	R&D, Most Recent Four Quarters
1	Microsoft	$7,420,000,000
2	IBM	$6,153,000,000
3	Intel	$5,755,000,000
4	Cisco	$4,730,000,000
5	Hewlett-Packard	$3,632,000,000
6	Oracle	$2,496,000,000
7	SAP	$2,296,330,000
8	Google	$2,120,000,000
9	Sun Microsystems	$1,937,000,000
10	Advanced Micro Devices	$1,847,000,000
11	EMC Corporation	$1,526,928,000
12	Yahoo!	$1,084,000,000
13	Seagate	$939,000,000
14	Symantec	$890,000,000
15	Apple	$844,000,000
16	Computer Associates	$657,000,000
17	Adobe Systems	$613,242,000
18	Intuit	$544,137,000
19	Cadence Design Systems	$494,000,000
20	Autodesk	$452,800,000
21	Network Appliance	$436,039,000
22	VMware	$285,941,000
23	BEA Systems	$240,578,000
24	McAfee	$218,000,000
25	Palm	$213,994,000
26	Novell	$208,370,000
27	BMC Software	$207,000,000
28	Citrix Systems	$205,000,000
29	Parametric Technology	$166,000,000
30	Verisign	$160,000,000
31	Sybase	$153,000,000

(continued)

Table 11-1 (continued)

Rank	Company	R&D, Most Recent Four Quarters
32	National Instruments	$127,000,000
33	Teradata	$126,000,000
34	Quest Software	$123,000,000
35	Compuware	$109,000,000
36	RealNetworks	$103,000,000
37	TIBCO Software	$92,924,000
38	Nuance Communications	$92,000,000
39	Red Hat	$91,125,000
40	Lawson Software	$81,488,000
41	Wind River Systems	$81,432,000
42	Progress Software	$80,345,000
43	Informatica	$70,000,000
44	Openwave Systems	$65,369,000
45	Salesforce.COM	$63,812,000
46	TriZetto Group	$62,000,000
47	Borland Software	$57,795,000
48	Silicon Graphics	$57,000,000
49	ANSYS	$56,000,000
50	MSC Software	$53,000,000

Sources: Company filings, Yahoo! Finance, ciozone.com

Avoiding Pitfalls

You create a highly marketable product. You have a strong system to sell it. You know how to innovate and are prepared to do so. Your business model is almost complete. Now you have to avoid pitfalls. Most business models can avoid all major pitfalls. However, the business environment is fluid and business models erode over time, so pitfalls are worthy of a quick discussion so you can ensure your business model remains problem-free. These pitfalls fall into three categories: excessive trend riding, overreliance on a few customers, and susceptibility to forces beyond your control.

Having pitfalls in your business model doesn't mean the model is bad. You simply need to be consistently aware of and plan for them. The danger lies in ignoring the pitfalls or using the ostrich plan (hoping they won't happen or believing things won't change). A fashion house understands that the hot new trend will last only a season and is already planning its demise. A company like Taser, in an overly litigious business, budgets a percent of sales for legal expenses.

Excessive trend riding

The Pet Rock was a big money maker — for a year. The Ruby on Rails software platform is currently hot, and many firms are cashing in. What happens when there's a new flavor of the month? It's fine to capitalize on trends. Trend riding can be a much easier way to grow sales than slogging through a stagnant market. However, you should remember that trends end, and you need to transition to a new trend *before* they do.

Overreliance on a few customers

Overreliance on a few customers is a common issue with second-tier automotive suppliers. I remember a gentleman telling me how he ran a company that supplied GM with the power antennas for Cadillacs. An entire plant made nothing but Cadillac antennas. Cadillac changed the design to a windshield antenna, making the power version obsolete. This gentleman was lucky. He jumped on a plane and begged GM to find another part for the plant to make, and GM did. If GM was less generous, he was out of business. Having an overreliance on a handful of customers doesn't ruin your business model; it just makes it weaker.

Susceptibility to forces beyond your control

Tourism businesses located near the Gulf of Mexico have had to endure the unpredictable wrath of Mother Nature many times in the past ten years. Another force beyond your control is the government. Susceptibility to governmental action or inaction weakens a business model. Consider the following:

✔ **Change in tax or other incentives:** As oil prices surged from $60/barrel in early 2007 to $145 by mid-2008, companies scrambled to profit from ethanol by building $100+ million refineries. The theory was that gasoline consumption could be shifted to a blend of 85 percent ethanol and 15 percent gasoline (E85) because ethanol was cheaper per gallon than oil. On top of that, the government subsidized ethanol an additional $0.45/gallon. However, oil prices dropped to $90/barrel and the government removed the ethanol subsidy. Less than five years after opening, many of these multimillion dollar plants have closed.

- ✔ **Infrastructure planning like moving a road, urban redevelopment, or road repairs:** It's tough to do business when no one can pull into your parking lot because the road is under construction.

- ✔ **Changing of laws or standards:** For instance, HIPPA compliance forced many small medical practices to cease operating or merge due to the forced technological upgrades.

- ✔ **Overly litigious businesses have a diminished business model:** This is the *Taser test*. Taser has a proprietary, industry-leading product that sells at a good profit but gets sued regularly for lots of money. Being sued often doesn't ruin Taser's business model; it just weakens it.

Chapter 12

Cashing In

· ·

· ·

*Y*ou may be asking why a chapter on selling your business is included in a business models book. If you're running a public company, feel free to skip this chapter. Capital markets provide public companies a ready-made exit strategy that smaller businesses can't access. I'm assuming that most people reading this book own or will be creating a mid-sized or small business.

At some point, you'll want to transfer operation of your business to others and collect the fruits of your labors. I call this a graceful exit. The design of your business model can facilitate a graceful exit or make it more difficult. Improper business model design at the early stages of business can significantly lessen your final payday. An estimated 35 percent of all small businesses are *never* sold. A buyer can't be found and the business simply shuts down — the antithesis of a graceful exit.

In order to have a complete business model, you must be able to successfully exit the business and receive a financial reward commensurate with your efforts.

In this chapter, you discover how and when to sell your business as well as how to maximize the sales price. I also introduce you to the concept of a graceful exit. Most people think the only way to exit a business is to sell it. But I tell you about another powerful exit strategy that could provide you a much larger payday.

Considering the Next Owner: The Best Business Models Have Transferability

One of the easiest ways to gauge a business model is by its profitability. A highly profitable business model must be a good model, right? It's possible, however, for a business model to produce excellent profits for decades but lack the ability to transfer this profitability to another owner.

Take a doctor's practice, for example. A doctor can earn excellent income for decades. The doctor can periodically improve her business model by adding additional revenue streams like testing or lab services. However, when the doctor retires, the business model falls apart.

You want to build your business model to be as valuable to the next owner as it is to you. The more seamlessly the business can be transitioned to a new owner, the better and more complete your business model.

Undermining the worth of your business model

Many business owners are so focused on building a profitable business today that they undermine the future value of the business. Ideally, you'll operate your business so that growing today's profits will also increase the future value of the business.

Lessons from the Rich Jerk

Lots of people sell educational materials telling you how to get rich or make money on the Internet. Some of these "gurus" make millions of dollars doing so. However, what happens when the guru in the video doesn't want to work anymore or wants to sell the business? He can't, because he's the face of the business and his personal brand *is* the business.

Enter the Rich Jerk (http://www.therichjerk.com). You may remember Tommy Vu, the real estate infomercial king. Vu was famous for challenging audiences with taunts like "Whazza matta, you chicken?" The Rich Jerk

is a harsher version of Tommy Vu for building Internet wealth.

Like or dislike the Rich Jerk's niche, the man (or woman) behind the business is a genius. Instead of building a personal brand that lives and dies with the individual, the Rich Jerk created a cartoon character to be the persona of the business. Just like Bugs Bunny lives on long after Mel Blanc passed away, the Rich Jerk has built a business model with a much more graceful exit than most of his or her competitors.

For example, Alan has a tendency to swoop into the sales process any time a big deal is brewing. Alan is a super-closer, so the deals get done. Everything seems fine today. Salespeople get commissions. Profits are made. However, by undermining the salesforce, Alan runs the risk that deals can't close without his personal efforts. Rather than training the sales force to close the tough deals, Alan is training them to be overly reliant on him. This system may maximize profits today, but it may cost Alan significantly when he sells the business because the new owner will be unsure whether profits can continue without Alan.

Several factors can adversely affect your ability to transfer the business to another owner and lower the sales value of the business in the process:

- ✔ **The owner holds the key customers, partner, and supplier relationships.** At best, the new owner will need to start at the beginning of the relationship-building process. At worst, these relationships will never be as strong as they were with the previous owner and the business will be negatively impacted.

- ✔ **The owner is personally responsible for a significant percentage of sales volume.** Any business whose number one salesperson is the owner has a transferability issue. When the business transfers ownership, the number one salesperson leaves.

- ✔ **Customers want to do business only with the owner.** This is common in personal services businesses. I love my local plumber, Betty. She always does great work. When Betty hires a second plumber, I don't want plumber #2, I want Betty.

- ✔ **Operations run smoothly while the owner is involved but fall apart otherwise.** This spoke-and-wheel type of operation has the owner in the center of everything. Even if the skills of the owner can be duplicated, she's involved in too many aspects of the daily operations. Changing the person at the center of the wheel is like trying to change the tires on a moving bus.

Most of these issues are the result of the business model being a personal brand of the owner rather than a standard business model. Until the business model is adjusted to remove the impediment of the personal brand, it will never reach its full potential.

Breaking away from a personal brand

Many mid-sized and small businesses leverage the personal brand of the owner for one reason — it works. Customers enjoy dealing with the person in charge. The owner is highly committed to every transaction working perfectly. Customers and stakeholders eventually realize they're getting that something extra from the owner's personal involvement versus dealing with an everyday employee. This translates into a better business for the owner — today.

Your business can operate profitably for decades with a strong personal brand at the core of your business model. When it comes time to exit the business, however, it may be time to pay the piper. Table 12-1 shows the total income earned by two plumbing companies, Best Local Plumbing and Sam's Plumbing. Sam's Plumbing relies upon the strong personal brand of Sam Smith, the owner. Sam is personally involved in the sales and service aspects of each job. Sam uses office staff and field support to assist him and complete the work.

Table 12-1	A Tale of Two Plumbers: Current Numbers	
	Sam	*Jane*
Sales	$2,000,000	$2,000,000
Direct marketing (10% of sales)	$200,000	$200,000
Cost of goods sold (15% of sales)	$300,000	$300,000
Labor (40% of sales)	$800,000	$800,000
Sales staff	$0	$100,000
Overhead	$250,000	$200,000
Profit	$450,000	$400,000

Jane, owner of Best Local Plumbing, takes a different approach. Jane doesn't want to be the "face" of Best Local Plumbing, so she has structured the model much differently than Sam. Some aspects of Jane's business are more challenging than Sam's. It's difficult to get an employee to take the care on a job that Sam will. It's difficult to find a salesperson who can sell as effectively as Sam can. It's more difficult to build loyalty for Best Local Plumbing than it is for Sam to build personal loyalty with his customers.

To Jane's credit, she has worked hard to overcome these obstacles and has built a business with the same sales volume as Sam's. Table 12-1 shows the current income of each operation. Note that Jane's sales expense is higher because Sam is filling the role of salesperson, and Jane must pay someone to fill this role. Jane saves $50,000 in administrative overhead expense, because she works in the office, and Sam must pay someone to fill that role.

From this perspective, Sam's business model looks superior because it produces more profit. However, the situation changes dramatically when Sam and Jane want to sell their businesses. Table 12-2 shows the likely selling prices for each business after profits have been normalized. For Jane, this normalization process is minimal because the marketing and operational functions of the business aren't dependent upon her. The new owner needs only to hire a person for the office to replace Jane. Because the business can run well without Jane's daily input, Jane will receive a higher profit multiplier when selling the business.

Table 12-2	A Tale of Two Plumbers: Selling the Business	
	Sam	*Jane*
Annual profit	$450,000	$400,000
Normalization of new salesperson	$(150,000)	$0
Normalization of additional overhead	$0	$(50,000)
Normalized profit	$300,000	$350,000
Profit multiple	3	5
Sales price	$900,000	$1,750,000

To normalize the profits of Sam's business is more complex. Because Sam is the key salesperson, the new owner must hire a highly skilled replacement. Good salespeople don't come cheaply, and Sam will have to pay more than the $100,000 per year that Jane pays her salesperson. Sam will receive a much lower profit multiplier than Jane, because the business carries his personal brand. The buyer will be forced to discount the buying price because he has the following questions:

✔ Will people still buy from Sam's Plumbing if Sam isn't around?

✔ Will a new salesperson be as effective as Sam?

✔ How much customer loyalty was to the business and how much was to Sam?

✔ How much will sales fall as a result of the change in ownership?

Sam may have banked $50,000 more profit each year, but Jane comes out ahead in the end. Sam's reliance on a personal brand may have produced additional profits for many years, but when Sam wants to exit the business, his personal brand will be a significant drag on the value of the business.

Jane's model has the added benefits of:

✔ **More potential for growth:** Jane isn't a "cog in the gears" like Sam. Her business had the potential to grow more easily than Sam's. This potential also makes Jane's business more salable.

✔ **Lower tax rates:** Sam pays ordinary income tax rates on the annual income he earns in excess of Jane. Jane will pay the lower capital gains rate on the increased sales value of the business.

✔ **Salability:** Sam's business may not be sellable at all. If Sam is the "face" of the company, or if the business is overly dependent upon his sales skills, a potential buyer may not want to take the risk of duplicating the model.

> ✔ **Vacations:** Jane can enjoy vacations. Sam is a vital employee of his business. When Sam doesn't work, the business doesn't work right. It's safe to bet that Jane took more personal time and enjoyed it more than Sam did.
>
> ✔ **Fewer hours:** It's probably safe to say that Sam works more hours per week than Jane does, because he's vital to day-to-day operations.

Taking lessons from Oprah

Oprah is rich for a reason — she's a savvy businessperson. Like many businesspeople, Oprah started out with talent and a strong work ethic. At 19, her hard work paid off, and she landed a job as co-anchor of the Nashville evening news. A series of upward moves landed her at *AM Chicago,* a struggling news show. Oprah's talents turned *AM Chicago* from an also-ran into a winner.

Eventually, *AM Chicago* was renamed *The Oprah Winfrey Show.* As a business model, Oprah still had nothing more than a personal brand.

At the Movies host Roger Ebert convinced Oprah to leverage her brand by syndicating it nationally. Oprah's personal brand was now national and Oprah was making millions annually. However, she was no different from a movie star. If she didn't work, she didn't get paid.

Oprah made a critical move that transformed her personal brand into an empire. She threatened to quit her show unless she could be the production company as well. Fearing the loss of revenue, *The Oprah Winfrey Show*'s owners conceded. Eventually, Oprah gained full production and distribution control of her show.

Oprah then leveraged her personal brand to build a business rather than just an income. As a result, Oprah's Harpo Productions has spawned several successful television shows, including *Dr. Phil, Rachael Ray, The Dr. Oz Show,* and *The Rosie Show.*

Despite her retirement from daily television, Oprah is consistently one of the top earners in Hollywood.

The lesson Oprah offers entrepreneurs is that a powerful personal brand isn't the end game. Instead, use a strong personal brand as a component of a larger business enterprise.

Selling Your Business Isn't the Only Exit Strategy

Most business owners think the best way to create wealth is to sell their business for a huge pile of money. Selling the business and collecting a multimillion-dollar check feels like the victorious crossing at the finish line. The journey has successfully ended, and the conquering hero gets a parade.

But what if your business can't sell for millions of dollars? According to data provider infoUSA.com, there are 17.6 million businesses in the United States. Only a small percentage of the business owners will collect a multimillion-dollar check when their business sells. The other businesses still need a viable exit strategy that will meet their financial needs. Enter the concept of the graceful exit.

A graceful exit from your business provides you with the income to live comfortably forever. There are two ways to gracefully exit a business:

- ✔ **Sell the business.** If you receive enough money from the sale of your business to live comfortably forever, that's a graceful exit. If you don't receive enough, it isn't a graceful exit; it's just an exit.

- ✔ **Create a CEO Emeritus role.** This is my favorite exit strategy. A *CEO Emeritus* is defined as someone who works as much or as little as he likes and continues to collect the same (or better) pay as when he worked full time. The business continues to serve as an income stream for the owner, as opposed to being traded for a cash asset in a sale.

Frequently, exiting the business as the CEO Emeritus is far more lucrative than selling the business. The ongoing stream of income from the business is, in many cases, significantly greater than the value of the lump-sum payment. Service businesses in particular should look closely at the CEO Emeritus option because the prices paid for these businesses tend to be lower.

Selling your business versus becoming CEO Emeritus

Whether to sell your business or keep it as the CEO Emeritus is a personal decision as well as a financial one. Tables 12-3 and 12-4 show some pros and cons for each.

Table 12-3	Pros and Cons of Selling the Business
Pro	**Con**
No more daily headaches	Trying to determine how to invest your money at 4% and still make the same income you made
Eliminates competitive, economic, and technological risks that could significantly hamper profits	Eliminates any upside of increased profitability
A feeling of victory/crossing the finish line	Trying to determine what to do with your time
Benefiting from insider information regarding timing of competitive landscape (take, for example, all the Internet companies, like Mark Cuban's broadcast.com or AOL selling at the absolute top of the market)	No downside
Having a large pile of money to invest elsewhere	You don't have any income from the business

Table 12-4	Pros and Cons of Keeping the Business and Acting as CEO Emeritus	
Pro	**Con**	
Keeping your nice paycheck	You will still have some involvement with the business — getting to zero is difficult	
Eliminates the inevitable boredom that business owners feel a year after selling	Find a better hobby so you don't get bored	
Provides continuity for employees	Potential lost opportunity for new ownership to shake up company culture	
Better wealth-building: The net present value of your income stream from the business is most likely higher than a lump sum payment due to today's low interest rates	No opportunity to invest in a new venture with proceeds of sale	

Comparing the financial benefits of exit strategies

In this section, I compare getting a large sum of money from the sale of the business to the ongoing income stream created from the CEO Emeritus plan. I use the example of a dental practice. Susan, the owner of the dental practice, currently does $1 million in sales and nets $300,000 per year. Typical selling price for a dental practice is 30 percent of annual sales. I double the sale amount just to be generous. I also cut Susan's CEO Emeritus pay to half her previous pay. Table 12-5 shows the analysis of Susan selling the business versus following the CEO Emeritus plan.

Table 12-5   Selling a Business versus Becoming CEO Emeritus

	Selling the Business	CEO Emeritus
Lump-sum payment	$600,000	$0
Taxes (25%)	$150,000	$0
Net investible assets	$450,000	$0
Investment Income (7%)	$31,500	$0
New personal expenses that used to be paid by the business (car, entertainment, dining)	($5,000)	$0
Emeritus salary	$0	$150,000
Annual income	$26,500	$150,000

As you can see in Table 12-5, the CEO Emeritus plan is far more lucrative for Susan. Of course, Susan has quite a bit of work to do to prepare her practice to run without her daily input. Looking at these numbers, you may wonder why anyone would sell their business for so little money.

If Susan can decrease her CEO Emeritus salary to only $100,000, she is still much better off than if she sold the practice. She'd need to sell the practice for $2,000,000, when the going price is only $300,000, in order to earn the same annual income. It's more likely Susan can make the CEO Emeritus plan work than find the world's dumbest buyer willing to pay eight times too much for the business.

Keep in mind, under the CEO Emeritus plan, Susan still owns the business and can sell it later. That is, Susan can collect the Emeritus income for years and still have the business available to sell if she wants to.

Improving Your Ability to Gracefully Exit

Whether you exit your business by selling it for a significant sum or via the CEO Emeritus plan (see the previous section), you can take steps to improve your payday. Creating a viable company instead of a personal brand can yield Oprah-like results (see the earlier section, "Considering the Next Owner: The Best Business Models Have Transferability" for details).

Relying on systems instead of people

This joke always gets a laugh. What's the definition of the perfect business? Answer: One with no vendors, no customers, and no employees. In particular, managing employees can be a challenge to a small business. Many business owners feel beholden to their employees. A business owner who feels this way is relying on his people to run the business. If you have any people problems, the business doesn't run right.

In his seminal book, *The E Myth* (Ballinger Publishing), Michael Gerber proposes, "The systems should run the business; the people should run the systems." By systematizing the operation of the business, the reliance on employees' whims is lessened, and the enterprise value of the business is increased.

McDonald's is a people-intensive business. Yet McDonald's isn't beholden to the skill, talent, and whims of its people. McDonald's has created vast systemization of every process needed to operate a restaurant — from the method of frying a hamburger to the places employees should stand during the lunch rush.

Systemization of your business can create a business that removes you from the day-to-day activities. This systemization allows the entrepreneur to build a stronger and more valuable business.

Focusing on enterprise value — not just profits

Public corporations are criticized for focusing too much on quarterly earnings rather than long-term profitability. Smaller businesses make the same mistake when they design their business model as a personal brand rather than an ongoing enterprise.

It's easy to understand why entrepreneurs fall into this trap. The benefits of the personal brand business model are many:

✔ Fewer operational headaches because the owner is intimately involved in all day-to-day aspects of the business.

✔ No bad decisions made by employees because employees aren't allowed to make any decisions. All decisions are made by the owner.

✔ Profits are at their absolute maximum because the owner is filling job positions that would normally be filled by paid employees.

✔ Customers enjoy dealing with the business owner who can wheel and deal, pull strings, and mobilize the entire enterprise if necessary.

✔ People like dealing with people. Putting a face on the company is appealing to many customers.

However, if entrepreneurs build businesses around themselves (personal branding), they have trapped themselves into building that brand rather than building an enterprise. When the time comes to sell, the value of the personal brand will be far less than the value of a true enterprise.

Selling at the right time

Most professional exit planners will tell you there is an ideal time to exit your company. Businesspeople looking to sell their companies for seven figures, eight figures, or more, spend years preparing the company for sale.

Just like investing in the stock market, timing is important to maximize your return.

The personal aspects of your exit plan are as important as the financial aspects. Many times a business owner's exit has more to do with nonfinancial issues than financial ones.

Selling for the right reasons

When you're ready to sell or exit your business, you want to do so for the right reasons. Certainly, collecting a huge check and becoming wealthy for the rest of your life is a great reason to sell. However, more often than not, business owners exit a business for nonfinancial reasons like frustration. Some good reasons to exit a business include

✔ **Starting another business.** You've spent five years growing this business. It's profitable. Now you're ready to pick up your chips and move to another table. This is a perfectly valid reason to sell a business.

✔ **Lost passion.** There's nothing wrong with the business, but you're just not that into it anymore. Owning a business is supposed to be fun. If you don't enjoy it anymore, sell it.

✔ **Geography.** You've decided you can't take the Cleveland snow anymore and want to move to Phoenix.

✔ **New phase of life.** The kids have graduated college and you're making significant changes in your personal life.

✔ **Big payday.** The business is profitable. The business is growing. The business model is outstanding. All the lights are green. Unexpectedly, a competitor calls and offers you $50 million for the business. You love the business but not enough to turn down $50 million.

✔ **Partnership issue solution.** Many partnerships involve a personal relationship as well as a business relationship. Most business owners work hard to preserve their personal relationship with a partner even if the business partnership is a mess. Selling the business to politely end the partnership is a viable option.

✔ **Adverse life event.** No one wants to think about it when things are going well, but life happens — and generally not at the time of your choosing. Poor health, family commitments, or the economy can bring unforeseen and untimely changes to your life and plans. These events are hard to anticipate and usually require you to, at the very least, examine and re-evaluate your options. Business owners could well face the possibility of having to make fundamental changes or even consider having to exit the business.

✔ **Benevolence.** You have owned a profitable business for 30 years. You have more money in the bank than you'll ever need. Your employees are like family. Many business owners in this situation perform a favorable employee buyout or sell the business with sweetheart terms to the key employee.

✔ **Timing.** All businesses have cycles. Remember the Palm Pilot? It was as hot as the iPhone. Palm Corporation would have realized a much greater sales price selling at the height of the craze rather than when it ended. You have a lot of inside information on your business. If you know things are only going to get worse, and you can realize a good sales price, now may be the time to exit.

Selling for the wrong reasons

If you read *Business Week* or *Fortune* magazines, you see many stories about large companies selling for large sums of money. In the mid-sized and small business world, these stories are less frequent. The reason for this is small business owners sometimes sell for the wrong reasons.

One of the reasons small businesses sell for too little is that business owners — like my dentist, Susan — are burned out. After 42 years of dentistry, Susan doesn't care about the money as much as she cares about just being done with it. This is a real shame. Susan has devoted 42 years of her life to building a nice dental practice. Now she's run out of gas and is going to sacrifice a significant amount of the equity she could have potentially built in the business, because she's sick and tired of being a dentist.

The following sections outline three bad reasons that business owners sell out.

Frustration

After 42 years practicing dentistry, there's a lot for Susan to be frustrated with. The receptionist was late yesterday, and patients were locked out of the office. No patients like coming to the dentist, so they're almost always grumpy. Insurance companies have become harder and harder to deal with. Patients don't want to pay their bills. Susan desperately needs a vacation but feels she can't take one. Does any of this seem familiar to you?

Rather than deal with these issues, Susan has found the ultimate solution — sell the business. After all, when she sells the business, all these problems will belong to somebody else. This solution sounds pretty good to Susan.

Of course, if the business has significant operational problems, any savvy buyer will find them. It may be nice for Susan to daydream about pushing these problems on someone else, but I've yet to see the "sell the business to someone stupid plan" work.

Frustrated or not, Susan needs to fix the issues with her business before selling. Her plan to find a buyer dumb enough to buy her problems isn't going to work. Under that plan, she'll waste valuable time finding potential buyers, only to have them exit the process when they uncover her skeletons.

No successor

As Susan gets older, a couple of things happen. First, she accumulates some wealth, which dissipates her need to work. Second, her desire to work lessens as time goes by. One day Susan wakes up and finds she's 70 years old. She doesn't want to be a dentist anymore, but she has no one to take over the practice. She doesn't have the time or patience to bring in a young dentist and train her. Instead, Susan sells the business for a pittance just to be done with it.

Five years before she wants to exit the business, Susan should begin transitioning the business. Susan could bring in a younger dentist and slowly transition her personal relationships to the new dentist. Alternatively, Susan could alter the areas of dentistry she practices so hygienists and assistants could do most of the work. Susan could lessen her workload by only performing dental procedures that take very little of her personal time.

Fear

There's a fine line between selling your business at the top of the cycle and being fearful of a downturn. If you guess correctly and sell at the top of the cycle, you're a genius. Guess wrong, and you're an idiot. This fear of being wrong motivates people to sell their businesses at the wrong time.

You should never sell your business if you're afraid of anything. It's one thing to make a calculated, intellectual decision and decide the time is right to exit. It's another to sell based on fear.

Chapter 13

Analyzing Your Business Model

*Y*our business model architecture is now complete. You have constructed a viable model by using the eight-component system that I cover in Chapters 6 through 12. Congratulations! Now it's time to review your model as a whole and gauge its strengths and weaknesses. In this chapter I show you how to assess and score your business model by using many of the same techniques professional business model analysts use. After you score your business model, you'll understand its strengths and weaknesses. I also offer suggestions on how to augment the strengths of your model as well as correct its weaknesses.

Comparing Live Business Models and Theoretical Business Models

Like any other theoretical exercise, creating and evaluating a business model is different in theory than in practice. The market will tell you the validity of your business model. Until that point, it's simply guesswork. At the same time, you can gauge the validity and potential success of your business model pre-launch. In this chapter I show you a quick and easy way to gauge your business model and how to identify areas for improvement.

Most business models created in the lab must undergo significant change as they're rolled out into the marketplace. Don't worry, this is perfectly normal. The act of rating the eight components of your business model will help you during this process. Knowing the core strengths of your business model can act as a compass during this time of much change.

This same process works for rating business models of existing businesses. If you're lucky enough to have an existing business, the process of scoring your business model can be quite valuable. You possess empirical market data for all eight areas of your business model. By objectively rating these components, you can assess your business model's strengths and weaknesses and home in on the best opportunities for improvement.

Using the Business Model Framework

Figure 13-1 shows the three areas of your business model — offering, monetization, and sustainability — and the eight components that comprise them.

Figure 13-1:
Business
model
breakdown.

To assess your business model, start with the big picture first.

✔ **What is your offer?** Briefly describe the key points of your offer and why they matter to customers. Ask yourself the following questions:

- What is your main product/service?

- Why does the customer need it?

- What does the customer do without it?

- Are you competing with non-consumption or existing competition?

- What makes your offering unique and different?

- How will you define and differentiate your offering?

- Who are your target customers?

- What value does your product/service deliver?

- Do you have a valid "Blue Ocean" strategy or a "Red Ocean" strategy? (See Chapter 7 for details on these strategies.)

✔ **How will you monetize it?** Will you make money by selling the item for a profit, or are there multiple income streams or creative revenue avenues to create profit? Here are some questions to ask yourself:

- Do you have a meaningful cost advantage?

- Can you flowchart your sales process?

- Are your products/services priced correctly?

- Does your business have an efficient value chain?

- Are there opportunities to grow or modify your value chain?

- Does your business struggle to grow consistently?

- Do you have a strong and proficient sales force?

- Are your revenues stable or predictable?

- Do you have a low break-even point?

- Are you able to borrow or raise funds from your investors?

- Is your business financially healthy or are you over-leveraged?

✔ **Can you effectively sustain it?** How will you deal with competition, innovation, and pitfalls, and successfully exit the business? Consider these points as you decide:

- How significant is your competitive advantage?

- Will you be able to maintain or grow your competitive advantage?

- Are you able to attract and retain a skilled workforce if needed?

- Do you have significant threat of new entrants entering the market?

- What are the barriers of entry to your designated market?

- Can you innovate more successfully than competitors?

- Does the negative impact of a pitfall kill the business?

- Do all the elements of the business model positively reinforce one another?

Figure 13-2 shows how to use the business model framework, using the online music service Spotify as an example.

Figure 13-2:
Defining the
key areas.

Working from the inside out

Just a quick description of each of the three categories is fine. After you complete these descriptions, you can begin work on the subcomponents of each. Start with market attractiveness and move clockwise around the graphic to note the key components, strengths, and weaknesses of each.

Chapters 6 through 12 offer details of all eight areas, giving you a deep understanding of how to assess these strengths and weaknesses. In the following sections, I also provide you with some lines of questioning to help you quickly assess each area.

In keeping with the Spotify example, Figure 13-3 shows a business model framework with notations for all eight sections of the business model.

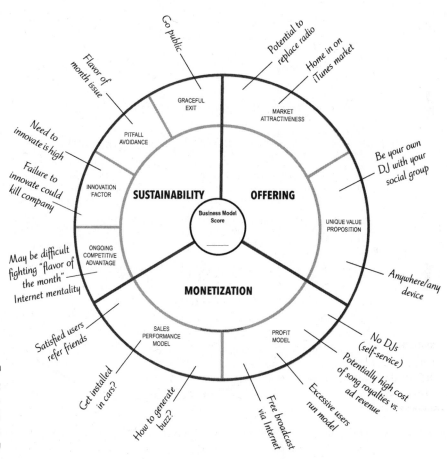

Figure 13-3:
Full business model analysis.

Answering questions about your business model

As you think about the eight areas of the business model framework, the following sections offer some considerations and lines of thought to help you better assess your business model. There are no wrong answers, but the more objective you are, the better your result will be.

Area #1: Market attractiveness

The attractiveness of the market is typically the most important component of the business model. See Chapter 6 for a more in-depth discussion. Considerations include:

- How large is the market?
- Is the market expected to grow within the next three to five years?
- Is the niche expected to grow?
- Are there any barriers of entry?
- Are your customers loyal?
- How do customers in this niche pay? Are they overly price sensitive?
- How competitive is your market niche?
- What is the size of your market?
- What are the typical margins within your industry?
- Do customers in this market tend to be loyal?
- Are industry margins increasing or shrinking?
- What is the general economic health of your customers?
- Are there any threats of any substitute products/services?

Area #2: Unique value proposition

Your unique value proposition (UVP) is a clear statement, in line with your market's challenges and desires, communicating the unique contribution your company, product, and services provide to your market that differs from your competitors'. Flip to Chapter 7 for more details. Ask yourself the following questions:

- How powerful and differentiated is your value proposition?
- Is your product/service easily marketable?
- Can your customers clearly differentiate your product/service from your competitors'?

✔ Is your brand meaningful in the customer's value/quality perception?

✔ How volatile is your market share?

✔ How important is the end benefit of using your product/service?

✔ How effectively can you convince a customer to buy from you and not your competitor?

✔ How is your ability to build relationships with your customers, suppliers, and employees?

Area #3: Profit model

In order to succeed in any type of business, it's important and vital to design and utilize a viable profit model. This involves a strategy that addresses all the core elements of the business operating system that go into making the company viable and profitable. See Chapter 8 for details on profit models.

✔ Do you have a limited profit margin due to the competitive nature of the market?

✔ How is the quality of your revenue streams?

✔ Have you maximized your gross profit margins?

✔ Are any of your revenue streams proprietary?

✔ Is your revenue recurring or one-time hits?

✔ How do your margins compare to your competitors'?

✔ Are there multiple vendors in your market or industry?

✔ Is your market overcrowded with competitors creating excess supply and limiting profit margins?

✔ Is your market industry highly competitive or is it unique?

✔ Are your customers price driven or value driven?

Area #4: Sales performance model

You can create a product that's well positioned and should produce outstanding margins *once it is sold*. Your business model needs to account for turning potential revenues into actual revenues. Chapter 9 offers additional details about the sales performance model.

✔ Can a salesperson of ordinary skill sell your offerings?

✔ Can a definable and repeatable sales process be created?

✔ Is the product marketed or sold? Products that rely on sales-intensive efforts should score lower.

✔ How well is the product/service marketed?

✔ How does your business's sales performance compare to competitors in your market?

✔ Do you have a sales pipeline model that can accurately predict future sales?

✔ How does the cost of customer acquisition compare to the lifetime margin generated?

Area #5: Ongoing competitive advantage

Ideally, your business model will create significant current advantage that you'll be able to sustain. By examining the finer points of competitive advantage, you can gauge the staying power of your model. See Chapter 10 for more information on maintaining a competitive advantage.

✔ Are you a cost leader in your market?

✔ Does your product/service have competitive advantage based on differentiation or focus?

✔ Do you have a skilled, loyal, and talented workforce?

✔ Do you have brand equity?

✔ Are there any existing threats from substitute products in your market industry? If so, how significant are they?

✔ Are the numbers of your competitors increasing or decreasing?

✔ Does your business have the creditworthiness to borrow funds if needed?

✔ Are you protected by customer-switching costs or is this a disadvantage?

✔ Are there financial barriers that help or hurt you?

✔ Is your bargaining power with your suppliers strong or weakening?

✔ Is the bargaining power of your buyers increasing or decreasing?

✔ How significant is the value and quality of your intellectual property?

Area #6: Innovation factor

To keep ahead of the competition and sustain your model, you will need to innovate. Every business — from mobile knife sharpening to integrated chip manufacturing — needs innovation. Different industries demand different levels of innovation to stay ahead of the competition. This component examines whether the model has proper balance between the need to innovate and the company's ability to innovate. Check out Chapter 11 for an introduction to your innovation factor; Part IV also delves in to the topic of innovation.

✔ How much do you need to innovate to keep pace with competition?

✔ Do you have the ability to innovate at that pace or better?

✔ How much of an advantage/disadvantage is this combination?

✔ How important is your product/service innovation to retaining or increasing your customer pool?

✔ Have you been successful when innovating your business model in the past?

✔ If you fail to innovate fast enough, how severe are the consequences?

Area #7: Pitfalls

A *pitfall* is a potential problem for your model. If the business is prone to litigation or governmental action or inaction, is faddish, or has other potential impediments, you must take these issues into account. A pitfall doesn't ruin a business model; it only weakens it. Fashion may be fickle, but many successful designers have navigated the industry for decades. Offshore oil drilling can create multibillion-dollar liabilities if things go wrong. Offshore oil drilling is still a viable business model, but you must take the potential downsides into account. Chapter 11 tells you more about avoiding pitfalls.

✔ Are you financially, strategically, and technically savvy?

✔ Are there any potential future threats from changing demographics, consumer behavior changes, and other trends?

✔ Is your business prone to potential government or regulatory policy changes?

✔ Is your business overly reliant on trends, fashion, or whims?

✔ Is your business location a strategic handicap?

✔ Do you have contingencies in place to protect your intellectual property?

✔ Is your overall business vulnerable to litigation or legal pitfalls?

✔ Is a large competitor entering your market a possibility?

Area #8: Graceful exit (mid-sized and small businesses only)

Some business models create excellent income but are tough for the owner to exit effectively. In order to maximize the benefits of your business model, it should be designed to allow the owner to make excellent income today as well as a profitable exit later. Take a look at Chapter 12 to work on creating a plan for your own graceful exit.

✔ Will you be able to sell your business for enough money to never need to work again if you choose?

✔ How reliant is sales success on owners' involvement?

✔ How many key partner, vendor, and customer relationships are dependent upon the owners?

✔ Is the business overly dependent on a few customers?

✔ Do you have an exit strategy in place should you need it?

✔ What happens if you "get hit by a bus?" (In other words, what if you immediately had to stop working in the business?)

Scoring Your Business Model

I guess I could ask you to pick a number between zero and 100 to represent the strength of your business model, but you've come this far, so I'll finish the job. By breaking the business model into components and drilling down into those components, you've explored all of its nooks and crannies.

Now you can add a numerical scoring model to the business model framework to create an easy way to gauge your model from 0 to 100. The upcoming sections walk you through a quick version of this scoring as well as offering details on a professional version.

I recommend you include business model scoring in your annual planning process. Have several key employees or advisors score your business model each year to see whether the model is increasing in effectiveness or needs innovation. The more quality input you get on your model, the better equipped you are to improve. Consider asking these people for help assessing your model:

✔ Key employees

✔ Trusted vendors

✔ Advisors like accountants, attorneys, bankers, and business coaches

✔ Business model consultants

✔ Shareholders

✔ Board of directors

For the best results, the person scoring the business model must have a deep and intimate knowledge of the business.

Quick-version scoring

Figure 13-4 shows the business model framework with scores for all eight sections added. These sections have scores from zero to varied maximums. The maximum scores vary to properly weigh the importance of that section.

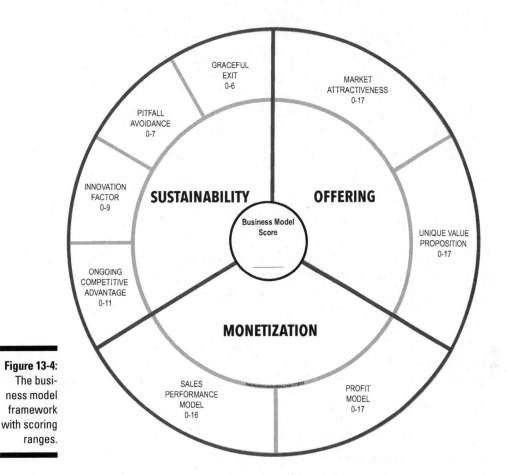

Figure 13-4:
The business model framework with scoring ranges.

By now, you've given a great deal of thought to each area of your model. Starting with market attractiveness at the top of the chart, write down your best estimate of the score for your business model. Next, score unique value proposition and move clockwise around the chart.

Then total each of the three section scores: offering, monetization, and sustainability. The maximum scores for each main section are 34, 34, and 33 respectively. Then total the three sections for your business model score.

Figure 13-5 shows the Spotify business model example from earlier in this chapter with scoring and comments on each of the eight sections.

Scores over 90 are exceptional, and a score of 80 or better is very good. Here's why: No business model is perfect. Even if the model was perfect, it wouldn't take long for competition to see the perfection and attack. If the business model score is below 50, you have some work to do, but you also have some big opportunities.

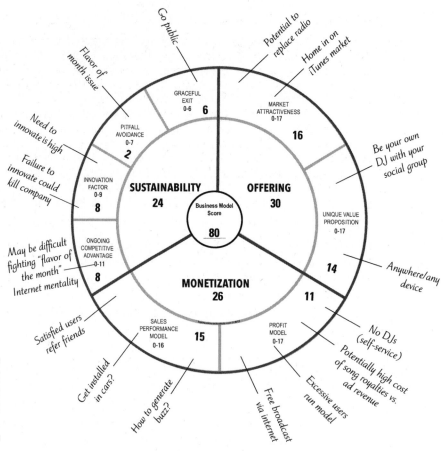

Figure 13-5:
Fully scored
model with
notations.

What to do about a high score

You just scored your business model, and you received a 95. Congratulations!
A Google-like score in the 90s represents a powerful business model. Step
one is to verify. A score this high justifies massive investment in the business
to fully benefit from the model. Before doing that, get some additional input
on the business model score. Have some folks with intimate knowledge of the
business — like employees, consultants, bankers, or attorneys — create their
own scores to make sure your assessment is accurate. When you verify the
accuracy, move briskly. Competitors will quickly learn from your business
model innovations and copy them. This development will probably weaken
your model. The sooner you can grab customers, create barriers, and create
economies of scale, the better.

What to do about a low score

If your score was lower than you hoped, don't worry. If your score is like Apple's business model was over time, there would be periods where the score was very high and periods where it was very low. What Apple and IBM have done so well is to innovate their business models. You can too.

Pick the areas of your business model where you scored poorly. Can anything be done to improve them? Take Spotify's business model. The biggest weakness is the "flavor of the day" mindset of the Internet. Remember MySpace? Newscorp paid $580 million dollars for a white-hot Myspace in 2007 and sold it at a fire sale to a group led by Justin Timberlake in 2012 for a paltry $35 million. Is Spotify a legitimate replacement for iTunes and radio, or is it a fad? The ability to fix this potential pitfall significantly improves the Spotify business model.

In Part IV, I go into great depth on how you can innovate and improve your business model.

Peak business model theory

Keep in mind that your business model score isn't static. As business conditions change, so does your score. Business models tend to increase in profit-making power, and then they peak. Unchanged, the model continues to erode and produce less and less profit, and your score drops. This process may take months or years for a technology company or decades for a brewery or paper mill. Figure 13-6 shows a depiction of this decline.

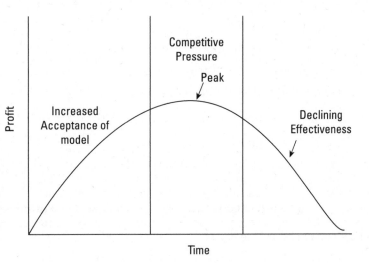

Figure 13-6: When your business model may be peaking.

Before your business model declines, fine-tune and innovate to power your model to the next level. Figure 13-7 shows how to time the process for maximum profit.

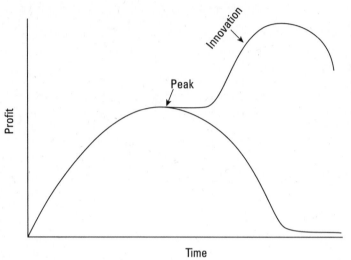

Figure 13-7:
Knowing
when it's
time to
innovate.

Professional-version scoring

Some businesspeople want to have the most accurate picture of their business model possible. If you're one of them, you'll be pleased to know that the Business Model Institute has created a professional version of the business model score. The professional version of the instrument has some of the same elements discussed in this chapter with these additional features:

✔ More than 100 criteria are analyzed.

✔ Scoring of the professional version accounts for an interrelationship among the eight areas rather than a linear-type scoring system. This proprietary system requires a software program to score the results. For instance, a model with a strong value proposition combined with significant pitfalls and weak ongoing competitive advantage could score radically lower than a similar model with strong competitive advantage.

✔ Only Certified Business Model Analysts (CBMAs) can score models on the software. Without significant training, scores would be nothing more than guesses.

If you want to know more about a professionally scored business model or becoming a Certified Business Model Analyst, visit www.businessmodel score.com.

Part III
Dealing with Change

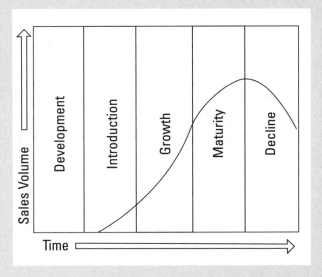

In this part . . .

✔ Deal with the inevitable changes caused by competitive, environmental, political, cultural, and economic factors.

✔ Know when your business model is weakening and when it's not. All business models weaken over time, but some indicators point to problem areas that you can fix before it's too late.

✔ Realize the consequences of leaving your business model unchanged. No matter how risky change seems, stagnating is worse. Take some risks and always be prepared to change course.

✔ Find the root cause of disguised business issues. *Hint:* It's probably a problem with your business model.

Chapter 14

Knowing that All Business Models Erode

*E*ventually your business model will be launched as a real-life business. Hopefully, your business will enjoy great success and prosperity. Unfortunately, the wear and tear of the marketplace takes its toll on *all* business models. Over time, the effectiveness of your business model will lessen. In this chapter I discuss the factors that erode business models and why it's not your fault.

There's No Shame in a Weakening Business Model

A weakening business model isn't a reflection of the skill of the businessperson. A weakening business model has very little to do with your talent and skill. Business models weaken because of market and competitive conditions, not because of any action or inaction you take. Reasons a business model can weaken are:

✔ **Competition:** Those pesky competitors just won't stand still. When you come up with a great idea, they will copy it, lessening your great idea's power.

✔ **Economics:** It's dangerous to blame the economy for the success or failure of your business model, but significant economic pressures can be disruptive.

- ✓ **Technology:** Kodak's film business was exceptionally profitable for decades. After digital photography reached similar photographic quality, the market for film evaporated.

- ✓ **Innovation:** Blockbuster Video succumbed to video streaming technology and thousands of Red Box video vending machines. Innovation doesn't have to be technological.

- ✓ **Buying habits:** As consumers continue to purchase more and more goods online, brick and mortar retailers fight this change in buying habits.

- ✓ **Government:** Your business model can suffer when the government makes decisions that impact it. Examples include a road being moved, changing regulations, new political leadership, and a variety of other factors beyond your control.

- ✓ **Market maturity:** Perhaps the most damaging factor is market maturity. As markets mature, the number of competitors increase, prices decrease, margins decrease, and competition intensifies. Many business models start out in an attractive market only to see the blue ocean turn red ten years later.

All business models deteriorate over time. It's not your fault. Time and competition are the culprit — not you. That said, it *is* your fault if you don't do anything about your deteriorating business model. By doing anything, I mean add, subtract, change, or innovate your business model.

Why companies miss threats

Business decisions are so easy in the rearview mirror, aren't they? The shoulda, woulda, coulda is always easier on someone else's business and looking backward. As a savvy businessperson, you need to be able to identify business model issues that are threats to your business before they impede profitability.

Here are some reasons business models can impede change:

- ✓ **Success:** Don't mess with success, right? It's difficult to sacrifice or cannibalize a successful model to attempt an unknown model. Generally, successful companies stick with their successful models until they receive firm data to contradict it. However, it may be too late to change. For instance, many brick and mortar retailers ignored the Internet threat until it was confirmed. By then, Internet retailers had changed customer behavior and garnered loyalty of their own.

- ✓ **Entrenchment:** Change is tough. It's also expensive and painful. Therefore, businesses avoid it. Why do businesses shrug off potentially damaging data? They have too much infrastructure in the current system, so they choose potential death by paper cuts rather than death by guillotine.

✔ **Varying goals amongst business units:** For instance, at Sony, the business model depended on the different businesses running like independent units — hardware had different objectives than software — so a specific business model risk was the lack of integration between the two when the market was demanding a complete, user-friendly customer experience.

✔ **Guessing poorly:** Sometimes companies try to innovate their business model and just guess poorly. They exhaust available resources chasing the wrong trends or innovations. It should be noted that no one can guess right every time, and errors of commission are always better than errors of omission.

✔ **Discounting competitors:** Can't you just hear a conversation at Borders or Barnes & Noble in 1997 regarding Amazon? It probably went something like, "Who wants to buy a book on the Internet?" Ten years later, Amazon was hosting Borders' online bookstore for them. Pooh-poohing nascent competitors with "crazy" ideas is very dangerous to your business. Many of these crazy ideas will be crazy, but pay attention to the ones that get traction and act accordingly.

Lessons from Apple and IBM

You don't have the luxury of writing your existing business model forever. Without business model innovation, your situation will gradually decline. It's a question of how fast, not if. Apple Computer and IBM provide great examples of how business models can be innovated and shifted to garner long-lasting success.

Apple: Coming back from the brink

It's hard to believe that Apple was near bankruptcy in 1997. The company was so desperate that it tried to merge with Sun Microsystems and had to borrow money from Microsoft. This same near-bankrupt company is now one of the highest valued companies in the world.

The business model lessons from Apple Computer are:

✔ Success number one doesn't guarantee success number two. The Apple II computer was a tremendous success, but Apple's business deteriorated rapidly afterward due to changes in technology, customer preferences, and competition.

✔ A bleak situation can be rectified. Even though Apple was on death's door in 1997, co-founder and CEO Steve Jobs was able to radically overhaul the business to engineer one of business's greatest turnarounds.

IBM: Anticipating problems and making the right changes

IBM is perhaps the best company in the world at business model innovation. IBM should have gone out of business half a dozen times. Unlike other businesses, IBM tends to innovate its business model before it has a problem and bet big when needed.

The learning opportunities IBM provides are many: You can always fix/improve your model, you need to always improve your model, and you can radically change your business and be successful. Over the course of 100 years, IBM went from time clocks and scales to green energy consulting.

The following sections offer an interesting rundown of the changes in IBM's business model.

Early business models

- ✔ In the 1880s the predecessors of IBM produced a wide range of products, including employee timekeeping systems, scales, automatic meat slicers, coffee grinders, and punch card equipment. At that time, their biggest customer was the government, who used the punch card system for the 1900 census.

- ✔ Many improvements to the punch card systems, like punchless "fill in the oval" systems, grew the business.

- ✔ IBM and its predecessor companies made clocks and other time recording products for 70 years. In 1958, IBM Time Equipment Division sold its assets to Simplex Time Recorder Company.

- ✔ In 1933 IBM purchased Electromatic Typewriter Co. to acquire important patents. Electric typewriters would become one of IBM's most successful products, and by 1958 IBM was deriving eight percent of its revenue from electric typewriter sales. In the 1960s IBM introduced the Selectric typewriter, which would eventually garner a 75-percent market share in the business typewriter market. IBM wisely exited the typewriter business by spinning it off as a part of Lexmark in 1991.

Early computer business models

- ✔ In 1952 IBM entered the nascent computer business with the 701. In the 1960s IBM introduced the revolutionary System/360, the first large "mainframe" computer to use interchangeable software and peripheral equipment. *Fortune* magazine dubbed it "I.B.M.'s $5,000,000,000 Gamble," because no one had a guarantee that the concept of computer compatibility was going to succeed in the marketplace. In order for the S/360 to succeed, it would have to cannibalize IBM's existing, revenue-producing computer product lines. The plan worked and the Big Blue empire was the result. The S/360 was such a competition killer, it spawned sayings like "No one ever got fired buying IBM," and "The 7 Dwarfs," referring to the seven computer companies of the era dwarfed by IBM's market prowess: Burroughs, UNIVAC, NCR, Control Data Corporation, Honeywell, RCA, and General Electric.

✔ Many additional business units were spawned as a result of IBM's computer success: Magnetic disk drives, magnetic strip cards such as the ones on credit cards (IBM's magnetic strip is the industry standard worldwide), computer chips, and computer memory.

Rise of personal computing

✔ IBM saw the threat the PC posed to its highly profitable mainframe business, so it jumped into the market. Unfortunately, IBM wasn't successful, because the company didn't follow an integrated architecture business model as it had on the S/360. IBM was late to the PC party, so it allowed outside vendors to supply components (open architecture) to increase speed to market. IBM had some early success in the PC market, but companies like Dell and Compaq came into the market with better business models for selling low-margin PCs and took most of IBM's share.

✔ Interestingly, if IBM had stuck with closed architecture, its PC venture had the potential to be hugely successful. Both Intel and Microsoft rode IBM's coattails on the open architecture PC and created profitable business models. If IBM had used its own microprocessors and operating system, perhaps it could have grown a PC processor division the size of Intel and an operating system division the size of Microsoft.

✔ After it became clear that desktop PCs were an unattractive business model, IBM shifted focus to more profitable laptops, developing the popular ThinkPad. In 2005, IBM gave up on PCs altogether and sold to Chinese manufacturer, Lenovo.

Refocus on profitable hardware

✔ In the early 1990s IBM was in big trouble. Its once profitable products had eroded into low-margin, transactional, commodity businesses. In 1992, IBM reported an $8.10 billion loss, which was the largest single-year corporate loss in U.S. history at the time.

✔ Under CEO Lou Gerstner, IBM divested itself of low-margin industries (DRAM, IBM Network, personal printers, and hard drives). Gerstner radically changed the business model away from separate business units, reintegrating IBM as a one-stop shop for corporate IT departments.

✔ IBM refocused on one of its core competencies — large-scale computing. Even with the significant computing power of networked PCs, some large-scale applications are too complex. IBM supercomputers are some of the most powerful computers in the world.

✔ Previous R&D investments allowed IBM high margins in specialized chip production. IBM-designed chips are currently used in PlayStation 3, Xbox 360, and Wii game consoles.

Rebirth as a service and software company

- IBM realized that hardware margins are quickly commoditized, so the company shifted its business model to focus on software and services.

- A key decision was to become brand agnostic. IBM integrated whatever technologies the client required, even if they were from an IBM competitor.

- In 1995 IBM acquired software developer Lotus Development Corp., beginning an effort to grow the software portfolio from one brand, DB2, to five: DB2, Lotus, Web Sphere, Tivoli, and Rational.

- IBM augmented its services business with the acquisition of the consultancy division of PricewaterhouseCoopers in 2002.

Be Proactive and Be Rewarded

Companies like IBM that have remained viable for long periods of time understand the importance of proactively changing their business models. The fact is, you usually can't see the destructive forces coming. In order to have the most profitable business model in your industry, you need to proactively change it from time to time.

Annual business model planning

Companies engage in annual strategic planning and annual business planning. Why not annual business model planning? If the business model is central to the profitability of the enterprise, then critical thinking about the business model is essential.

I recommend an annual business model review. During this review you should:

- Evaluate your business model based upon the eight-part framework. See Chapter 5 for an overview of this framework.

- Assign someone on your team to play devil's advocate. This person is in charge of pooh-poohing every idea and making you prove the validity of it. This person should also assume the mindset of your competitors. Seeing your ideas through the lens of your competition can be difficult. When you're so focused on making your own ideas successful, you may forget that your competitors are trying to stop these ideas from becoming successful.

- Analyze the aspects of your business model that are improving. Why are they improving? What can you do to augment or enhance this improvement? Will they continue to improve?

✔ Analyze the aspects of your business model that are deteriorating. Can you rectify the problem or only slow down the deterioration? If the problem can't be fixed, should you bother slowing down the deterioration or give up?

✔ What untapped revenue sources can be garnered from the model? Have you accessed all proprietary revenue streams?

✔ If you knew with 100-percent certainty that your business model would stop working completely in three years, what would you do?

✔ If you knew with 100-percent certainty that your business model was a home run, what would you do?

✔ Ask the Brewster's millions question. If someone gave you $10 million with the condition that you had to invest it in your business model, how would you best make use of this money?

✔ What small business model experiment can you make in a different business? It doesn't matter whether this business is in a related or unrelated field.

Start over every five years

Unmodified, your business model will stop working well. For the lucky businesses, this process takes 20 years. For most businesses, it takes only ten years. For technology businesses, it may take only two or three years.

Rather than slowly boiling your frog, start over with your business model every five years. You now understand how to create a powerful business model (if you don't, spend some time looking over Part II). Rather than innovate or tweak your existing model, erase the whiteboard and start over completely.

I'm not suggesting that you ditch your existing business model or stop your existing business. I am suggesting that you go through the exercise of pretending to start over with no encumbrances. This isn't an easy exercise. Pretending that you don't have any encumbrances or any business is difficult. If you can put your creative energy into the exercise, however, you should garner many creative ideas that can radically improve your business model.

Example: Sony

Sony has a reputation for cannibalistic innovation. Sony doesn't wait for a competitor to beat its product offering, it beats the product offering itself. When most companies create a feature or product that would severely damage their existing offering, they kill the product or slow its introduction to market. Theoretically, this maximizes the economic return of the product. Sony takes the opposite approach by rushing the product to market, killing its own existing offering.

Sony's theory is that if it doesn't out-innovate itself, competitors will. Sony may be cutting off profitable revenue streams of existing products, but Sony consistently produces innovative new products ahead of competition. New products tend to command greater margins than older/mature products. As long as Sony's innovation cost is lower than the profits cannibalized, this is a great strategy.

Aim to innovate your business model as Sony innovates products. Rather than trying to squeeze every last drop of juice out of your business model, self-cannibalize and move on to a better version of your model.

Chapter 15

Looking for Signs that Your Business Model Is Weakening

. . . .

In This Chapter

▶ Spotting the signs your business model may be weakening

▶ Painting a target on yourself by generating superior margins

▶ Persisting through the hard times may be a bad idea

▶ Trying easy instead of trying hard

. . . .

*B*y nature, business is competitive. Like a boxer, your competition weakens you as the fight goes on. Sometimes it's tough to know when your weakened state is reasonable and when it's not.

In this chapter, I show you how to recognize when the competitive fight is getting the best of your business model and when the cause is business execution. I discuss four of the most common signs that your business model may be losing its effectiveness: decreasing margins, prolonged minimal profitability, persistent flat sales, and a general dissatisfaction with your business. More importantly, I show you how to spot these trends and offer suggestions on how to best fix them.

Decreasing Margins

I can't emphasize this point enough; great business models have superior margin. You should gauge your margin two ways. First, gauge margin with no regard to competition. A business with a 90-percent margin probably has a better business model than one with a 15-percent margin. Second, gauge margin against companies in the same industry. It's possible your margin percentage could be declining but increasing compared to your competition. For instance, your company's margin could decline from 40 percent to 30 percent, while the average industry margin declines from 35 percent to 20 percent. Your business model would be in better shape than the competition's, but your model would still be weakening.

Any decrease in margin percentage should be viewed as a warning sign. A common tendency among business owners is to pump up sales to compensate for decreasing margin. Sometimes this solution is the right one — and sometimes it isn't. Defaulting to the increasing sales option can create a slippery slope. There are always more sales to get, so it always seems like the best option. Before taking that tact, explore why margins have decreased and attempt to fix it.

Great margins paint a target on your back

Creating a product with great margin acts like a magnet pulling competitors toward you. If you do your job well and create a product or business innovation with outstanding margin, competitors will be envious. They'll see this innovation as a way to improve their own business models. Unfortunately, doing a great job on your business model paints a target on your back. This is why business model innovation is so important (see Chapter 11 for more on the importance of innovation). The inconvenient reality of competitors copying your best ideas forces you to out-innovate them. May the best innovator win.

Aside from innovation, here are a few additional things you can do to slow down the competition's assault on your model:

- **Protect your intellectual property:** Innovation is about ideas. Protect your intellectual property like Apple does. Expect employees to keep new developments confidential. Use nondisclosure agreements with employees, vendors, and partners.

- **Make sure your purchases are important to your vendors:** Vendors are looking for the next piece of business — not to help you protect your innovations. Make sure you're a "big fish" to your vendor, so you can demand secrecy and/or exclusive contracts.

- **Hang on to your key employees:** One of the easiest ways for the competition to catch up is to remove a star player from your team and put her on their team.

- **Tie up key assets:** McDonald's has an entire department devoted to site selection. Most of this team's efforts focus on finding great locations before the competition. McDonald's uses sophisticated data analysis for this purpose. When Apple releases a new product, it secures a multi-year exclusive contract from vendors of key components. This tactic eliminates the competition's ability to play copycat.

- **Market like a tidal wave:** Instead of throwing out a trial balloon for your innovative new product, keep it a secret. Wait until the last moment to make your innovation public, and then market the daylights out of it. This tidal wave marketing approach can act as a moat against competition.

Product lifecycles and your business model

Your ability to generate enough margin depends in part on the product life-cycle. Generally, the early stages of the lifecycle offer higher margins than the later stages. During the later stages, many competitors have entered the market but few have left, leaving an imbalance of supply and demand. Many times the end of cycle offers both lower sales volume and lower margin due to excessive competition. However, it's possible to experience higher margins at the end of cycle if competition radically decreases. For instance, when the Yugo halted automobile sales in the U.S., a savvy parts company bought all remaining parts and is now the only source for Yugo parts in the U.S. (www.yugoparts.com). These parts are slow movers but command a nice margin. Figure 15-1 shows how sales volumes increase during the product lifecycle. Increasing sales volumes attract competition and drive margins down.

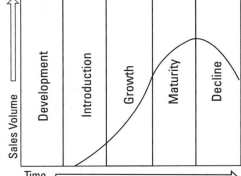

Figure 15-1:
Typical
product
lifecycle.

The following sections give you a quick breakdown of the product lifecycle, using the example of UGG boots. Margins in the early phases of the product cycle are significantly better than margins at the end. That doesn't mean you can't have a good business model with mature offerings. Many of the success-ful products offered by Procter & Gamble are mature. However, Procter & Gamble expends significant effort on creating new products, adding improve-ments to existing products, and extending its brands. This enables Procter & Gamble to extend the period of time where margins are strong.

Stage 1: Development

During the development stage, the product isn't available for widespread pur-chase. The company fine-tunes the offering prior to introduction.

Stage 2: Introduction

The introduction phase is when the offer is first taken to the marketplace. Potential customers see the product in stores and advertisements and compare the offer to existing options.

During this phase, companies tend to use one of two pricing strategies. They either set prices high to recoup development expenses, or they use penetration pricing that prices the product artificially low in hopes of building volume to cover the development expenses. When cellphones were first introduced in the 1980s, the Motorola DynaTAC 8000X, popularized by Michael Douglas in the movie *Wall Street,* cost $3,995 (that's $9,065.69 in today's dollars). Initial purchasers of cellphones paid for the development costs. As these costs were recovered, the cost of cellphones has dramatically decreased.

New prescription drugs use the subsidized approach. The drug companies know the lifespan of the product because their patent will expire on a specific date. The drug company estimates the total lifetime sales of the product and prices the first pill sold at the same price as the last pill sold (barring a similar drug entering the market and creating pricing pressure).

Like any innovative product, the introduction of UGGs was a slow process. Early adopters of UGG boots were primarily California surfers. Because volume is low and the product innovative, margins were high and competition low. For UGGs, this period lasted for more than ten years. Sales increased — but slowly — during this period.

Stage 3: Growth

The growth phase is when sales and profits for the new product begin to rise. Most companies keep product prices stable during this phase to maximize earnings and market share. Distribution channels will most likely expand. For instance, Kashi cereals were originally available at health food stores. As the product grew in popularity, mainline retailers like Walmart and Kroger started carrying the product.

For UGGs, the growth phase was ignited by *Baywatch* star Pamela Anderson getting caught on camera wearing the boots. Other celebrities started wearing the boots, and a national trend began. As the only player in the sheepskin boot market, UGGs was able to maintain prices and capture nearly 100 percent of the market growth.

Potential buyers of UGGs saw Pamela Anderson wearing the boots, but so did potential competitors. A few competitors created lookalike products, cutting into UGGs' market share. However, the market was growing so rapidly that these competitors made only a small dent in UGGs' profitability.

Stage 4: Maturity

The maturity stage begins the downward march of margins. Competitors who saw an attractive market in the growth phase finally have their product on the market. Combined with that, sales begin to flatten out, which creates an imbalance of supply and demand (excessive supply). The buyers are now in control and margins fall.

The effect of all these sellers coming into the marketplace can lead to price wars and intense competition. The market can become saturated and the bigger players may leave the market because the margin produced by product sales is no longer worth the effort.

UGGs haven't hit full maturity yet. Sales aren't occurring at the frantic pace they were previously, but they're still robust. UGGs are still selling at full retail price, and discounting is uncommon. When UGGs begin to lose sales to knockoff brands that cost one-third as much, the maturity phase will be in full swing.

Stage 5: Decline

As sales volumes begin to decline, the imbalance of supply and demand takes its toll. The market is now saturated with entrenched competitors fighting for ever-decreasing volume. The war of attrition, in which all combatants lose, is in full swing; and prices, as well as margins, continue to drop.

A common mistake entrepreneurs make is viewing the exit of a large competitor as a positive event. Their logic goes: "This means more market share for everyone else, including me." This logic makes sense, but it doesn't work that way. The big company is smart enough to exit the upcoming war of attrition. Sometimes, the right move is for you to follow suit.

When decreasing margins are tolerable — and when they aren't

Competition and decreasing margins are a fact of life. How do you know whether or not decreasing margins should be moving you to change? Ultimately, the decision rests upon your ability as a businessperson. Consider these factors:

 ✔ **Velocity of the decrease:** When IBM entered the PC market in the mid-1980s, a desktop computer cost around $3,000. By the mid-1990s a desktop computer cost around $1,000, and today you can buy a decent desktop system for $400. Interestingly, one of the core components in the IBM 8086 was the Intel 8086 chip. This chip cost around $350 at the time. Today's equivalent Intel chip is the i7, which costs about $300. If your margins are decreasing at the pace of IBM's, the analysis is much different than if they're decreasing at Intel's pace.

✔ **Reason for the decrease:** A margin decrease due to an economic decline or something temporary is much different from a decline due to far too many entrenched competitors insisting on a war of attrition. Decreasing margins are a fact of life. Small decreases for good reasons can be tolerated.

✔ **Likelihood of increasing margin in the future:** When oil dropped to $30 per barrel in the 1990s, oil companies kept drilling because they knew oil would sell for more in the future.

✔ **Stage of the product lifecycle:** If you're in the maturity phase of the product lifecycle and margins are decreasing, it's expected. If you're in the introduction phase or early growth phase and margins begin to decrease, it can be cause for concern. (See the previous section "Product lifecycles and your business model" for more on these phases.)

✔ **Your ability to innovate:** 3M Corporation understands that the product lifecycle curve cuts into margins. 3M is a perpetual innovation machine that strives to get one-third of its revenue from new products because these new products will always carry better margin than their mature lines. 3M doesn't kill off mature lines; it augments them with innovative variations or new products.

✔ **Expected number of competitors entering the market or leaving the market:** Currently, UGGs has only a few competitors. What if a dozen new competitors entered the market? The most likely effect is dramatically increased competition and price cutting.

✔ **Your ability to decrease costs:** Walmart and Amazon have been successful in markets with significant downward margin pressure by becoming ever more efficient. These companies have matched margin pressure with costs savings to preserve the strength of their business models.

✔ **Sunk cost:** This one's a trick. Sunk cost should have nothing to do with your analysis. The reason sunk cost made the list is that businesspeople treat it as a consideration when they shouldn't. Just because you invested a lot of time and money in a product doesn't mean you should keep fighting a bad market. That's not to say you should walk away from your investment; just make sure you make a rational decision based on the other factors and leave sunk cost out of the equation.

Example: Memory chips

Intel was formed on July 18, 1968 as a memory chip provider (SRAM and DRAM). The founders of Intel came from Fairchild Semiconductor, an industry leader. Intel skipped the introductory phase of the memory chip business and jumped in during the growth phase. Over the next few years, Intel grew nicely. But the growth phase didn't last long due to many large Japanese companies entering the market.

Frustrated with the low margins in the now mature memory chip business, Intel executives Gordon Moore and Andy Grove bravely decided to exit the memory chip business. Intel refocused its efforts from DRAM to emerging central processing unit (CPU) technology. The resulting 8086 processor became the standard for the burgeoning PC market and led to Intel's dominance in the chip manufacturing market.

As you can see from the Figure 15-2, Intel's decision to exit the memory chip market was extremely wise.

Intel Memory Market Share and Sales
(Adopted from Burgelman, 1994; Grosvernor,1993)

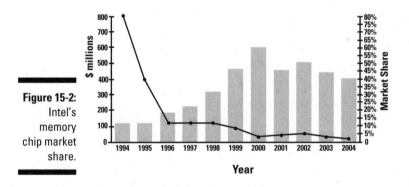

Figure 15-2:
Intel's memory chip market share.

Figure 15-3 clearly shows why Intel was anxious to leave the flat-lining memory business in exchange for the rapidly growing microprocessor business.

Esitmated Memory Sales and
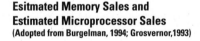
Estimated Microprocessor Sales
(Adopted from Burgelman, 1994; Grosvernor,1993)

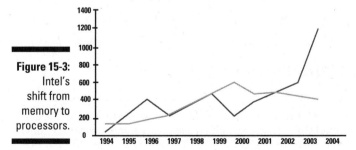

Figure 15-3:
Intel's shift from memory to processors.

Prolonged Minimal Profits

Prolonged minimal profits tends to be a small-company problem. Large companies have several lines of business and can afford to shift resources to their highest and best use, resulting in increased profitability. What if you're a local diner that can turn out only a small profit each year?

Sam runs a local diner and works hard. Sam's best year was 1997, three years after opening, when he netted $65,000. Last year, Sam made $52,000. He has averaged $54,000 per year in profit.

After 20 years in business and 20 years of consistent profits, it's clear that Sam will continue to net a modest $50,000 annually. Here's the issue: businesses move forward or backward; there's no equilibrium in business. Sam may think he's holding pace, but in business, holding pace is really moving backward.

Sam may get lucky and be able to finish his career at his diner, and then sell it for a modest sum. More likely, Sam will hit a speed bump and it will severely damage his business.

Sam has a business model issue. His business model only allows a hard-working man to earn a modest living. That's all this business model has to give. Sam is talented enough to do better but won't without some innovation of his business model.

The fine line between almost turning the corner and stupidity

Sam the diner owner must be from Chicago. Lifetime Chicago Cubs fans like Sam and me are affected by "wait 'til next year" syndrome. How many years has Sam toiled away with the hope that next year will bring the big payday? Sam's tenacity and hard work are to be admired, but Sam's delusion that his profits will magically improve is nuts.

Sam's profits aren't going to radically improve, because Sam has empirical evidence that he's getting everything the current business model has to give. Without changing his business model, Sam is living the Benjamin Franklin quote, "The definition of insanity is continuing to do the same thing and expecting a different result."

Don't be like Sam. Persistence in business should be rewarded with an improving business model and profits. Without that improvement, it's stubborn pigheadedness.

Don't become an indentured servant to a bad business model

When someone like Sam the diner owner insists on working harder at a flawed business model instead of improving it, he winds up being an indentured servant to his bad model. Here's how it happens:

1. **Sam creates his business model and works hard to successfully launch the diner.**

2. **The diner passes the make-it-or-break-it point and operations get more profitable.**

3. **A few years pass and nothing really changes — for better or worse.** Sam relaxes and feels stable and secure. Sam enjoys the break after the difficulty of launch.

4. **Something begins to decay Sam's business model.** It could be economic, the opening of a competitive restaurant, or customers wanting a change. Sam has hit a fork in the road. He must either innovate his business model or keep the same one. Sam opts for the "try harder" plan, keeping the same model. After all, changing the business model is risky and difficult.

5. **Sam's frog begins to boil.** Every erosion of business conditions causes Sam to "try harder." Sam continues to work harder and harder for the same results, becoming an indentured servant to the business. Sam stops taking vacations, works seven days a week, and stops enjoying business ownership as a result.

Nobody wins the war of attrition

A *war of attrition* is one in which the combatants fight furiously for long periods of time but no one wins. The sides grind each other down until one party runs out of resources. You don't want to get into a war of attrition because even the winner loses.

A client of mine sold parts to the automotive aftermarket. Only 50 companies were in this business. During a three-year period, 25 of these companies exited the business by choice, bankruptcy, or merger. My client was excited. After all, many of these companies folded their tents. This meant more business for the remaining players, right? Wrong.

It's been 15 years since this shakeout and the industry still stinks. My client's company still fights hard for every customer and has constant downward price pressure. Remember the card game, "War"? Most kids stopped playing it because no one ever won. It was boring and wasn't fun. The same thing is true in business. If you're in a game of War, don't try to figure out how to win; just don't play!

The try-easy plan

Exiting a bad business easily isn't always possible. Sometimes the business model can't be successfully innovated. For situations in which it's not practical to abandon a business model, the *try-easy plan* is a good option. What's the try-easy plan?

1. **Acknowledge that some of your hard work has minimal reward.**

2. **Find the point of diminishing return where your hard work doesn't add much value.**

3. **Work hard up to the point of diminishing return and stop.**

4. **Let go of perfectionist habits.** This step is the hard one. When you stop working as hard as you used to, small things will go wrong. These little imperfections will annoy you. Let them be imperfect. You're leveraging the Pareto principle (also known as the 80/20 rule). By definition, you're doing 80 percent and letting go of 20 percent. Within that 20 percent, some things won't go perfectly. So what? The cost of fixing the 20 percent far exceeds the value of perfection.

5. **Use the time you save from implementing Step 4 to create new revenue streams, new products, or a completely different business, or to innovate your business model.** The benefits gained from these activities far exceed putting the time into the old business model.

Flat Sales Trend

It's a pretty safe assumption that you're constantly trying to improve your sales. If these efforts fail to meaningfully raise sales, your business model may be weakening. Flat sales are a lot like a hole in a rowboat. Your sales efforts feverishly bail the water, but the hole in the boat lets in as much water as you bail out. Any gains resulting from increased sales efforts are offset by erosion of the business model.

If you experience a long-term, flat sales trend, look at potential business model issues first and then — and only then — make an operational push to increase sales.

Two big box mall retailers currently have this issue. Both JCPenney and Sears have had flat sales for years. To their credit, both retailers have recognized the fundamental market changes affecting their business model and realized the need for big changes.

JCPenney has radically overhauled its pricing structure, eliminating all sales in lieu of a low-price-every-day model. JCPenney has also created stores within a store to improve its offerings. It's too early to see whether this model will work, but give JCPenney credit for trying a new model.

Sears has taken a much different approach. Several years ago Sears purchased Land's End in an attempt to improve already profitable clothing sales. The Land's End experiment has worked, but not well enough to fix Sears's problem. Currently, Sears seems to be slowly dismantling the company in order to preserve equity. Sears sold a large portion of its Canadian stores, sold prime real estate, spun off the Hometown stores, focused on licensure of its popular brands such as Craftsman, and refuses to reinvest in its stores.

The difference between the Sears model and the JCPenney model is that JCPenney is trying to survive as a reinvented form of a big box retailer. Sears seems to be attempting to sell off assets piece by piece, leaving a gutted, non-functional retailer to go bankrupt at the end. It will be interesting to see which model works the best. If JCPenney fails to reinvent itself successfully, the Sears approach could be the better method to preserve shareholder value.

General Dissatisfaction

General dissatisfaction with your business is probably the least accurate predictor of an issue with your business model, but it can be a predictor. There are hundreds of reasons to be dissatisfied with your business that have nothing to do with your business model. The following reasons tend to be issues with your business model rather than just day-to-day issues:

- **Inability to find good employees:** Why can't you find good employees? Probably because you can't pay enough to get good employees. Why can't you pay enough? You don't have enough margin. You don't have enough margin because of your business model.

- **Inability to retain key employees:** Employees may not know they do this, but subconsciously employees gauge the quality of your business model. They understand that a job at Google pays better than a job at Yahoo! The company with the better business model usually pays better and provides more job security. When employees discover an employer with a better business model, sayonara.

- **Difficulty increasing sales:** It's the components of the business model of your offering that are making it difficult to sell. Fix those components and it won't be so difficult to increase sales.

- ✓ **Getting tired of dealing with competitors:** You're probably tired of dealing with competitors because you have too many of them. This overly competitive marketplace smacks of a bad business model or bad market niche. Again, the problem is with the business model.

- ✓ **Having customers who don't want to pay their bills on time:** Customers have an amazing ability to prioritize bill paying. They pay the bills they absolutely have to first and stall as much as possible on the nonessential vendors. If the customer is paying you slowly, it means you're a nonessential vendor. The problem is that your business model has you positioned as a nonessential vendor, not that the customer doesn't want to pay you.

- ✓ **Being sick of all the changes brought on by the Internet:** I agree, all the operational and marketing changes brought about by the Internet are daunting. I'm guessing that if you're sick of the confounded Internet, you're probably fighting the trend, not riding the trend. The fact that you're fighting a powerful trend indicates that you have a problem with your business model.

- ✓ **Becoming tired of fighting the fight:** As you can see, most business issues are rooted in a business model issue. Treat these problems as a gift — not a curse. If you take the time to explore the business model root cause, you can make your business enjoyable again.

Business ownership is supposed to be fun

Owning a profitable, successful business should be one of the most enjoyable endeavors of your life. Ask any business owner who's done so, and I bet she'll agree. I've seen business owners get beaten down by their businesses. What really has these business owners beaten down is their business model — not their business. Please use the lessons in this book to fix what's wrong with your business model. Business ownership can and should be fun!

Chapter 16

Detecting Hidden Problems and Adapting before It's Too Late

In This Chapter

▶ Working on your business model (It's like a magic wand!)

▶ Looking at common issues like the need for more sales and the need for more time

▶ Identifying the root causes of everyday business issues

▶ Adapting your business model while you still can

Sometimes everyday business problems really are more of a problem than they seem. Many times these problems are symptoms of a deeper business model issue. By learning to recognize the root cause of these everyday problems, you can save yourself tremendous grief. If you address the business model as the root cause of the issue, you'll find that many problems simply disappear.

In this chapter, I tell you about some of the common symptoms of business model issues and their solutions. Be prepared for a bit of a shove toward confronting and dealing with these issues now rather than later. Then I discuss the process of business model erosion and how to mitigate its effects. By counting on change, you can maintain a stronger business model than your competition.

Fixing Your Business Model to Make Other Problems Disappear

I always joke that there is no magic wand in business. However, the closest thing to the elusive magic wand is addressing a root business model issue effectively. When you solve a root business model issue, ten other so-called problems magically disappear.

The best way to explain this phenomenon is to use an example. Occasionally, many business owners get frustrated with employees' poor performance. They say things like, "How hard is it to . . .," or "Why anyone can't just . . .." I call the issue "inferior work by employees." The root issue here isn't dumb or lazy employees; it's more likely a combination of poor pay and lack of training.

Don't stop there. Assume the business in this example is like most small to mid-sized businesses and can't afford to pay top-shelf compensation packages. If the business could recruit better qualified people, job performance would improve. It sounds simple; pay more and get better people. Why didn't these owners think of that sooner? They didn't think of it, because the current business model doesn't support paying more. If the true root of the problem is the need for a higher caliber employee, the business model must support the pay of the more expensive person. Currently, the business model doesn't support the higher pay, ergo the performance issue.

If you believe the pay level and caliber of the staff isn't the issue, then the staff's poor performance is probably rooted in lack of training. More than 90 percent of mid-sized and small businesses significantly shortcut training or skip it altogether. You can assume that an outstanding training program would solve or significantly mitigate the performance issues, because it would.

You probably understand the importance of training. It's hard to argue that inadequate or bad training beats quality training. So why shortcut the training? Necessity, that's why. The time and human resources necessary to train the employees simply weren't available.

Most business owners and their staff are time starved. They're time starved because they're paying for the staffing level the business model can bear. Change the business model to generate more margin, and — poof — the problem disappears.

Examining Some Disguised Issues

Sometimes what ails a business is exactly what it seems. If you need more customers to buy your products, the obvious solution is better or additional marketing. If you want to expand but don't have the capital, finding a willing lender is a good option.

However, sometimes the obvious solution to a business problem is a symptom and not the root problem. A business can need capital for many reasons: capital expenditures, expansion, funding receivables or inventory, or buying a competitor. These are all good reasons to need additional funds. In some cases, however, the business needs funds because the model isn't generating sufficient profits. The loan doesn't fix this problem; it only artificially subsidizes the weak business model.

This section describes several instances in which "the problem may not be the problem" and is more likely a business model issue.

Disguised issue: The need for more sales

There's no such thing as a successful business model that doesn't have a successful sales model. If you can't sell a product profitably, you won't stay in business very long. Although sales are fundamental to a successful business model, many entrepreneurs overemphasize the idea that simply increasing sales will solve all problems. The salespeople are underpaid? Sell more. The business is losing money? Sell more. Customers demand more for less? Sell more.

It's difficult to find a business owner who doesn't say, "We need more sales." After all, additional sales can provide much needed cash and margin. Additional sales volume greases the wheels of business, including yours.

However, your bills are paid with gross margin. Consider these formulas:

Sales – Cost of Goods Sold = Gross Margin

Gross Margin – Administration and Overhead – Interest = Net Margin (also called Net Profit)

Additional sales volume doesn't always translate into more net profit. Trading $1 of sales for $0.80 in cost generates cash flow, but it may not generate enough of what you really need — profit.

The real issue is that you need more profit! Yes, adding more customers is one way to get more profit. If getting more customers was simple, though, wouldn't you already have done so? The real issue is a problem with your business model.

In many cases, the sales volume of the business is acceptable. Sales can't be *easily* increased. For instance, a plumbing contractor with an eight-percent market share may be doing pretty well. All the low-hanging fruit has already been picked. Increasing sales means increasing market share from an already respectable eight percent and working to attract ever more difficult customers. This plan may increase sales, but the ever-increasing cost of customer acquisition may outweigh this gain.

Additional sales may not be the best way to increase profits. In fact, the lack of new customers is a less likely cause of the root business model issue than a financial issue, such as:

- ✔ A cost structure that's too high for the current sales level

- ✔ A competitive disadvantage regarding cost (think of Walmart versus a local grocery store)

- ✔ Total margin that's simply too low for a viable business model

- ✔ Cost accounting issues or not properly accounting for margin

For example, many car dealers sell vehicles for "below invoice." Theoretically, this appears to be selling the vehicle for less than it costs. However, dealers get multiple rebates and kickbacks worth thousands of dollars per vehicle. So what's the margin per car, $0 or $2,000? It all depends on how you choose to do your cost accounting.

Figure 16-1 shows what raising prices can do for your margins. At a 20-percent margin, a price increase of only two percent allows you to lose nine percent of your business and make the same profit.

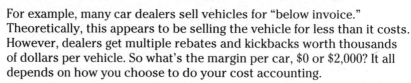

IMPACT OF PRICE INCREASES

if your present margin is

And you increase prices by	20%	25%	30%	35%	40%	45%	50%	55%	60%
	To produce the same profit your sales volume must be reduced by:								
2%	9%	7%	6%	5%	5%	4%	4%	4%	3%
4%	17%	14%	12%	10%	9%	8%	7%	7%	6%
6%	23%	19%	17%	15%	13%	12%	11%	10%	9%
8%	28%	24%	21%	19%	17%	15%	14%	13%	12%
10%	33%	29%	25%	22%	20%	18%	17%	15%	14%
12%	38%	32%	29%	26%	23%	21%	19%	13%	17%
14%	41%	30%	32%	29%	20%	24%	22%	20%	19%
18%	44%	39%	35%	31%	29%	26%	24%	23%	21%
18%	47%	42%	38%	34%	31%	29%	26%	25%	23%
20%	50%	44%	40%	38%	33%	31%	29%	27%	25%
25%	58%	50%	45%	42%	38%	36%	33%	31%	29%
30%	60%	55%	50%	46%	43%	40%	38%	35%	33%

If your margin is 30% and you increase price by 10%, your volume can go down by 25% before your profit falls to the earlier level. (If all customers bought the same, you could lose 1 in 4 customers and still make the same profit).

Figure 16-1:
Impact of pricing on margins.

Perhaps the answer *is* adding new customers. Sometimes, you want to attract new customers but can't seem to do so. You try and try, but sales increase only marginally. You continue to press on the sales gas pedal when it's already floored. The real issue is that your existing sales and marketing system isn't working, yet you insist on trying to squeeze more sales from it.

To fix the root cause, stop trying to work a flawed sales system. Address the underlying issue. Most likely, it's one or more of the following:

- ✔ An undifferentiated or "me-too" product or service. Premium pricing is difficult to command from a "me-too" product or service. For instance, most consumers don't care what brand of gasoline they purchase because gasoline brands are undifferentiated.

- ✔ Poor marketing of a good product/service.

- ✔ An under-leveraged brand.

- ✔ A sales or marketing effort that's failing to sell a sellable product or service.

Blindly chasing more sales only exacerbates the real problem. It doesn't fix it. Generally, one of two fundamental business model issues is at the root of the problem:

- ✔ You're not generating enough margin from existing sales.

- ✔ You have an issue with the salability of your product.

Fix these issues and your "we need to sell more" issue will disappear.

Disguised issue: The need for a 26-hour day

One of the traits I most admire in business owners is their dogged persistence. You are one hard-working group. Many times I hear, "If I only had a 26-hour day . . ." Wouldn't it be wonderful to be Samantha on *Bewitched*? Wrinkle your nose and everyone around you freezes while you keep working. Implicit in this wish is the knowledge that your business isn't performing as well as you know it could. If you only had more time, you could tackle all those big opportunities.

It's probably safe to assume that you're the most valuable person at your business and that your time has the highest per-hour value. If your time is the most valuable, the obvious solution is to delegate some of your work to your subordinates. Shoot, why didn't you think of that before? Oh, you did, but you have no one to delegate to. You have no one to delegate to because you lack the funds to pay someone to do the work. Your solution is to donate your extra time for free to the business.

This issue is so common that I have a name for it — The Big Subsidy. The logic goes something like this: "I don't have the money to pay someone to do this task, but I'm on salary, so I'll do it." The business model can't support paying the required staff to complete the work, so you jump in and donate your personal time for free. Now you're trapped doing $12-per-hour work instead of more important tasks.

The solution to the The Big Subsidy is to challenge your business model instead of your work ethic. Why doesn't the model generate enough margin to pay the $12-per-hour person? Fix the business model issue and you won't need a 26-hour day.

Ignoring Business Model Issues Only Extends the Pain

In *Secrets of the Millionaire Mind* (HarperBusiness), author T. Harv Eker points out that if you tend to the roots of the tree, the fruit harvest is bountiful. However, if you tend to the fruits and not the roots, eventually, your harvest will decrease and your tree may die.

The same is true for your business. The profits are the fruits, but the business model is the roots. If you don't tend to the roots, your problems will not simply go away.

If you insist on tackling the obvious issues instead of their root business model causes, you will suffer unnecessarily. At some point, you'll need to tackle the root cause(s) regardless of how difficult it may be to do so. Instead of viewing a business model tune-up as daunting, view it as the chance to create a competitive advantage. Be willing to do the work your competitors aren't willing to do. While they're sitting on their laurels, you'll be fine-tuning your business model. Use your knowledge of business model design and innovation to outsmart your competition.

As a consumer, you can spot root business model issues a mile away. If the retail store is dirty or the parking lot is empty, you subconsciously know that the problem isn't the parking lot; there's a business model issue. Spotting problems with your own business, however, is much more difficult. Take heed when any issue arises, and if need be, make sure you dig all the way to the root to fix it.

Considering the Consequences of Not Adapting

In order to keep your business model working at its best, you need to innovate, adapt, and be flexible. Building a business isn't like building a house. When you build a house, you get to cut the ribbon on the front porch when you're done. Building a business model is more like building a sandcastle. You finish and then the tide comes in and knocks some or all of it down. The issue is how fast the tide comes in — not whether it comes in.

Your job as a savvy businessperson is to understand the tides and proactively move your sandcastle where the tide won't destroy it.

Your model is eroding, but how fast?

All business models erode — some fast, some slow. How quickly your business model erodes depends on a variety of factors:

- **Use of technology in the industry:** Technology tends to cause disruption and create competitive advantage. If the industry has a general propensity to leverage technology, count on your business model eroding faster.

- **Competitive intensity:** Fiercely competitive industries are always scratching and clawing for a better, faster, or cheaper way to do business. Many of these turn into business model innovations and work to erode yours.

- **Economic factors:** A good economy may either slow down or speed up the erosion of your business model. For instance, a strong economy spurred massive investment in Internet-related businesses, causing excessive competition and eroding otherwise good business models. A good economy made the entire construction industry fat and happy and lessened competition. The same can hold true for a bad economy. A bad economy may cut risk-taking and extend the life of your business model, or it can cause competitors to deploy unused resources toward innovation.

- **Convergence of industries:** The digital camera business isn't being eroded by a better digital camera or an innovation. It's being eroded by cellphones. The two businesses are converging, and cellphones are eroding the digital camera market significantly.

- **Industry attractiveness:** High profile investments in Facebook had many venture capitalists, technology entrepreneurs, and well-established companies looking for new business models in social media. A highly attractive market created a highly competitive market.

- ✔ **Barriers to entry:** Industries that require hard-to-find skills, large sums of capital, or other barriers to entry can expect their business models to erode more slowly than others.

- ✔ **Dependence on trends:** A business model dependent on trends will usually erode faster than others. That doesn't mean a trend-dependent business model is a bad one. Companies like Ralph Lauren, Chanel, and Tiffany's have successfully navigated fashion trends for decades.

- ✔ **Availability of information:** One of the huge advantages early social media companies like Facebook had was the dearth of data available for competitive analysis. The industry was so new that no meaningful data existed. Lack of information causes uncertainty. Uncertainty raises risk. Increased risk lowers the entrance of competitors and makes the business model last longer.

- ✔ **Stodginess of industry:** Banks have a reputation for stodginess; marketing agencies have a reputation for the opposite. If your industry operates like bankers, expect business model changes to come more slowly.

- ✔ **Risk aversion of industry:** Large pharmaceutical companies spend hundreds of millions of dollars every year trying, and sometimes failing, to develop new drugs. You can assume large pharmaceutical companies aren't risk averse. Insurance companies employ armies of actuaries to assess and avoid risk and have entire departments dedicated to risk avoidance. You can assume insurance companies are somewhat risk averse. If your industry is full of insurance companies, your business model will erode more slowly than if it's full of pharmaceutical companies.

Change always seems risky

Change stinks. You toil away for years building a great business model and a great business, and then change comes along and messes with it. In business models, the devil you know always seems better than the devil you don't know.

Eventually you will need to change your business model. It's not a question of if; it's a question of when. So the hundred-thousand-dollar question isn't "Should I change?" The question should be, "Is it riskier to change now versus later?" Generally, it's less risky to change too soon than too late even though it doesn't feel that way.

After World War II, a devastated Japan was looking to rebuild its industrial base. Clamoring for any edge, Japanese manufacturers turned to W. Edwards Deming's statistical quality control methodologies. For years, Deming tried to convince U.S. manufacturers to adopt his process to no avail.

The Japanese used Deming's techniques to create radically superior manufacturing processes, which resulted in higher-quality products produced at a lower cost. Large American manufacturers were profitable and growing, so the addition of Deming's process was an annoyance.

In the early 1980s, Ford dealers discovered that among models with U.S.-made and Japanese-made transmissions, customers requested models with the Japanese-made transmissions much more often. Customers were even willing to wait for long periods to avoid the U.S.-made version. After record losses in 1981, Ford called upon Deming to bring his practices to Ford. While U.S. automakers were languishing, Japanese automakers were flourishing due to lower costs and higher quality production.

This example may seem old, but U.S. automakers are still paying the price for their slow adaptation. U.S. automakers viewed change as dangerous because their existing business model was quite profitable. Their unwillingness to change resulted in a 30-year head start for the Japanese. When weighing risk, make sure to account for competitors who are willing to take the risk you aren't.

Not changing may be worse

An inherent part of human nature views change as risky or bad. Famed psychologist Abraham Maslow theorized that one of a human being's core needs was safety. Maslow also stated that higher-level needs, like belonging or self-esteem, were impossible to achieve *without* an individual's safety needs being met. Figure 16-2 shows Maslow's Hierarchy of Needs. I have to believe this hierarchy affects the behavior of businesspeople — safety good, risk bad. In other words, change is bad, no change is good.

Figure 16-2:
Abraham Maslow's Hierarchy of Needs.

SELF-ACTUALIZATION
Pursue Inner Talent, Creativity, Fulfillment

SELF-ESTEEM
Achievement, Mastery, Recognition, Respect

BELONGING - LOVE
Friends, Family, Spouse, Lover

SAFETY
Security, Stability, Freedom from Fear

PHYSIOLOGICAL
Food, Water, Shelter, Warmth

Case study: Blockbuster Video

A good example that illustrates the danger of not changing is Blockbuster Video. Blockbuster grew from a handful of stores in Dallas to a worldwide video rental powerhouse with 6,500 locations. Blockbuster dominated the video rental industry until the mid-2000s, peaking at a market share over 50 percent. Through a series of nonsteps, not missteps, Blockbuster is now irrelevant. Clinging to its hugely successful retail movie rental model was the primary culprit in Blockbuster's demise. In 2001, Dish Network purchased the assets of Blockbuster from the bankruptcy court for $320 million. Here are some of the action opportunities Blockbuster missed:

- 1999: Netflix was formed. Blockbuster let Netflix operate without competing against it until 2004, when Blockbuster started its DVD-By-Mail service.

- 2002: Redbox was created, not by two guys in a garage, but with the blessing and funding of McDonald's. Rather than participate in the venture, Blockbuster waited until 2009 to roll out 9,000 Blockbuster Express units to compete with the 30,000 Redbox units operating at the time.

- 2005: Coinstar bought 47 percent of Redbox for a paltry $32 million. Blockbuster's total market capitalization at the time was $7.35 billion. Why did Blockbuster sit idly by? It would seem that half of Redbox would have been worth more to Blockbuster than to Coinstar. Blockbuster could have rebranded the Redbox machines or closed them down, forcing people back to its stores. Blockbuster's existing business model centered around its massive retail presence. What was it supposed to

do, close all its stores? The inertia of their store-based model caused Blockbuster to play ostrich (burying its head in the sand) and hope the problem wouldn't grow.

- 2007: Netflix mailed its one billionth DVD. Blockbuster continued to arrogantly assume it could beat Netflix despite a five-year head start. Again, Blockbuster's business model strength, its stores, became its weakness. A mail-based model like Netflix cannibalized stores, so Blockbuster protected its stores by downplaying the importance of mail-based DVDs. At some point, the big mistake Blockbuster made was not buying Netflix. When it was clear the Netflix model was winning, Blockbuster should have conceded and crushed the competition by buying Netflix.

- 2007: Redbox captured a 34.5-percent market share, passing Blockbuster. In no rush, Blockbuster waited two years to launch its vending service. In an ironic twist, Redbox bought all 10,000 Blockbuster Express kiosks in 2012 for $100 million.

It's clear that Blockbuster was lulled to sleep by its dominant market share and brand presence. The entrenchment in a highly-profitable retail business model made Blockbuster complacent. This complacency caused the company to delay tough decisions and leave the business model experimentation to the "little guys." Unfortunately, Blockbuster is the little guy now.

As an interesting aside, Netflix tried to do what Blockbuster should have done: gently transition from business model #1 to business model #2. In 2011, Netflix CEO Reed Hastings possessed a profitable DVD mail service and a growing video streaming service. However, Hastings saw the writing of the wall — DVDs were going away — and knew he had to transition to a streaming video model.

Hastings split Netflix into a mail DVD service under the existing Netflix name and moved the streaming to a new company, Qwickster. Unlike Blockbuster, Hastings was disrupting his own business model. However, the move angered customers. Splitting the companies required two separate logins and two separate bills. In addition, Hastings raised prices 60 percent in conjunction with the split. The result was catastrophic and fast. In four months, 800,000 Netflix subscribers quit the service and the stock dropped 77 percent.

Hastings quickly recovered, nixing the Qwikster service and apologizing to customers. He didn't reduce pricing, because Hastings felt Netflix still offered the best value in the marketplace. Netflix continues to try to gently transition from a mail-order business model to a streaming business model.

In business, situations are fluid, not static. Safety today may be risk tomorrow. Risks taken aren't permanent. If you make a significant change to your business model and get evidence it's a bad idea, you can adjust. Business models are molded out of clay, not chiseled out of marble.

Part IV
Business Model Innovation

Getting in the Insurance Business

Risks Clients are forced to accept	Would they pay to mitigate?	How much?	Potential insurance policies	Our cost	Additional profit
Is the plumber well-skilled?	Yes, the time needed for a poorly skilled technician could add hundreds to the bill	10% - 20% more	Self-certify plumbers as ABC Plumbing Gurus/Master Technicians. Hire only plumbers with 5 years or more experience and advise accordingly. Have a fix it the first trip guarantee	1/2 or less the additional revenue gained	50% margin on upsell
Will I have to take off work and wait on the plumber?	The cost of the inconvenience is significant for some customers	$20 - $50 per job	Do better than the 1 hour windows promised by the other companies. Guarantee the plumber will be there exactly on time. It's simple, under-schedule not over-schedule. Budget slack time so the plumber can be on time. Charge customers if they are not on time too. Companies employing this strategy can command rates 25% -50% higher than market.	30% of additional revenue created	70% margin on business created
Is the plumber honest or will he sell me things I don't need?	Over-selling is a big fear in service industries	5% - 25% more	Gather dozens of video (not written) testimonials with happy customers discussing this issue	$1500	Margin generated by additional sales
Will the plumber be "casing" my home?	May not be reasonable for the customer to feel this way but some have this sinking feeling	A little	Background check all employees, run employee's credit scores every 6 months to ensure they are not having financial issues. Create a "We watch our employees so you don't have to" campaign where employees wear wireless helmet cams monitored by the home office.	$5000 - $10,000	Margin generated by additional sales
Does the plumber have the right tools and parts on their truck?	Customer does not want to pay $150/hour for a trip to Home Depot for a $2 fitting.	5% - 10% more	It's impossible to always have everything on the truck, but it is possible to have everything 90+% of the time. This one is a classic opportunity missed. Because it's impossible to always have everything on the truck, plumbers give up on guaranteeing it. The answer is simple, upcharge for the guarantee and eat the cost of the times you don't have everything. You can have a driver fetch parts so the plumber doesn't have to leave or offer customers a $100 discount if you do have to leave.	10% - 50% of additional revenue generated	This feature could attract new customers or get existing customers to pay more, so the profit potential is significant
Does the plumber have a next job or will they try to drag this one out?	A plumber with a busy schedule probably completes the job with briskness. A plumber wondering where his next gig will come from might stretch this one out.	5% more	Flat rate	Cost of poorly estimated jobs	Improves profitability via more closed sales from comfortable prospects.
Will this repair fix the problem permanently or will I be calling them in 6 months for "round 2"?	Most customers want to understand the total cost to fix the problem, not just the cost today.	A little	Create a "One and done" or "5 year guarantee" to make the customer comfortable that you have completely solved the problem. You don't have to give it on all jobs. If a customer has a 100 year old house, nicely tell them that you cannot guarantee any pipes over 20 years old.	Minimal because our high-quality work already should last 5 years.	Margin generated by additional sales
How long will this repair take at $150/hour?	That feeling of clicking the stop watch and knowing every minute the plumber scratches his head and says "Hum" costs you $2.50 stinks.	Potentially a lot more because the customer has no idea how long the job should take. If the customer thinks 5 hours is reasonable but the job will only take 1 hour, the margin opportunity is significant	Flat rate	Cost of poorly estimated jobs	Game-changing

In this part . . .

- ✔ Tune up your business model through innovation. True innovation involves more than just tweaking your current business model.

- ✔ Determine how and where to begin the innovation process. When innovation is part of your model, you're more likely to reap the rewards of this tactic.

- ✔ Check out examples, exercises, and tools that can help you begin the innovation process.

- ✔ Understand the secrets of disruptive innovation as a technique to radically transform your model for the better.

- ✔ Consider advanced business model innovation techniques, which are some of the best tricks in my bag — they've made my clients millions.

Chapter 17

Figuring Out Where to Begin the Innovation Process

In This Chapter

▶ Avoiding the mistake of simply adjusting your existing model

▶ Using the crystal ball exercise

▶ Getting past the fear of being wrong

▶ Understanding the beauty of a cheap fast failure with upside

▶ Learning to version your business model

*H*ow do you fix a business model? You innovate. Done right, innovation not only repairs a broken business model, but also makes it better than it was before. The innovation process for a business model is similar to any other innovation process. Innovation takes a dash of creativity, a dash of guts, some futurism, and a bunch of business experience put together to create a beautiful new model.

Many businesspeople understand the importance of fine-tuning the business model through innovation, but they don't know where to begin. This chapter discusses the process to start improving your business model through innovation. I demonstrate why tweaking your old model rarely works, how failure can be your friend, and the importance of predicting the future.

Adjusting Your Old Model Rarely Works

Emily owns a spa in an affluent suburb. For the past ten years Emily has enjoyed a great deal of success. A few years ago Emily's business dropped 20 percent due to the recession. Emily made a few changes to gain back some sales and aggressively cut costs. With these changes, her business was still quite profitable. Then a Massage Envy franchise opened down the street. Massage Envy uses a unique business model that doesn't require appointments and uses a health club membership model rather than the standard pay-per-use model. More than 40 percent of Emily's business was massage, and that segment of her business was cut by half.

Emily knew she needed to change her business model. She made a list of the customers she served and the types of services offered. Emily methodically analyzed how she could better serve these customers and sell more of these services. Emily came up with dozens of changes, very few of which worked.

The problem with Emily's business model innovation plan wasn't the quality of Emily's ideas, it was the way Emily went about the innovation. All Emily did was play around the edges of the existing model. Much like sanding off the rough spots of a board, the wood is still the same length, width, and shape when you're done sanding. It's just missing the rough spots. Emily needed more than removal of the rough spots. She needed a vastly improved business model, and she wasn't going to get one tinkering around with her existing model.

Looking forward, not backward

You achieve business model innovation by looking forward, not backward. Looking backward gets you what Emily got — sanding off some rough spots. If you're looking for significant innovation, ignore your current situation and look into the future.

To look into the future, you must use a clean slate. When Emily innovated her business model, she made several presumptions:

- ✔ **Emily's current lines of business should be grown and made more profitable.** Did Emily consider the possibility that greater profitability could be obtained by shrinking or dropping some of these lines of business? Probably not, because she started with the presumption that she should grow the lines instead of using a clean slate.

- ✔ **The objective of the business model innovation was to fight back the advance of Massage Envy.** This is a defensive position. Business model innovation done for defensive purposes yields different results than innovation done for offensive purposes. Typically innovation done in an attempt to lead a market is more profitable than innovation designed to fight back competitors. Emily would have been better served to design her innovation to leapfrog over Massage Envy with something spectacular rather than trying to catch them.

- ✔ **She must compete with Massage Envy.** Because she started with the existing paradigm, several options never entered her mind, like co-locating with Massage Envy, buying a Massage Envy franchise, or partnering with them.

- ✔ **She must operate from a physical location.** Over the past 20 years, many business models have been created for mobile operation of formerly fixed locations.

If Emily had used a clean slate and future focus, her business model innovation would have been significantly better.

Example: McDonald's global business model

McDonald's operates 31,000+ locations in more than 100 countries. Part of McDonald's successful business model outside the United States is using a clean slate rather than dropping in a standard U.S. McDonald's and tweaking it.

In Thailand, McDonald's serves Samurai Pork Burgers and Thai Spicy Fish McDippers. In the Philippines, customers can purchase sugar-soaked spaghetti, tuna pies, and seaweed flavored fries. European McDonald's serve beer. In the Northeast U.S., McDonald's serves Newman's Own coffee to cater to local preferences.

Some McDonald's don't serve Big Macs, French fries, or Coca-Cola. In fact, the most common item across all McDonald's menus is a milkshake. Milkshakes are available in all of McDonald's global markets except for Argentina, Paraguay, and Guatemala.

McDonald's has been successful in a wide variety of cultures and geographic locations, because it designs a business model specific to each one.

Predicting the Future

Nothing is better for your business model than correctly predicting the future. By correctly predicting the future, I mean predicting the business environment variables that will affect you in the future. If you can accurately predict these key variables, your business model will be vastly superior to your competitors'. Here's why. Your competitors likely won't try to predict the future at all. Their meandering, combined with your correct prediction, equals a bonanza for you. If your competitors bother to guess and guess wrong, you win again.

When trying to predict the future business environment, look into the crystal ball. Then take action. After all, the best way to predict the future is to invent it.

Gazing into the crystal ball

A fortune teller looks into the crystal ball and tells you your future. To innovate your business model, you need to do the same thing. Look into your crystal ball and make your best guess regarding these variables:

✔ **Interest rates:** Not long ago the interest rate for business borrowing was nine percent. Businesses have been spoiled by historically low lending rates. A significant increase in the prime rate could have a significant impact on your business model.

✔ **Economic growth:** Will the economy grow or shrink, and by how much? How will the local economy be affected by the national economy?

✔ **Real estate values:** Many businesses are affected by the value of real estate. Will real estate prices in your area rise or fall? How does this fluctuation affect your business? What can you adjust accordingly?

✔ **Price and availability of labor:** Will a sufficient labor pool with the skills you need be available? Will the cost of this labor work within your existing business model?

✔ **Price and availability of extremely talented labor:** McKinsey & Company made the term "war for talent" famous. McKinsey's research showed there will be worldwide competition for the most talented employees. It doesn't matter if you're a biotech company or a landscape contractor, extremely talented employees are rare and difficult to find. Will you be able to find such employees? If you can't, how do you need to change your business model?

✔ **Technological changes that affect the industry:** Many experts feel the days of credit cards are numbered. Near-field communication chips in cellphones may take the place of credit cards. How does this change affect the business model of companies like Walmart, American Express, and banks? Every industry is affected by technology. Don't think you're not affected just because you're not a technology company. Mobile restaurants have been very disruptive to brick-and-mortar restaurants.

✔ **General technological changes:** Ten years ago, no one had a smartphone or an iPad. Now every business must deal with these technological tsunamis. How will society's technology habits change and affect your business model?

✔ **Changes in buyer behavior:** In 1978 Americans ate out 15 percent of their meals. By 1995 this percentage rose to 29 percent. This trend is great for restaurants but bad for grocery stores. What significant trends in buyer behavior can you foresee?

✔ **Demographic changes:** The massive buying power of the baby boomers created entire industries. How do upcoming demographic changes affect your business model?

✔ **Changes in marketing methodologies:** Direct mail is dying. The post office may not even be around in ten years. Telemarketing to consumers is illegal in many states. Online advertising can be tricky. Social media advertising feels like a crapshoot. How will you navigate the changing landscape to market your products? What new trends do you foresee? How can you capitalize on these trends?

✔ **Overall growth of your industry:** Will your industry grow or shrink?

- ✔ **Growth of your niche:** Will your niche grow or shrink?

- ✔ **Potential competition entering the market:** Do you see competition entering the market? Who? Don't forget indirect competitors.

- ✔ **Convergence of industries:** No one predicted that cellphones would compete against digital cameras ten years ago. What industries have the potential to converge with yours? If a battle ensues, who will win?

- ✔ **Success of your current initiatives:** Which of your current initiatives works well and which doesn't? How does this answer affect your future business model?

In order for this exercise to work, you must guess. Saying something like, "I think the economy will be okay" isn't a guess. "I think the economy will grow two to three percent" is a guess you can take action on.

Overcoming the fear of being wrong

Businesspeople don't like the crystal ball exercise in the previous section, because they don't like being wrong. Here's the rub; guessing wrong is almost always better than not guessing. Your guesses aren't chiseled in stone. You'll just be heading in a new or different direction. If it becomes clear you made a wrong turn, you can correct it.

Perhaps the crystal ball exercise can be categorized under trying too hard versus not trying hard enough. Failure to guess at the future is not trying hard enough and doesn't yield the best business model innovation. If you're brave enough to engage in the crystal ball exercise, most of your guesses will be close to correct. That alone will put you light years ahead of the competition.

Practicing trend extrapolation with a dose of creativity

Sometimes analytical types, like accountants and engineers, have a hard time performing the crystal ball exercise. Sorry ladies and gentlemen, you still need to do it. If you're having a hard time being creative, try to creatively extrapolate a current trend. Bill Gates and Paul Allen didn't invent the PC operating system that made them rich. They saw an article in *Popular Mechanics* touting an operating system for the Altair computer. Gates and Allen took this nascent trend and extrapolated it, a lot. As it turns out, they were right. The trend was huge and their correct prediction created a powerful business model.

Predicting home security trends

Back in 2005, despite his reluctance, I made a client in the home alarm business go through the crystal ball exercise. He spent the first 30 minutes of our meeting complaining about several negative trends appearing in the industry. Several cities had instituted large fines for initial false alarms and misdemeanor offenses for excessive false alarms, and police had become reluctant to respond due to the high rate of false alarms. The city of Las Vegas stopped responding to alarms altogether, forcing homeowners to employ private security companies to do so.

I asked the client to look into the crystal ball and paint me a picture of what the home security business would look like in five years. Here's what he said:

- All cities would operate like Las Vegas, with no police response to alarms.

- High fines would continue and most likely get worse.

- These two factors would discourage homeowners from getting alarm systems. I had him guess at the percentage decrease in installations this change would cause. He estimated a 30 to 50 percent decrease.

- Wireless technology would allow unskilled installers to easily equip homes. This issue was significant because his business catered to high-end homes with complex installations done by a highly skilled staff. Wireless technology would make less skilled installers competitive with his highly skilled staff.

- Recently, Internet Protocol (IP) IT companies began competing in the video surveillance business. Video surveillance

represented 25 percent of his business. At the time, he hadn't lost many significant bids to an IT company. However, because cameras were IP devices for most users, some prospects viewed the IT company as having superior skills with this technology versus his company's video expertise.

This report doesn't sound very positive, does it? It was clear that his existing business model was in danger of stagnation or erosion. However, he had a profitable business built around the existing infrastructure in which the wired-system-based alarm company installed the system, a monitoring company responded to intruders and filtered false alarms, and the police arrested the perpetrators.

Everyone in the existing ecosystem was happy except the police. It was also clear that wired technology would eventually be replaced with wireless technology, rendering the client's most skilled workers under-utilized and under-valued by the marketplace. The client needed to create a new business model that leveraged the changes in the marketplace instead of fighting them.

After brainstorming for an hour, we hit up on an interesting topic — self-service monitoring. Anyone who has had an alarm has had a false alarm. The homeowner wants to call the police only if there's an intruder. Unfortunately, alarm technology was based upon window sensors and motion sensors, both of which are blind. A motion sensor has no idea whether a bird went down your chimney or an intruder is stealing everything you own. The alarm just goes off. The concept of self-service monitoring involves using streams of video of your house to every smartphone you designate. You can take a quick look to see whether it's an intruder or a bird and push a button to notify the police if it's an intruder. Effectively, the call center that monitors alarms and automatically calls the police is replaced by the customer. This new business model solves the Las Vegas problem, plus it provides a variety of additional features because of the video feed. I'm sure you've seen commercials on television for systems like this one, but they didn't exist in 2005.

By looking into the crystal ball and extrapolating current trends, this business owner was able to accurately predict the future and create a business model to capitalize upon it.

Failure Can Be Your Friend (As Long As It's Cheap and Fast)

Inside Silicon Valley, failure is viewed as a badge of honor. A failed entrepreneur is thought to have battle scars and wisdom that can't be attained through the easy road of success. Everywhere but Silicon Valley, failure is a Scarlet Letter — a sign of a poor businessperson.

I dare you to name a business model that worked perfectly on the first try. You can't do it because there isn't one. The first version of *every* business model fails. Doesn't this fact make you feel better? Knowing that whatever model you roll out will have something wrong with it is a relief. It takes the pressure off and makes perfectionism seem silly. Why bother trying to make the model perfect when it's impossible?

Rather than try to make your business model perfect, try to get to the perfect version faster. Business models are iterative. You try, you fail, you tweak. Rinse and repeat. Eventually, after many iterations, you get your perfect model. The savvy business model designer moves through the iterations quickly rather than focusing on perfection.

I suggest you follow a rule I call "cheap fast failure with upside." As long as your business model tweak has some upside, limited downside, doesn't cost a lot, and can be tested quickly, go for it.

Redefining failure

I suggest that you redefine failure. All the revisions to your business model will be "failures" if you define failure as non-perfection. Instead, define failure as something that doesn't eventually move you forward.

If you still believe in your overall business model concept, and you try a business model revision that doesn't work, take the Thomas Edison approach; consider yourself one step closer to success because you've eliminated that option.

Even trials that end in "failure" can sometimes be the most valuable learning experiences on the path to even greater success. If you read interviews with successful businesspeople, many list "failures" as key in their ultimate success. Many times, success isn't as good a teacher as failure. Find a way to pull the silver lining from failure, and apply it to the next version of your model.

Examples: Failure as the first step toward success

After spending $100 million to develop the Newton tablet computer, Apple appeared to be left with nothing but the distinction of coining the term "PDA." The Newton was an abject market failure. Apple scrapped the project but had learned many valuable lessons, including handwriting recognition and creation of a new operating system.

Conventional wisdom at the time said Newton was ahead of its time. Apple took this wisdom into account and applied the Newton technology to a Macintosh tablet computer. Apple applied for several patents for this tablet but never released it. This Macintosh tablet later turned out to be the Apple iPad, which currently runs Apple's proprietary iOS System Software, a direct descendant of the Newton operating system.

Ice cream entrepreneurs Ben Cohen and Jerry Greenfield originally opened an ice cream parlor in a renovated gas station. Two months later they closed down, realizing they had the wrong business model. They shifted their focus to packaging pints of ice cream and franchising stores as a model instead of running their own ice cream store. This new model created an empire. Ben and Jerry have never been afraid of experimentation as some of their oddball ice cream flavors — like Oh Pear, Economic Crunch, Peanut Butter and Jelly, and Schweddy Balls — make clear.

The United States of America failed at its original business models, including the Articles of Confederation. Eventually, the model was changed to the Constitution and the existing structure of government with success.

Steve Jobs purchased the Graphics Group from the Computer Division of Lucasfilm limited. George Lucas was going broke funding the exciting technology and couldn't turn it into a profitable business model as a toolkit for movie special effects. Jobs paid Lucas $5 million and put another $5 million of working capital into the Graphics Group and renamed it Pixar Studios. The business model and technology created by Lucas were changed from a special effects focus to an animation focus and yielded many profitable movies.

The Post-it Note was created with a glue formulation that failed its original purpose.

Hundreds of successful companies were jettisoned from larger organizations as losing business models only to thrive as independent businesses. Stock market darling Intuitive Surgical purchased the intellectual rights to the da Vinci Surgical System from nonprofit research institute SRI International. SRI was trying to create a device that could perform remote battlefield surgery. This model failed but Intuitive Surgical has been wildly successful selling the system for laparoscopic surgery.

Pipeline powerhouse Kinder Morgan was created because of founder Richard Kinder's philosophical business model differences with Enron's Ken Lay. Kinder was the President and COO of Enron from 1990 to 1996 and helped Enron build a small pipeline division. Lay wasn't interested in "hard asset" businesses because they didn't offer the astonishing profits Enron was making by trading energy. In 1997 Kinder left Enron to start Kinder Morgan. It turns out Kinder's hard asset business model was vastly superior to Enron's. Today Kinder is the 41st richest person in the U.S., worth more than $9 billion.

Former Pepsico divisions Frito-Lay and Yum Brands (Taco Bell, KFC, and Pizza Hut) are functioning better with an independent business model versus as a division of a larger corporation.

The lesson from these examples is that sometimes apparent failures are merely bumps in the road on the way to success. These bumps are failures only if you stop innovating.

Staying viable with business model versioning

In order to stay viable, all business models must undergo constant innovation. Much like the evolution of software, business models have versions. Every time you make a change or adjustment to your business model, you're creating a new version.

The software versioning process goes something like this:

- ✔ Dot.0 releases represent significant changes to the software. Windows 7 had significant updates, changes, and technology from its predecessor Windows XP.

- ✔ Point releases represent upgrades or tweaks to a dot.0 release. The lower the numeric value of the point release the less its significance.

> Windows 3.1 was the first significant improvement to Windows 3.0, whereas Windows 3.11 was a much smaller change. Software releases such as Windows 3.1118 are minor and probably represent nothing more than a bug fix.

The business model versioning process is exactly the same. Large sweeping changes to your business model are similar to dot.0 software releases. Smaller changes are just like point releases.

Figure 17-1 shows the business model evolution of a lawn and garden equipment manufacturer. Several significant business model changes have been made over the company's long history. In addition to these dot.0 changes, the company made many point releases to its business model.

There's no right answer to how often you should version your business model. The only certainty is that not versioning your business model will eventually destroy it. Generally, a new dot.0 release of your business model should occur every ten years or less. Each year you should make some point release change or changes to your business model in order to keep it fresh.

Apple's business model versions

I could write an entire book on Apple's business model and a detailed analysis of its gyrations. Here I do a quick review of Apple's business model history instead.

✔ **Version 1: Garage computer company.** Only 200 Apple I computers were built. Steve Wozniak hand built each of them. The experiment worked, and Apple moved on to Version 2 of its business model.

✔ **Version 2: Burgeoning PC manufacturer.** It wasn't clear whether personal computers were for consumers or businesses at this time. The Apple II computer wasn't the top-selling brand. It was in third place behind Commodore and Tandy, but Apple caught a lucky break. The Apple II was selected as the platform for VisiCalc software. Many experts credit the rise of the PC to the "killer application" VisiCalc.

✔ **Version 3: Entry into business computers.** The success of the IBM PC made it clear that business use of PCs would exceed home use. Not wanting to miss this large market, Apple made two failed attempts at this market — the Apple III and the Lisa.

✔ **Version 4: Finding a niche.** The failed Lisa computer led directly to the successful Macintosh. Unable to compete against IBM PCs and their clones, Apple found devoted and loyal niche users in graphics-intensive industries. These loyal Apple users carried the company through its most difficult decade.

✔ **Version 5: Gadget company.** As iPod sales eclipsed Macintosh sales, Apple continued to focus on profitable consumer device sales such as iPhones (an iPod with a phone) and iPads (a giant iPod) for record profits.

Figure 17-1:
Business
model
versioning
example.

Model Version 1.0
Controlled distribution to single customer

Model Version 1.1
Purchase first machine

Model Version 1.2
Move out of repair shop to facility

Model Version 1.3
Stock inventory and create catalog

Model Version 2.0
Transition to traditional 3-step supplier

Model Version 2.1
Buy lots more machines

Model Version 2.2
Switch pay to piecerate

Model Version 2.3
Hire plant manager from competitor

Model Version 2.4
Implement competitor's best practices

Model Version 3.0
Ooops, 3-step distribution dying

Model Version 3.1
Hire more reps

Model Version 3.2
Prettier catalog and marketing materials

Model Version 3.3
This isn't working. Keep 3-step customers we have and focus on better model

Model Version 4.0
Ooops V2, let's try 2-step distribution

Model Version 4.1
Find reps for 2-step distribution. Oops, there really aren't any

Model Version 4.2
Owner becomes sales rep.

Model Version 4.3
Discovery: Ooops, this isn't an unserved or unserserved market, now what?

Model Version 5.0
Manufacture weather enclosures for OEM tractor manufacturers at ALL costs
Description:
Several Universal cabs entering market vs. our model specific units. Competitive product showing up in Sears and other mass merchandisers

Model "Secret"
Stick with OEM vs move to dealer-direct model as cost of marketing deemed to be excessive vs. margin gain

How did it work?
Not well. OEMs kept beating on margin to the point it became break even in a good year.

Model stopped working because?
Margin erosion, competition

Model Notes
1966–1990

Model Version 6.0
Mitigate seasonality of business by expanding into sun shades.
Description:
That was 6 months on, 6 months off business so it became difficult to maintain key employees and profitability suffered because of low output during off-season

Model "Secret"
Reduce seasonality

How did it work?
Well

Model stopped working because?
Loss of major customer and marriage to OEM model which competitors destroy by direct sales model

Model Notes
1990–Present

Model Version 7.0
Leverage excellent reputation in the marketplace to sell directly to dealers
Description:
This was a difficult decision as OEMs are needed to provide advance blueprints of new models for design process. Losing OEM support could be catastrophic. That said, decision was made that the category was insignificant in sale to OEMs but they needed to offer the product and would "wink" at the channel conflict.

Model "Secret"
Increase margins, leverage Rolodex

How did it work?

Model stopped working because?
Model was never truly successful because they were 5 years late for the party (remember Parade Timing)

Model Notes
2000–Present

Chapter 18

Starting the Innovation Process

. . . .

In This Chapter

▶ Knowing what type of innovation you need

▶ Benefitting from both marginal and quantum innovation

▶ Learning to love crazy ideas

▶ Keeping your innovation process on track

. . . .

Many businesspeople don't know where to begin the innovation process. Innovation doesn't really have a standard formal process, so some people feel like innovation is nothing more than whipping up some ideas.

Without innovation, your business model will stagnate and become less and less effective. Like it or not, at some point you need to give serious thought to the innovation of your business model. When that time comes, the better your innovation process, the better the outcome will be.

In this chapter, I discuss the process of innovation and the differences between marginal innovation and quantum innovation. I show you the benefits of bringing in outside talent and some of the tools you can use in your innovation process.

Comparing Marginal Innovation and Quantum Innovation

This statement may be an oversimplification, but innovation can be put into two categories: marginal innovation (also known as incremental innovation) and quantum innovation. Both forms are important to your business model but serve very different functions.

Quantum innovation involves radical departures from the existing norm and tends to be far riskier. As I discuss in Chapter 17, quantum innovations are the dot.0 releases of your business model. *Marginal innovation* improves existing aspects of your business model or makes minor additions/subtractions. Marginal innovations are the point releases of your business model.

When you need each

So how do you know when you should be focusing on a quantum innovation or a marginal innovation? The need for innovation can be compared to a drive for a touchdown in football. On third down and two yards, you need just a short run to keep moving. When you have a free play, because the other team jumps offsides, you try a deep pass.

Figure 18-1 shows the best timing and type of innovation. During the growth phase of your business model, consistent point release innovations always make sense. These innovations are similar to short runs that keep a drive going for the offense.

When your business model is proven and going strong, you have the equivalent of a football free play. You can take some big chances — quantum innovations — with minimal risk. Go big now, before it's too late. When you realize your business model is rapidly declining, innovation may take too long to work to fix the issue. You always want to be innovating before you need to.

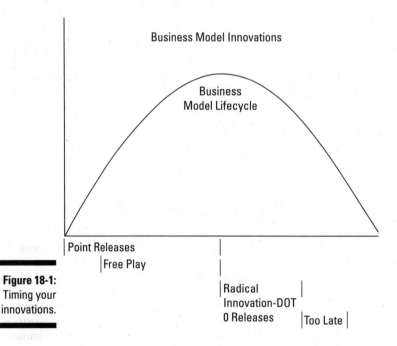

Business Model Innovations

Business
Model Lifecycle

Point Releases
Free Play

Radical
Innovation-DOT
0 Releases

Too Late

Figure 18-1:
Timing your
innovations.

Benefits of marginal innovation

The primary benefit of marginal innovation (point releases) is less risk. I hope I have convinced you of the danger and extreme risk of no innovation. Marginal or incremental innovation offers you the ability to stay ahead of the competition without great risk. Many marginal innovations lead you to quantum innovations later.

The Apple Lisa Computer was a quantum innovation that failed in the marketplace. The hugely successful Macintosh computer wasn't a quantum innovation. Apple simply took the quantum innovations from the Lisa and repackaged them in the Macintosh. The real innovation of the Macintosh was dramatically lowering the price from the Lisa and streamlining the feature set.

It can be argued that all of Apple's super-successful products are marginal innovations of the iPod. The quantum innovation was either the original iPod or the iPod touch — depending on your point of view. The iPhone is an iPod touch with a phone; not a huge stretch. The iPad is a giant iPod; even less of a stretch. Yet both of these products have made tens of billions of dollars for Apple.

Apple provides several lessons to businesspeople:

- ✔ It's amazing how far you can ride one winning innovation (like the iPod).
- ✔ Innovative marketing can be as important as innovative products or offerings.
- ✔ Stick with your winners. Just when you thought the iPod was dead, Apple offered new colors, sizes, and features.
- ✔ Keep innovating. Every year, Apple makes changes to all its winning offerings. Rather than rest on its laurels, Apple keeps innovating.

Benefits of quantum innovation

Quantum innovations are empire makers. It's rare to find a stellar business that didn't have a quantum innovation at some point. Apple has built an empire based upon one quantum innovation — the iPod.

If you want to build a business model that will make you truly wealthy, you need quantum innovation. People throw around terms like "thinking outside the box" when referring to quantum innovation. Sometimes it's hard to know what qualifies as quantum innovation. Ultimately, it's subjective, but most quantum innovations create a great deal of discomfort. If you're not uneasy or uncomfortable, the change is probably not risky enough and not quantum innovation.

These well-known companies were all jumpstarted by a quantum innovation:

- ✔ **Sony** brought the first transistor radio to market. Leveraging the disruptive power of the transistor versus the vacuum tube, Sony gained a significant foothold in both radios and televisions.

- ✔ Budweiser beers have been the top seller for decades. **Anheuser-Busch** was the first U.S. brewer to use pasteurization to keep beer fresh, the first to use mechanical refrigeration and refrigerated railroad cars, and the first to extensively use bottles.

- ✔ **Google** was the 18th major search engine for the Internet but defeated all competition because of one idea — PageRank. Every other search engine used the data on the target website to yield search results. Google added the dimension of interplay and linkage between websites to create the PageRank criteria, vastly improving the quality of search results.

- ✔ **CMG Worldwide** created a multimillion dollar intellectual property rights management firm representing the estates of famous deceased people, including Mark Twain, James Dean, and Lou Gehrig. The company pioneered the representation of deceased celebrities.

- ✔ **Kellogg's** built the world's largest cereal company as the direct result of Kellogg's Corn Flakes.

- ✔ **Procter & Gamble** has consistently used innovation to outmaneuver its archrival Colgate-Palmolive. Crest overtook Colgate toothpaste with the addition of fluoride to toothpaste. In the 1920s, Americans used soap flakes to clean their laundry. The flakes performed poorly in hard water, leaving a ring in the washing machine, dulling colors, and turning whites gray. Procter & Gamble created a powdered formula, Dreft, that that pulled the dirt away from clothes, and suspended it until it could be rinsed away. This formula plus the introduction of Tide ten years later put P&G ahead of Colgate-Palmolive for good.

- ✔ You may think innovation can't apply to a boring business like steel, but you'd be wrong. **Bethlehem Steel** was the first to produce wide-flange structural shapes in the U.S. (H-beams). The H-beam is credited with starting the skyscraper era and made Bethlehem Steel the leading supplier to the construction industry. Bethlehem steel was used in the Empire State Building, the Chrysler Building, the Golden Gate Bridge, Madison Square Garden, the Merchandise Mart, Rockefeller Center, Alcatraz, and the Hoover Dam.

- ✔ **Campbell's Soup** was a very ordinary canning company until 1897 when an employee developed a commercially viable method for condensing soup.

✔ **Johnson Controls, Inc.** ranks #67 in the Fortune 500, and is a global leader in energy management, batteries, and automotive interior systems. The genesis for this global giant was the 1883 invention of the first electric room thermostat by the company's founder Warren S. Johnson.

✔ **Nike** built a $24 billion a year business starting with a pair of running shoes made with a waffle iron.

The danger of marginal innovation is you always start with the status quo. Quantum innovation ignores the status quo. Starting with a clean slate leads to radical and disruptive change.

Perhaps the best way to demonstrate the power of quantum innovation is through the example of Google and the Encyclopedia Britannica. When I was 12 years old I needed to write a report on Thomas Jefferson. Most of the knowledge I needed was garnered from the Encyclopedia Britannica. Thirty years later, my daughter needed to write a report on Thomas Jefferson. She gathered the information she needed from the Internet, in particular from Google.

When I was 12 years old, the leading company in the Thomas Jefferson information providing business was the Encyclopedia Britannica. Thirty years later, Google was the leading company in providing information on Thomas Jefferson. This leads to the question, who should have been Google? The answer is the Encyclopedia Britannica.

It's probably safe to say the folks at the Encyclopedia Britannica were incremental innovators, not quantum innovators. They probably viewed themselves as book publishers, not information providers. When the new technology of the Internet came out, they saw through the lens of their existing book publishing business rather than the blank canvas of the Internet.

Discovering the Correlation between Craziness and Innovative Genius

All innovation is theoretical and untested. The more radical the innovation, the crazier it seems. Human beings are wired to dismiss crazy ideas as bad ideas. In order to be a successful innovator, you need to temper this behavior.

Most highly successful innovations are dismissed as crazy initially. In general, the more people like your idea, the less likely it is to be a powerful innovation. A few freakishly loyal advocates are all that's needed for a powerful innovation to take hold. Figure 18-2 shows the relationship between popular acceptance of your idea and the likelihood that your idea will be a powerful innovation.

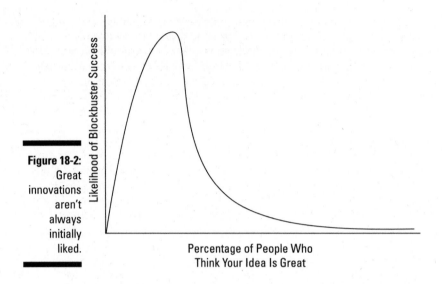

Differentiating crazy ideas from genius

How do you know whether your crazy idea is genius or just plain crazy? You don't. During the innovation process all you're doing is taking your best guess. The market will tell you whether your crazy idea is genius.

Part of the innovation process is testing your idea in the marketplace. True quantum ideas rarely have fast, massive acceptance. More likely, radical quantum innovations create a handful of loyal, evangelistic fans. These evangelicals create the foundation for the product's growing acceptance. When attempting a quantum innovation, always aim for rabid fans rather than mass acceptance. If your offer can't create rabid fans, your idea is probably crazy. If you can create rabid evangelicals, you have a chance to be a genius.

Knowing that patience is a virtue with innovation

Innovative offerings rarely hit the market and explode in popularity. More often, an innovative offering creates evangelical fans and grows slowly over time. If the entrepreneur remains patient through this phase, the innovation can explode in popularity at a later time. From the outside, these offerings look like overnight successes. In reality, the entrepreneur has patiently toiled for years to gain this "overnight" success.

If you want to garner the most from your innovations, be patient. Overnight success is so rare, you should probably pretend it doesn't exist. A far more successful option is to patiently wait for your innovations to take hold. Again, pay attention to whether you have evangelical fans. If you do, be patient as long as they stay evangelical. If you don't have evangelical fans, adjust your offering until you do. Without these evangelical fans, patience may not be a virtue.

Travelocity was the first travel site to offer a calendar feature showing airfares by date. Low price matters in the world of online travel, so this powerful innovation was a game changer. No one used the calendar feature. Online travel booking was just catching on, and customers weren't ready for an advanced feature such as visual calendar booking. A few years later, this feature was added with great success. The lesson: Just because your innovation isn't catching on today doesn't mean it won't later.

Keeping the Creative Process on Track

Creative innovation is difficult for most business owners, so don't be discouraged if the process is challenging. Business ownership can be lonely. Many times business owners have no high-quality sounding board for their ideas. If you're fortunate enough to have the availability of a team to help you brainstorm innovative ideas, consider yourself lucky. Many mid-sized and small businesses don't have the executive talent to create a brainstorming team.

Bringing in outsiders

It's difficult to have a highly creative idea in a vacuum. The best creative process is a group process, not an individual process. This fact presents a challenge for mid-sized and small businesses where the owner may be the only executive. If you lack the staff to create an innovation team, consider bringing in outsiders. Outsiders can not only fill empty seats on your team, but also bring a fresh perspective that insiders lack.

The value of fresh eyes

The process of innovation requires different thinking and unique perspective. It's very difficult to get a unique perspective from someone inside your organization. It's like the perception of a child's growth from the eyes of the grandparents versus the parents. The parents see the child every day and subtle changes blend together and become the norm. A grandparent who sees the child a couple of times a year sees dramatic changes in the child.

The grandchild has grown several inches, has a more extensive vocabulary, and seems more mature each time the grandparent sees the child. The growth and development of the child is the same; however, the perception of this growth is far different for the parent and grandparent.

Because of their different perspectives, sometimes the grandparents' opinions on child rearing are more valuable than the parents'. In business, you want to harness this same effect. An outsider brings a grandparents' set of eyes to your business. Plain and simple, the outsider sees things that an insider simply can't see.

Best options for help

When innovation becomes a priority, you want to create a high-quality innovation team. Most likely the best team will be augmented by outsiders. You can find quality outside team members in a variety of places. Good candidates for your innovation team include:

- Business model or innovation consultants
- Business coaches or consultants
- Marketing consultants or agencies
- Branding consultants or agencies
- MBA students or interns
- Friends or colleagues who own a business
- Board members

Points of resistance

I could go on and on about the benefits of bringing in outsiders. The upside is tremendous, yet most mid-sized and small businesses don't do it. The list of reasons is long, but here are the usual suspects:

- **Cost:** Outside expertise has a cost. The benefits typically outweigh the costs multiplied several times over, but the benefits always seem unpredictable or tenuous. Known cost plus unknown benefits stops some entrepreneurs from investing in outside help.

- **Confidentiality:** Businesspeople don't want to share sensitive information with strangers. Somehow, it feels safer not sharing the inside scoop. Any outsider will be willing to sign a standard non-disclosure.

- **Theft:** What if the outsider steals my ideas, people, customers, or other valuable property? Okay, but what are the odds? Most people are ethical and honest. Plus, you can get a non-disclosure and/or non-competition agreement just in case.

> ✔ **It's just one more thing to do:** In the already-too-busy world of entrepreneurs, getting input (whether good or not) from outsiders seems like too much work. Of course, this attitude violates the "stop trying harder rule" I discuss in Chapter 15.

Of course the biggest culprit is accountability. Outsiders force you to refine your ideas and select the best ones for action. After some time has passed, the outsiders may even ask, "How is that important initiative going?" Face it, one of the best parts about being an entrepreneur is having no one to answer to. Having outsiders feels too much like having a boss to some. What these entrepreneurs are losing is immeasurable. Like it or not, there is a straight-line relationship between accountability and performance. The higher the accountability, the higher the performance.

Using tools during the process

The most important tool you use during the innovation process is the brainpower of your team. You also want to employ some tools and techniques during the innovation process. Consider the following:

> ✔ **Use templates.** www.innovationinpractice.com suggests using four templates to spur innovation: Subtraction, multiplication, division, and task unification.
>
> - **Subtraction:** Removing an essential component and keeping only what's left. The Jitterbug cellphone for seniors removed many features not used by folks over 50.
>
> - **Multiplication:** Making a copy of a component but changing it in some way. The current razor blade wars are an example of this template. Gillette creates a three-bladed razor, so Shick innovates with a four-bladed razor.
>
> - **Division:** Dividing a component out of the product and putting it back somewhere else, or taking the component and physically dividing it. MP3 players replaced all-in-one boom boxes but sold the headphones/speakers separately.
>
> - **Task unification:** Assigning an additional task to an existing component by giving it a new job in addition to its existing job, such as using cellphone cameras for virtual real estate tours.
>
> ✔ **Innovation is a multistep process.** Start at the highest and broadest level at the first meeting and gradually filter ideas in subsequent meetings.
>
> ✔ **Follow brainstorming rules during the initial meetings.** It's difficult not to critique ideas. However, if you allow discussion on the merits of an idea, you'll stifle additional ideas. Don't do it.

✔ **Buy a brainstorming toolkit.** You can find a variety of flash card kits, board games, and other gadgets to assist in the brainstorming process.

✔ **Use a good business model framework.** Dr. Alexander Osterwalder's Business Model Canvas can serve as a good business model framework at the beginning of the innovation process.

✔ **Leverage your local business schools.** Most MBA or undergraduate business programs are looking for interesting real-world projects. Have a student sit in on your innovation team meetings or have students research or vet your ideas.

✔ **Use the cheap fast failure with upside approach.** The Pet Rock taught businesspeople that there's no such thing as a stupid idea. The market will tell you whether your idea is genius or stupid. When innovating, keep in mind the cost of market trial. An innovative idea that requires a significant investment for trial may be the wrong idea.

Chapter 19

Using Disruptive Innovation

In This Chapter

▶ Discovering the power of disruptive innovation

▶ Understanding why the disruptor usually wins

▶ Targeting non-consumption

▶ Knowing when to swing for the fences

onsistent incremental innovation is vital to the success of your business. However, at some point you'll want, or need, to swing for the fences. Game-changing innovations remake competitive landscapes and create fortunes for business owners.

Quantum, game-changing innovation can take a variety of forms. Here are a few interesting examples:

✔ Delta Airlines purchased a refinery to arbitrage jet fuel and potentially save more than a billion dollars annually.

✔ Hospitals created adjacent surgery centers with private rooms and concierge service to cater to the growing outpatient surgery market.

✔ General Electric leveraged its knowledge of engine technology to become a dominant player in the emerging wind power market.

✔ Toyota and Honda created high-end brands Lexus and Acura to grab a profitable share of the luxury car market.

✔ Google is constantly experimenting in seemingly unrelated fields, looking for the next big idea. Google has dabbled with mapping, space travel, wind farms, 3D glasses, and phone service.

✔ A local coffeehouse divided its space in half and has a brewpub/coffeehouse combination.

✔ A San Antonio diner closed its retail location, moved into a giant-sized mobile home, and moved to the Permian Basin oilfields where customers gladly pay twice as much per meal.

✔ A frustrated lawyer quit practicing law and refocused on trust-based financial planning, doubling her income.

Quantum innovation can take an infinite number of forms. However, the best opportunity for radical, quantum innovation comes from disruptive innovation.

The Disruptive Innovator Usually Wins

To paraphrase Harvard innovation guru Clayton Christensen, a disruptive innovation is one that creates a new market and a new value network. Over the course of time, this disrupts existing markets and value networks and eventually replaces them.

Disruptive innovations create seismic shifts in existing markets by changing products or services in ways the market didn't expect or even deem possible. A disruptive innovation is like moving a road; if all the traffic stops, the business dependent upon the traffic dies. Many disruptive innovations have technology at the core, but a disruptive innovation doesn't have to center around technology. Panera Bread and Chipotle have disrupted the fast food business by offering higher quality food, not technological superiority.

Table 19-1 shows some examples of disruptive innovations and the markets that they radically changed.

Table 19-1	Disruptive Innovations
Innovation	*Disrupted Market*
MP3	Records
Automobile	Railroads
Drugstore mini-clinics	General practitioners/doctors
3D printing	Factories, machine shops
Redbox	Video stores like Blockbuster
Hybrid automobiles	Oil
Personal computers	Mainframe/minicomputers
Desktop publishing	Offset printing
Zipcar	Car rental, trains, buses
Linux	Traditional operating systems like Microsoft Windows
Digital camera	Film
Telephone	Telegraph
Outpatient surgery centers	Hospitals

Innovation	*Disrupted Market*
Model T	All other automobile manufacturers, horses
YouTube	Traditional advertisers and content providers
Medical tourism	Surgeons
Google	Yellow Pages
Skype	Long distance carriers
Web conferencing	Airlines
World Wide Web	Travel agents and more
Smart meters	Utility workers
Crowdsourced financing	Banks
Craigslist	Newspapers
Online learning	Universities
Home medical testing	Laboratories

Disruptive innovation often offers a less expensive way of doing business, but not necessarily a better method. A web video conference isn't superior to a live meeting, but it costs 50 times less. A digital picture is inferior to a film picture, but it costs almost nothing and is vastly more convenient. Linux has far fewer features than Windows, but costs nothing to buy. Typically, these disruptive innovations offer acceptable quality and features for a vastly cheaper price. This combination tends to capture large swathes of the market.

Occasionally, a disruptive innovation is cheaper and better. Skype offers video and phone conferencing for far less than long distance phone-only service. MP3 files can be used on dozens of formats and have portability, which CDs do not. Redbox video rental costs one-fourth what Blockbuster charges and has many more locations for pickup and drop-off. Google search results are fine-tuned for the user versus a generic phone book.

Whether the disruptive innovation is better or slightly inferior in quality to the existing offering, the disruptive innovation almost always wins.

Lessons from the innovator's dilemma

How do powerful industry leaders like Kodak, Blockbuster, *The Chicago Tribune,* Bethlehem Steel, Circuit City, and the R. H. Donnelley Company get toppled in a few short years? They get toppled by powerful disruptive forces that move the road. Like many entrenched companies, they couldn't react to the disruptive forces.

The preeminent authority on disruptive innovation, Harvard professor Clayton Christensen, explains how industry leaders fall prey to the innovator's dilemma. Industry leaders establish large market shares from large, high-profit customers. In order to meet market growth expectations, the company innovates at the high end of the market, creating products and services that generate superior margins and sell for high prices.

Lesson #1: A strong competitor may be just what you need

As firms dominate a market, the thirst for ever-increasing margins allows for disruptive innovation. As established competitors strive for ever-increasing margins, an opportunity to serve customers at the low end of the market opens. These customers are viewed as unattractive to entrenched firms chasing better and better margins from bigger and bigger customers.

Prior to 1975, full-service brokerages like Merrill Lynch were the only option to purchase stocks. Large commissions were based on the dollar amount of stock purchased and could reach thousands of dollars for a single transaction. Commissions also had fixed minimums that ended up excluding small investors. At the time, most Americans didn't own stocks.

On May 1, 1975, the minimum commission limit was lifted, allowing discount brokers like Charles Schwab to offer commissions that were 70 percent less than full-service brokers. Schwab tapped the market of small investors who were unable to pay large minimum commissions. These customers were ignored by the large firms because they had only small amounts to invest and weren't willing to pay the high commission rates the large firms were used to receiving. Like many disruptive innovations, what starts off as a small, unattractive market grows into a much larger, more attractive one. Today, Schwab has 8.2 million clients. Other discount brokers like E*TRADE, Scottrade, and TD Ameritrade have millions of clients as well, proving the market was far larger than full-service brokers imagined.

Lesson #2: Free rein

Entrenched companies know about disruptive innovation but often choose to ignore it. Along comes a potentially disruptive innovation that offers lower sales prices and lower margins. Why would the successful firm blow up its business model in exchange for a smaller, lower-margin market? The answer is that it usually doesn't. The firm stays with its existing winning formula just like the full-service brokerage houses did.

By ignoring the potentially disruptive and unattractive market, the established companies allow new entrants free rein and virtually no competition during the early phases. If the disruptive innovation takes hold, it may be too late for the established firm to participate in the new market.

Mail delivery of video and video vending machines were a disruptive force for retail video stores. Netflix offered to sell itself to Blockbuster for $50 million during its early years. Blockbuster scoffed at the idea because its retail business model was far more lucrative. However, Blockbuster failed to see the disruptive force of the innovation and by the time Blockbuster realized the road had moved to non-retail delivery of videos, it was too late.

Lesson #3: Disruption as annoyance

Established firms dismiss disruptive innovation as a low-margin annoyance. Long-distance providers said things like, "Who wants to use their computer as a phone?" Integrated steel mills were happy to let mini mills chase low-margin rebar sales. Kodak dismissed digital picture quality as too low to affect its film market. Blockbuster wondered why anyone would want to wait for a movie to be mailed to them instead of picking it up immediately in a store.

When mini steel mills started appearing in the early 1960s, big integrated steel mills like U.S. Steel were unconcerned. Unlike integrated mills, mini mills had small electric furnaces that were capable only of melting scrap steel and turning it into low-margin rebar for construction. Rebar was the lowest margin item integrated mills produced (five percent), so they were glad to let the mini mills have this item. Because the margin at a mini mill was 20 percent, they gladly grabbed the lion's share of the rebar market. After conquering that market, they moved up the food chain step by step. All but one integrated mill is now out of business, and mini mills have grabbed 60 percent of the steel market.

Lesson #4: Disruptor becomes competitive

The disruptive innovator finds a way to fix problems. Mini mills eventually created a direct strip casting process that allowed them to make highly profitable sheet products. Prior to this innovation, only the integrated mills could produce these products. When mini mills, with a 20 percent lower cost of operation, could manufacture the same product, it was game over.

Netflix found a way to get DVDs to most customers the next day, making it more — not less — convenient than running to Blockbuster. Broadband Internet and the prevalence of Wi-Fi networks made Skype just as convenient as a landline. Betting on the clunky disruptive process staying clunky is a bad bet.

Lesson #5: New market outgrows existing market

By the time the entrenched competitor realizes the disrupted market will exceed the size of its old market, it's too late. Google does more business than the Yellow Pages ever did. Discount brokers expanded the number of investors to levels unimagined by Merrill Lynch and the other full service houses. Kodak's peak film sales were about $3.5 billion in the early 2000s. Every day 200 million digital photos are uploaded to Facebook and another

300 million are uploaded to Instagram. If Kodak had focused on the photo market instead of the film market, it could have benefited from the explosion of photo-taking.

Additional examples of disruptive innovation include:

✔ **Newspapers:** When Craigslist, `Monster.com`, and `Autotrader.com` entered the market, an Internet ad was less effective and more expensive than a Sunday classified ad in a newspaper. Newspapers stuck with their existing business model, choosing to keep prices and margins high to maximize profits. As use of the Internet exploded, advertisers shifted their spending from newspaper to Internet advertising. This shift increased the cost effectiveness of Internet advertising and placed the newspapers' business model on a slippery slope of ever-decreasing effectiveness and advertising revenue. From 2000 to 2011, newspaper classified advertising declined 70 percent.

✔ **Yellow Pages:** Similar to newspapers, Yellow Pages enjoyed a profitable near-monopoly. Yellow Page providers tried to create an online version to counter Google's attack, but it failed because the Yellow Page providers tried to create a competitor to Google on business listing searches rather than all searches. Google captured the market because clients were using the site for *all* searches. Why would consumers leave Google to use a specialty Yellow Page search site? Answer: They wouldn't, and they didn't.

✔ **Full-service homeowner's association management:** Software-based tools allow homeowners to perform 90 percent of the functions traditionally performed by property managers. Full-service property managers using the old business model are chasing fewer and fewer customers who require fewer and fewer services.

How to benefit from disruptive innovation

If the disruptive innovator typically wins, and the new market created by the disruption can exceed the size of the old market, it pays to be the disruptor. Professor Christensen delineates several tactics to effectively innovate.

Compete against non-consumption

Disruptive innovations offer less expensive options to consumers. Therefore, look for non-consumers who would gladly purchase if the price were lower. Be careful. This step sounds easy, but lower pricing doesn't always equate to a customer purchase. I don't own a cat. I'm a non-consumer of cat food. No radical price decrease will get me to buy a cat or cat food. However, dramatically lower the cost of an electric car or a vacation, and I will buy.

Charles Schwab provided a low-cost option for stock market investors who couldn't afford to buy under the restrictive rules of full-service brokers. The millions of tiny commissions discount brokers earn add up to billions more than those earned by full-service brokers.

Items that competed against non-consumption include the following:

- ✔ **3D printing:** 3D printing allows companies to make dies and molds for low volume production at a cost-effective price. Prior to 3D printing, production of these parts and their corresponding dies was cost prohibitive.

- ✔ **Cellphones:** A cellphone wasn't a better phone. It was a way to be more productive in the car and a safety device. Prior to the cellphone, these needs weren't being met.

- ✔ **Model T Ford:** Henry Ford was competing against travel by horse, not other cars.

- ✔ **Southwest Airlines getaway fares:** Prior to high oil prices, Southwest's $49 last-minute fares enticed passengers to visit Grandma or Las Vegas instead of staying home.

- ✔ **Web conferencing:** It may cost $200 for a video conference of 20 executives versus $20,000 for a live meeting. The meeting is important, but not $20,000 worth of important.

Attract overshot customers

Overshot customers are buyers of a current offering who are unwilling to upgrade to premium options. They fall into two categories

- ✔ Consumers who aren't willing to upgrade because they can't afford it

- ✔ Consumers who feel the current product offers a weak general solution to a specific need, but no niche solution exists

As an example of the second category, consider the many seniors who own cellphones that can perform hundreds of functions they don't want or need. The Jitterbug phone removes most of these unwanted features but offers big buttons, a large keypad, and a bright color screen, making it the perfect cellphone for seniors.

The rule to follow for overshot customers is "Good enough is good enough." Offer a good enough option at a great price, and you can attract these overshot customers.

Examples of companies catering to overshot customers are:

- ✔ **Oracle's Open Office** offers bare-bones spreadsheet and word processing programs for free download. The product is targeted at many customers who use only one percent of the available features of Microsoft Excel and/or Word. Despite the fact that most customers use only a fraction of the Word or Excel program features, Microsoft releases a new version every few years. Microsoft has created a hole at the low end of the market for software such as Open Office.

- ✔ **37 Signals** offers basic Internet-based software for project management, customer relationship management (CRM), and collaboration. Unlike other software companies, 37 Signals insists software must be so simple that no manual or training is required to use it. Its strategy is to target the overshot customers of other CRM and project management software companies.

- ✔ **Apple** used the iPad to prove there was a market of overshot laptop and desktop computer users. The iPad offered a cheaper and easier way to access the Internet and e-mail for these users.

- ✔ **Online universities** cater to students who value a degree more than the entire college experience. Many students don't care about fraternities, football games, or big-name-university alumni associations. They just want the sheepskin.

- ✔ **CVS' Minute Clinic** offers a few bare-bones services — such as vaccinations, strep tests, and diagnosis of basic illnesses — in a more convenient format than traditional doctors.

- ✔ **Prepaid debit and credit cards** tap the large market of the un-banked. These consumers typically pay cash but still need a credit card for Internet purchases, car rentals, and other credit-card-only purchases. Full service banks offer too many services at too high a cost for these customers.

Segment by customer utility

Businesses tend to place customers into demographic segments like income, age, gender, or location. A customer doesn't buy a product because he's a middle-income, college-educated homeowner. According to Christensen, the consumer "hires" a product because there's a job to be done. You hire McDonald's to stop the rumbling in your stomach, not because you're a 26-year-old male in the right demographic.

Christensen teaches this point in his MBA course with the example of a milkshake. A fast food restaurant wants to improve its milkshake sales. First, the company segments the market by both the product (milkshakes) and demographics (the profile of an average milkshake drinker). Then the marketing department asks people within the demographic to list the characteristics of an ideal milkshake (thick, thin, chunky, smooth, fruity, chocolaty, and so on). The company makes adjustments to the milkshakes based upon the suggestions, but milkshake sales don't improve.

Then the company switches its approach to focus on the job a customer "hires" the milkshake to do. After a study, the restaurant discovers something surprising; 40 percent of milkshakes are purchased first thing in the morning by commuters ordering them to go.

The restaurant interviews customers who purchased a morning milkshake and asks why they purchased them in the morning. Most buyers said they were facing a long, boring commute and wanted something to occupy their time, could be eaten with one hand so they wouldn't mess up their work attire, and would help hold off hunger until lunchtime.

It turns out the job the milkshake was hired to do was more about solving boredom of a morning commute than the taste. Because the commuter wants the milkshake to last the whole trip, the thickness of the milkshake is important. The company made morning milkshakes thicker and more interesting by adding chunks of fruit. This change significantly increased milkshake sales.

When you think about the job the customer needs done, you may get a creative spark or find a completely new angle. You don't want to buy gasoline; you want to buy your car moving down the road. The following products created unique offerings by using the job to-be-done approach:

- **Brita:** The water purification creates drinkable water. For many customers, the job to be done is eliminating plastic bottle waste, not filtering water.

- **Hallmark cards:** When you care enough to send the very best. The job is to show love, caring, and affection at the highest level. The words on the card matter far less than the gesture.

- **Hipmunk.com:** This company carved out a niche in an already crowded travel site industry by doing a job other sites couldn't — comparing departure times and price rather than just price. The job to be done on Hipmunk is to schedule the most convenient travel, not the cheapest.

- **Muscle Milk:** The job to be done is providing a convenient, good-tasting protein after a workout rather than being a milkshake wannabe.

- **Netflix and Redbox:** These services both rent DVDs but do different jobs for the customer. Netflix provides a convenient stream of entertainment from your movie queue delivered to your door. Redbox provides cheap entertainment *now*.

- ✔ **Nike:** A Nike team jersey isn't just a shirt; it's a source of pride and belonging.

- ✔ **Nintendo Wii:** This product has created a huge audience with grandparents. Grandma doesn't want to play a video game; she wants a shared activity with her grandkids.

- ✔ **Olé:** The hearing aid for people that don't want to wear one. The job to be done isn't hearing better. The job to be done is hearing better without anyone knowing you're using a hearing aid.

- ✔ **Whole Foods:** This grocery store offers natural foods. The job to be done is living healthier. The customer accomplishes this job by purchasing items found at Whole Foods.

- ✔ **Zipcar:** The job to be done isn't renting a car more easily; it's an augmented bus or train. You can't carry five bags of groceries or a sofa on the bus.

Most of Your Existing Model Works Fine: Don't Throw Out the Baby with the Bathwater

Over-innovation is possible. Much like the analogy of digging up a plant to see whether it's growing, too much change can damage your business model. Coca-Cola thought it was losing ground to Pepsi and decided to change the 99-year-old formula. New Coke was a PR and marketing disaster. Only 79 days after New Coke was released, Coca-Cola quickly reversed course and brought back the original formula as Coca-Cola Classic.

Comparing under-innovation and over-innovation

Coca-Cola over-innovated. It can be difficult to find the proper balance of innovation and change. You have the potential to over-innovate by

- ✔ Messing with trusted brands, like Coca-Cola did.

- ✔ Falling victim to bright shiny object syndrome. New ideas that are unencumbered by the annoyance of execution always look more interesting. Focusing on the next big thing sometimes takes focus away from the last big thing.

✔ Having impatience for growth. Sometimes companies can push too hard for growth and over-innovate their way to failure. Internet grocery provider Webvan had success in a select few markets but pushed its business model to the breaking point by expanding into marginal cities.

✔ Having impatience for profits. Twitter has yet to make a profit but boasts 140 million users sending 340 million tweets each day. It's debatable whether Twitter will ever be a profitable business model, but the company has been patient for profits and hasn't over-innovated the business model.

More often, companies under-innovate. Their business model begins to work well, and then they get complacent. Along comes a disruptive innovator and pummels them.

Innovation involves risk. Generally, entrepreneurs avoid risk and therefore shy away from innovation. If in doubt, shoot for over-innovation. Here's why. What feels like over-innovation probably isn't.

Here are some signs you may be under-innovating:

✔ **Declining margin percentage:** New innovative products have higher margins. As markets mature, competition intensifies and margins begin to fall.

✔ **Intensified competition:** Innovation is the best defense against competitive pressure. If you're feeling intense pressure from competition, it may be time to fight it with innovation.

✔ **Lack of growth:** Slowing growth means the maturity phase isn't far behind. Rather than deal with the negative consequences of maturity, like price pressure, innovate.

✔ **Lack of new products:** Over-tweaking old products or simply riding your existing offering will eventually catch up with you.

✔ **Boredom:** If you're bored with the business, it's safe to assume your customers could be bored with your offering.

✔ **Quality team members leaving:** Your best team members value new challenges and a chance to demonstrate their creativity. Lack of innovation denies them the opportunity to shine. They'll leave to find a company that can give them this opportunity.

Knowing what parts of your model to keep and what to throw out

How do you know what parts of your model require innovation and what parts don't? In general, if something is working, incremental innovation is the best option. If you sense decay, it's time to stop tinkering and try quantum innovation.

When deciding what parts of your model to keep and what to radically change, consider these factors in your decision:

- ✔ **Future potential of the offer:** Fighting hard for market acceptance of a potential billion-dollar product is different from fighting hard for a $100,000 opportunity.

- ✔ **Acceleration:** If progress is accelerating, it's probably best to leave things alone. If progress is decelerating rapidly, it's time for quantum innovation. RIMM, the maker of the BlackBerry device, is currently in this position. Its market share is shrinking precipitously. At times like these, "If in doubt, throw it out."

- ✔ **Sales volume:** Apple is finally seeing iPad sales acceleration slow. iPads are a multibillion-dollar product; Apple has no need to panic about the deceleration. Incremental innovation is more prudent when large sales are at stake and deceleration is mild.

- ✔ **Market share:** Starbucks experiencing declining sales is different from a year-old coffeehouse beginning to see sales soften. Starbucks may be best to wait things out or adjust the model slightly. The new coffee shop may need to radically adjust. Protecting a large market share justifies additional conservatism.

- ✔ **Market cycle:** The stage of the market cycle can help you determine whether you should be patient, adjust slightly, or radically innovate.

- ✔ **Previous incremental innovation:** If you haven't tried any minor innovations, it's probably better to start small than to radically change your model. On the other hand, if you've tweaked the same issue for years and been consistently unsuccessful, it's probably time to go big.

Chapter 20

Crowdsourcing as Advanced Business Model Innovation

. . . .

In This Chapter

▶ Discovering the power of crowdsourcing

▶ Looking at ten things you didn't know were crowdsourced

▶ Harnessing the power of crowdsourcing to improve your business model

. . . .

*I*f you've ever posted a video on YouTube, voted for an American Idol, read the Oxford Dictionary, or commented on Yelp.com, you've seen crowdsourcing firsthand. Merriam-Webster defines *crowdsourcing* as "the practice of obtaining needed services, ideas, or content by soliciting contributions from a large group of people and especially from the online community rather than from traditional employees or suppliers." Put in simple business terms, *crowdsourcing* gets many people, from customers and vendors to complete strangers, to contribute to solving a common task.

Typically, these "contributions" from the crowd are free. You can see how getting free anything from the crowd, versus paying employees or vendors, could radically impact your business model. Innovative companies from the Fortune 500 to mom-and-pop shops have used crowdsourcing to speed innovation, keep in touch with customers, create new products, find creative solutions, raise capital, and more.

The concept of crowdsourcing was coined by Jeff Howe in a 2006 *Wired Magazine* article. Howe puts crowdsourcing into four main categories:

✔ **Crowd creation uses the masses to add value to the product.** Examples include:

   • NASA's Clickworkers, in which space enthusiasts help categorize crater patterns on Mars

- Open source software such as Linux

- `Threadless.com`, which allows consumers to propose T-shirt concepts for sale

- iStockphoto, which uses amateur photographers to provide low-cost, high-quality stock images

- The Rally Fighter Car, which was the first crowdsourced "creative commons-like" car. More than 35,000 designs by 2,900 community members from more than 100 countries contributed to the design.

✔ **Crowd voting leverages technology to garner input from the masses, and then makes the results available as output.** Howe notes the 1/10/89 Rule: One percent of participants will create something valuable, like a well-written review, ten percent will vote and rate, and 89 percent will consume content. Examples of crowd voting include:

- Reality TV voting

- `Yelp.com`

- Movie rating sites like Fandango

- Digg

✔ **Crowd wisdom.** This principle attempts to harness collective knowledge of many to solve problems or predict future outcomes. Howe states, "Given the right set of conditions, the crowd will almost always out-perform any number of employees — a fact that many companies are increasingly attempting to exploit." The concept of democracy is centered on the wisdom of the general public to know how to best select leaders. Yahoo! Answers and open innovation leverage the wisdom of the crowd as well.

✔ **Crowdfunding cuts out traditional lending institutions as an unnecessary middleman.** Borrowers unable to secure funds through traditional sources can use a collection of hundreds of individual lenders to meet their financing needs. `Kiva.org` uses crowdfunding to make micro-loans to entrepreneurs in developing nations. `Kickstarter.com` funds a variety of startup projects from movies to inventions to businesses.

In this chapter, I discuss the powerful business model innovation strategy that is crowdsourcing. I explain that it isn't a fad, and I give you potentially surprising examples of crowdsourcing. I also do my best to convince you that your business model can benefit from crowdsourcing, while making sure you're aware of the downside.

Advanced business model innovation

There is no limit to the number of ways you can innovate. Many innovations are inspired by another company's great idea. The innovator gets the spark from the other company, and then manipulates the idea a bit so it works for his. These types of innovations have built many great companies and industries. Steak and Ale founder Norman Brinker is credited with inventing the salad bar in the early 1960s. Dozens of restaurant innovations have been hatched based upon Brinker's salad bar.

Sometimes a relatively mundane tactic from one industry is transformed into a business model blockbuster in another. The assembly line transformed the manufacturing industry, and then became ubiquitous. Since then, the assembly line has been used in hundreds of non-manufacturing environments, from McDonald's to offices. Other innovations are based upon broad business model techniques that can be used in limitless business scenarios. The freemium business model strategy has been creatively used by thousands of companies, including cereal companies, car dealers, and Internet information marketers.

Three broad, yet powerful, business model innovation strategies are crowdsourcing (the subject of this chapter), sales virtualization (check out Chapter 21), and insurance (flip to Chapter 22). These strategies are broad but can apply to any company. Any one of these strategies has the ability to radically transform a business model and make it better.

Crowdsourcing Is Here to Stay

Ten years ago, a handful of crowdsourcing applications like YouTube, Elance, and American Idol tapped into the power of the crowd. Today thousands and thousands of companies use crowdsourcing to

- ✔ **Create products.** Giving consumers "a hand in the brand," Frito-Lay created the "Do Us a Flavor" contest. This contest, a first in the United States, is already a hit in other countries. Some of the funky flavors suggested include Chili & Chocolate, Caesar Salad, Late Night Kebob, and Cajun Squirrel. These contests have generated more than eight million chip flavor ideas globally. The contest winner receives $1 million.

- ✔ **Vote on new product options.** The Frito-Lay contest entrants get vetted by a celebrity panel to a handful of options, and then consumers vote on the winner.

- ✔ **Utilize a real-world ad agency.** Global consumer powerhouse Unilever recently decided to fire its ad agency of 16 years, turning to crowdsourcing platform IdeaBounty to create ideas for its next television campaign. Coca-Cola's Sprite brand ran a contest among film students for its most recent TV spot. This campaign did more than just generate ideas; students submitted finalized commercials ready to air.

✔ **Rate products in real time versus a focus group.** If you've watched a recent political debate, you've seen the graph on the bottom of the screen moving like an EKG. Selected voters rate their satisfaction or dissatisfaction of the candidate's comments in real time. In the old days, audience members were pulled into a room, where they were surveyed or interviewed, and then feedback was interpreted by political gurus.

✔ **Create a suggestion box on steroids.** Customer comments and suggestions have always been valued by businesses, but most suggestion boxes garnered very few comments. The ease and massive scope of the Internet allows comments and suggestions to be crowdsourced for greater accuracy and volume.

✔ **Pull collective wisdom from around the world.** One of the tenets of crowdsourcing is that the crowd is almost always right. This premise has been heavily researched and proven true. By leveraging this collective wisdom, companies can more accurately predict the success of new product introductions. Fandango.com posts both moviegoer and critic reviews. Which do you trust more, the collective score of 10,000 moviegoers like you or that of a handful of critics? Most movie patrons trust the collective wisdom of the crowd to better predict the quality of a movie than the opinion of critics.

✔ **Break work into manageable pieces.** Finnish company Microtask uses crowdsourcing to complete extremely dull tasks that are tough to stomach 40 hours a week. For instance, the company is digitizing the archives of the National Library of Finland by breaking scanned documents up into millions of little pieces. Those pieces are placed within a game called Mole Bridge. Players read the tiny pieces — which are just images of individual words — and type what they say into a window. Players move forward in the game as a result. Microtask combines the data and gets free typing and translation services.

✔ **Allow customers to co-create products.** CafePress, a popular custom T-shirt and gift site, claims 11 million unique visits per month and more than 250 million different products on its site. T-shirt designers create their own designs and post them for other visitors to purchase. Designers earn a royalty on any sales.

✔ **Raise money.** Crowdfunding sites like zopa.com and kickstarter.com can raise hundreds of thousands of dollars in days.

Business model architects can't afford to treat crowdsourcing like a fad. The cheap and easy transfer of data made possible by technology has created this powerful business tactic. It's here to stay.

Ten Things You May Not Know Were Crowdsourced

Leveraging the power of the crowd is more common than you may think. Here are some everyday examples of crowdsourcing you may not have known about:

- ✔ The Green Bay Packers have been saved by crowdfunding twice. The team was nearly bankrupt, and no bank or investor would step in. So, in 1923 local merchants raised $5,000 by selling 1,000 shares for $5 apiece to the local community, and in 1935 $15,000 was raised.

- ✔ Toyota's logo. In 1935, the company held a contest that received 27,000 design entries from which the logo was chosen.

- ✔ TomTom GPS units use a user input system called Map Share that allows corrections and additions to the TomTom map. Millions of map corrections have been logged by users, improving the overall experience for all.

- ✔ Twitter paid around $6 for the crowdsourced bird logo.

- ✔ Your iPhone is a radar detector. The Cobra iRadar is a radar, laser and speed, and red light camera detection device that communicates with your iPhone through a special app that shows hotspots on a GPS map. Users report police activity into the app, effectively crowdsourcing speed trap detection.

- ✔ Citibank crowdsources its customer service. Rather than house reps in a large office and source talent locally, thousands of reps from around the world log into a web-based system where calls are bullpenned. Then the calls are distributed to the best available reps based on a rating system that weighs their upsell history, customer satisfaction, average time per call, and so on. Reps are paid based on this scale as well.

- ✔ Salesforce.com's Jigsaw sells crowdsourced data. Customer A inputs data that isn't currently in the database for consumption by Customer B. This business model differs greatly from that of data providers such as Dun & Bradstreet who build their own databases via phone books, Internet directory mining, and phone calls.

- ✔ Harley-Davidson's recent television ad, "No Cages," was crowdsourced.

- ✔ McDonald's recently launched a crowdsourced burger, the Pretzelnator, in Germany.

- ✔ Google results are effectively crowdsourced. The key ranking factor is PageRank, which takes hundreds of factors into account but primarily weighs hyperlinks from other sites. Where do hyperlinks come from? They come from the mass of Internet users recommending the site to others via a hyperlink.

Your Business Model Can Benefit from Crowdsourcing

Many businesspeople treat crowdsourcing as "something for the other guys." They don't fully understand crowdsourcing, so they treat it like a foreign language — something they hear about but don't understand. The fact is that most businesses can benefit from some form of crowdsourcing. Crowdsourcing has the potential to speed development, generate creative ideas, and lower costs. Crowdsourcing is a potentially disruptive innovation for businesses that can effectively leverage its power. (See Chapter 19 for more on disruptive innovation.)

Crowdsourcing is 1,300 times faster

A crowdsourced product can be created in a fraction of the time of a traditionally created one. Crowdsourcing eliminates layers of bureaucracy, allows vast numbers of participants, and uses transparent information that can't be rivaled by a single organization.

Since its first printing in 1771, The Encyclopedia Britannica has created more than 65,000 articles in its collection. Since January 2001, Wikipedia has amassed nearly 3.9 million articles. Put another way, the Encyclopedia Britannica has averaged adding 270 articles per year while crowdsourced Wikipedia has added an average of 354,545 annually — or 1,313 times more.

The nature of dark matter stumped astronomers for decades, so NASA created a dark matter competition to crowdsource answers. Martin O'Leary, a British glaciologist from the University of Cambridge, won the contest. His solution was a mathematical model for the tiny distortions in images of the galaxy, thought to be dark matter. NASA, the European Space Agency, and others had been working on the problem for years, but O'Leary found the solution in a week and a half.

Crowdsourcing creates a new meritocracy

In a crowdsourced environment, barriers are reduced and access to resources increased, creating an equal and unbiased playing field. Take, for example, the NASA contest from the previous section. Who knows whether user name Joe5434 is a 12-year-old in Tulsa, Oklahoma or a 62-year-old, out-of-work welder in Wales? It doesn't matter. Information typically shared only with insiders is available to all, and may the best ideas win — regardless of their source.

Historically, a variety of barriers kept talented players off the field. You couldn't write for a major newspaper without a journalism degree. Today, blogs and news aggregation sites like `digg.com` allow anyone to publish. The crowd votes with views, comments, and ratings to allow the cream to rise to the top.

Picking winning stocks has long been the sole domain of well-educated and skilled market mavens employed by Wall Street firms. These firms sold their ability to pick winners for billions of dollars via newsletters, commissions, private banking, and fees. Using crowdsourcing, The Motley Fool has disrupted this profitable industry. Using an investor community of 170,000, the Motley Fool's CAPS rating system lets the crowd vote on stocks from zero to five stars.

The patented CAPS system has been proven accurate. Five-star stocks have performed better than 4-star stocks while zero-star stocks underperformed, supporting the crowd's prediction. The Motley Fool also ranks its nearly 75,000 members' individual stock-picking ability. Top stock picker bbmaven isn't a Wall Street guru; he's an ordinary guy from Massachusetts. However, bbmaven's stock-picking record is better than many million-dollar, salaried fund managers, including *Mad Money*'s Jim Cramer. The Motley Fool has emulated Cramer's stock picks, and he has an 82.52 score while bbmaven has a score of 99.9.

Reality TV can be seen as a form of crowdsourcing. Previously, only a handful of famous actors in Hollywood could be selected as the star of a new television series. Now, everyday people — like *Jersey Shore*'s Snooki, Mike Rowe of *Dirty Jobs*, *Deadliest Catch*'s crab fishermen, Honey Boo Boo, *The Real Housewives*' Bethenny Frankel, and *Jon & Kate Plus 8*'s Kate Gosselin — can enjoy fame and fortune.

Crowdsourcing can generate superior ideas

Sun Microsystems cofounder Bill Joy famously pointed out, "No matter who you are, most of the smartest people work for someone else." If only you could access these smart people, right? You can via crowdsourcing.

Canadian gold mining company Goldcorp was building a new plant for the conversion of gold ore and needed to know how much gold was in the ground. The company's internal geologists couldn't provide the answer. Founder Rob McEwen stunned the gold mining industry by sharing his company's proprietary geological data, so people all over the world could do the gold prospecting for him.

The Goldcorp Challenge offered $575,000 to the winner. A team of two Australian firms created a 3D model of the mine and created the winning plan out of thousands of entries. Their plan identified more than 110 sites for exploration, and 50 percent of them were previously unknown to the company. More than 80 percent of these new sites yielded significant gold reserves. Goldcorp made millions from this data.

The Encyclopedia Britannica boasts articles from 110 Noble Prize winners and five U.S. presidents, yet many experts view Wikipedia as a superior source for information. In this case, quantity *may* beat quality. While the Encyclopedia Britannica boasts more than 4,000 article authors, Wikipedia has more than 750,000 contributors. Your next door neighbor may not be able to outsmart a Nobel Laureate on an IQ test, but I bet he or she knows more about household cleaners or automotive repair.

Many computer professionals prefer the open source Linux operating system to Windows. Linux advocates note that Linux is more stable, has fewer viruses, and doesn't slow down over time as advantages over Windows. Like Wikipedia, Linux is a free platform that has been upgraded and refined by thousands of programmers.

Crowdsourcing lowers costs

Frito-Lay may be paying $1 million for a new chip flavor (see the earlier section "Crowdsourcing is Here to Stay" for details), but this amount is cheap compared to the alternative. If Frito-Lay created a new chip flavor the old-fashioned way, it could spend tens of millions of dollars and have less of a chance for success. In Table 20-1, I compare the old product development process to crowdsourcing, using the Frito-Lay chip flavor contest as an example.

Table 20-1   Frito-Lay: The Old Product Development Process versus Crowdsourcing

The Old-Fashioned Way	Crowdsourcing
Get a team of scientists, food science experts, and marketers to brainstorm ideas for product flavors. Imagine the cost of these high-talent professionals generating ideas for a few months.	Offer a $1 million "prize" and get millions of flavor ideas for less than the cost to develop them internally plus tons of PR for free.
Make prototype chips and have multiple focus groups evaluate them.	Prototype only a few vetted options.

The Old-Fashioned Way	*Crowdsourcing*
Take the suggestions of the focus group back to the product creation panel and make adjustments.	The crowd acts as the ongoing focus group, filtering out bad ideas and reinforcing the good ones.
Continue this process until satisfied with the product.	This step not needed.
Market the product to the public and hope they like it.	The contest markets the product, so it needs far less marketing when the product is live.
Repeat the whole process if the product fails.	Chances of market acceptance are much better because consumers created and voted on the product. In addition, allowing consumers input/buy-in for the product vests them in its success.

By crowdsourcing the new flavor, Frito-Lay saves development costs, accelerates development, gains invaluable PR (the contest crashed its Facebook site), gets to pre-market the product effectively, and exponentially increases the odds of the product's success.

Table 20-2 illustrates additional ways crowdsourcing can lower costs.

Table 20-2	**Lowering Cost with Crowdsourcing**	
Crowdsourcing Option	*Lowers Costs By . . .*	*Examples*
Crowd testing	Quickly tapping worldwide resources.	utest.com
Vendor crowdsourcing	Offering access to worldwide resources. Matches supply and demand. Hungry vendors can quickly access projects.	elance.com, 99designs.com, guru.com
Volunteerism	Allowing for free products. Everyone needs a hobby, and crowdsourced creations allow for free products.	Linux

(continued)

Table 20-2 *(continued)*

Crowdsourcing Option	Lowers Costs By . . .	Examples
Clever work chunking	Breaking large tedious tasks that would be too expensive or cumbersome to complete into small tasks done by many.	Amazon Turk, Captcha transcription
Surveying	Giving instant feedback from a significant number of users, which leads to better decision-making.	American Idol, `Feedback army.com`
Co-creation	Removing tasks from the firm, increasing the odds of market acceptance, and increasing customer loyalty. All this is possible when the firm and customer work together to create and customize offerings.	Nike gives customers tools to design their own sneakers
Crowdfunding	Removing the traditional lending institution as middleman. Opens markets to nontraditional lenders as well as marginal loan customers.	`zopa.com`, `kiva.org`, `kickstarter.com`
Users helping users	Providing customer service for free. Why have a customer service staff when the best service can be provided by other customers for free?	Countless Microsoft forums, Yahoo! Answers
Contests	Using the crowd to do it better, faster, and cheaper when internal resources may not be able to solve the problem.	Netflix's $1 million prize to help improve its collaborative filtering algorithm, Goldcorp Challenge
Open innovation	Accessing some of the brightest minds in the world for moonlighting prices. Companies can do this by sharing formerly sacred data.	Eli Lilly uses the InnoCentive platform to solve complex drug creation problems
User data compiled and fed back to users	Obtaining data more quickly. Cellphone GPS systems submit a user's current speed, and then combine this data with other users' speeds to yield a traffic map. This data is more accurate and timely than the old method, a traffic helicopter and radio broadcasting.	GPS traffic applications

Naming a new division

A company wanted to create a new division and needed to name it. There were no wrong answers and no way to grade the quality of a name, but the owner had a feeling that he shouldn't name the new division. He was leaning in one direction but decided to let his customers name the new division. The business owner provided approximately 20 clients with a list of possible names and asked them to rank their top three choices. The clients had a clear choice. The owner went with his clients' pick even though he disagreed with it. Ten years later he's elated he went with the wisdom of the crowd instead of his own opinion.

By finding ways to use crowdsourcing in your business model, you can move faster, lower costs, and access new talent. Any of these benefits can create new and meaningful competitive advantage.

Crowdsourcing simply works better sometimes

If you want your business model to perform at its best, you need to be open to the possibility that crowdsourcing may be more than a novel way to do business. In some cases, crowdsourcing exponentially works better than existing methods. Many open innovation projects — like the Goldcorp Challenge or Eli Lilly's call for drug research innovation — overcome problems not easily solved by the organization.

Many prize-based contests like Frito-Lay's Do Us a Flavor or `99designs`' graphics design bring so much additional brainpower to a problem that previously unimagined solutions become real.

In other cases, the crowd can tackle a massive task that's too big for one company. By digitizing books one Captcha at a time, entire libraries can be quickly transcribed. Facebook is using the crowd to translate the site to various languages. The cost of translating millions of web pages to dozens of languages would prove cost prohibitive and would deny Facebook to users in their native language. Highly accurate traffic data accumulated from thousands of user's GPS phones furnishes instant, accurate data instead of helicopters observing some traffic jams and missing others.

The crowd can also provide speed. If you discover that your website has a nasty virus at 3 a.m. and want it fixed immediately, good luck rousing your webmaster. Post the project on Elance or Rentacoder, and the problem could be fixed before your webmaster's alarm clock rings. For tasks that can be crowdsourced, the availability of a large, eager pool of talent can benefit your business. iNews reporters get breaking news to consumers much faster than commercial news outlets. As the democratic movement was taking place in Egypt, Twitter was a superior source of news versus CNN. Five dollar donations texted by millions of cellphone users sped relief for Superstorm Sandy victims compared to a Red Cross telephone campaign or telethon.

Crowd wisdom can exceed individual wisdom in some cases. Motley Fool CAPS readers pick stocks better than many professionals. For many moviegoers, Fandango users rate movies better than professional critics. Knowing when to leverage the wisdom of the crowd can improve your business.

Potential Downsides of Crowdsourcing

Crowdsourcing has many potential benefits. Some potential negative effects of crowdsourcing are also worth mentioning. Consider the following:

- ✔ **Low cost can equal low value.** For every $35 Nike logo, hundreds of low-quality logos are created.

- ✔ **Lack of continuity.** Many of the crowdsourcing platforms businesses find useful leverage freelance designers. If you use a single ad agency, it may be more expensive, but you get consistent branding and continuity. Using the crowd may be cheaper, but you sacrifice continuity and may have to manage the brand yourself.

- ✔ **Facilitates the "race to the bottom."** Crowdsourcing pundits claim that bidding free-for-alls drive down prices and lower wages for providers.

- ✔ **Option overload.** The sheer volume of the crowd can be overwhelming. Having one design firm may not result in the best logo, but you have only five options to consider. Create a logo design contest and you have to choose from hundreds of options. The additional options may not always be worth the additional time needed to manage them.

- ✔ **Difficulty managing the crowd.** Starbucks created the crowdsourced platform MyStarbucksIdea to solicit feedback and ideas from customers. However, only 0.05 percent (one out of every 2,000) of the ideas have been implemented. If you ask for ideas and don't implement them, the crowd may turn angry or view the program as a marketing ploy.

- ✔ **The 1/10/89 rule.** Only one percent of the crowd makes meaningful contributions to sites like Yelp, Zagat's, and Google Places. You may call the other 99 percent complacent. They ate a meal, it was good, and they went home. They have no need to log in and write a review. So who does take time to write reviews? Angry people, that's who. Ask any business owner the ratio of upset customers who write reviews to happy customers who do. It's exceptionally lopsided. This trend makes the crowdsourced rating system inherently negatively biased. Some businesses have resorted to phony positive reviews to combat this negative bias. This tactic further destroys the validity of the system.

Crowdsourcing may have some drawbacks, but crowdsourcing has triggered a dramatic shift in the way work is organized, talent is employed, research is conducted, and products are made and marketed. Find a way to leverage it into your business model.

Chapter 21

Utilizing Virtualized Sales Processes

A *virtualized sales process* leverages recent technological advances, particularly the Internet, to make the sales process more cost effective and productive. The process of sales virtualization began with the printing press. Prior to Gutenberg, the only way to entice a buyer was face to face. The printing press allowed merchants to create sales messages and transfer some of the in-person selling to the printed word. The telephone provided even more sales virtualization by allowing in-person selling to be performed over phone wires. Corporations set up massive appointment setting and telemarketing staffs to capitalize on the savings and increased productivity this virtualization provided.

The Internet and all its related sales tools — e-mail, video streaming, podcasts, search engines, websites, RSS, and webinars — provide the opportunity to dramatically transform sales processes.

In Chapter 9 I tell you that the sales performance model significantly impacts your business model. Leveraging sales virtualization can innovate your model for the better. Right now you may be saying, "Yeah, I have a website and we do webinars; so what's the big deal?" Sales virtualization is more than hosting a webinar. Sales virtualization radically shifts the early stages of the sales process to less expensive, non-human methods. You nurture leads by using Internet tools until they become more "sellable." When the leads are ready, you pass them on to the sales force. This process is significantly cheaper to administer and more effective if done right.

Understanding How the Internet Changed the World of Sales

Thanks a lot Internet. Before you, selling made sense. There were only a few ways to market: television, radio, direct mail, print ads, telemarketing, cold calling, and the Yellow Pages. Now it seems like there are thousands of methods: banner ads, pay-per-click, search engine optimization, videos, and countless social media outlets.

The old methods didn't go away; they just stopped working as well. Here's a secret. It's not the shift from old line media to new that matters to your business model. Business trends are constantly shifting and moving just like the world rotating on its axis each day. The planet is moving at 1,070 miles per hour, but you adjust and don't even feel like it's moving. The changes brought by the Internet are more like an earthquake. The Internet has jolted not only marketing methods but buyer psychology as well. It's the radical change in buyer psychology that creates the need for a virtualized sales process.

Don't sell like it's 1985

If you're over 35, you remember those good old days before the Internet. It felt like it was easier to sell back then, and it was in many ways. In 1985, when the Internet wasn't around, buyers behaved differently. Imagine it's 1985, and you want to shop for a new Cadillac. What do you do? You stroll into the dealership, figuratively "raise your hand" and say, "Hey, over here. I need some information because I'm a prospect." Information wasn't conveniently available to consumers any other way, so you needed a salesperson to get the information you wanted.

Fast forward to today. You're shopping for a Cadillac. Do you go to the dealer for information, or do you sit down at your computer and obtain it from the web? Most people shop extensively on the web before visiting a dealer. More importantly, they shop anonymously. The dealer may not know you're a prospect until you come into her dealership ready to buy. I just bought a car like this. I went to the dealer and said, "I want this one." The salesperson had no idea who I was until I bought. I "hid in the bushes" until I was ready to come out of them.

This is the way things are bought and sold today. Customers hide in the bushes until they decide they want to expose themselves to your sales process, and there's nothing you can do about it. So how do you sell things to buyers you may not know exist? The answer is in all those Internet options that may be driving you crazy. Changes in buyer psychology (rather than buyers' technical savvy or love of smartphones) make them necessary. Table 21-1 further compares sales techniques past and present.

Table 21-1   Comparing Sales Techniques Past and Present

1985	Today	Comment
Salespeople are valuable sources of information	Salespeople are annoying and disregarded	Buyers want to be educated before being sold. If you try to sell them before they're educated, you're less likely to get the sale.
Buyers interact with a potential vendor to discover how a product may suit them	Buyers surf the web anonymously	Buyers know they don't need to identify themselves as potential prospects until later in the process. As with deer hunting, if you move too soon, they'll run away.
Limited number of vendors	Seemingly unlimited vendors	Name an industry with too few firms. There aren't many. Globalization has created excess demand in most industries.
Buyers consider selling to be a necessary evil to get what they want	*Sell* is a four-letter word	Especially with the younger generations, anything deemed to be selling is frowned upon. Pre-Internet generations are used to getting valuable information from salespeople, so they tolerate them better. The younger generations have always self-educated and self-sold themselves, so salespeople are viewed as pushy, annoying, and unnecessary.
Negotiation for best price	Amazon Price Check	Buyers are capable of getting a great deal by clicking their mouse and don't need an uncomfortable negotiation.
Confrontational format	Buyers opt out if they sense confrontation or an uncomfortable environment	"Come on, you know you want it" doesn't work these days.
Secrets	Transparent information	Buyers are armed with your costs, company history, product and customer reviews, and comparison pricing. Transparent information greatly favors buyers and strengthens their feeling of control during the sales process.
Interruption marketing	Permission marketing	Not long ago, hundreds of firms generated billions in profits by cold calling people during dinner. Now cold calling is illegal in many countries.

(continued)

Table 21-1 *(continued)*

1985	Today	Comment
Peer referrals are less important than advertising	Reputation management	If your plumber did a poor job in 1985, you complained to a few neighbors. Today you post a negative review on sites like Angie's List or Google Places, and then you tweet about it, killing 100 deals for the plumber.
Limited advertising methods	Unlimited advertising methods, resulting in too much noise	The average person saw 500 advertising messages per day in the 1970s and sees as many as 5,000 per day now. Consumers' answer to this overload is to tune it *all* out.
Sellers in control	Buyers in control	The free flow of information, too many competitors in each market, and social media have put buyers firmly in control.

Check out Figure 21-1, an actual sign in a doctor's office. Drug reps used to be viewed as a valuable source of information on new drugs and technical information. This information could still be potentially lifesaving to a patient, yet the doctor refuses to get this information from a pharmaceutical salesperson. Because the doctor has the ability to self-educate and self-sell via the Internet, information delivery from a salesperson (even if it could be superior) is frowned upon.

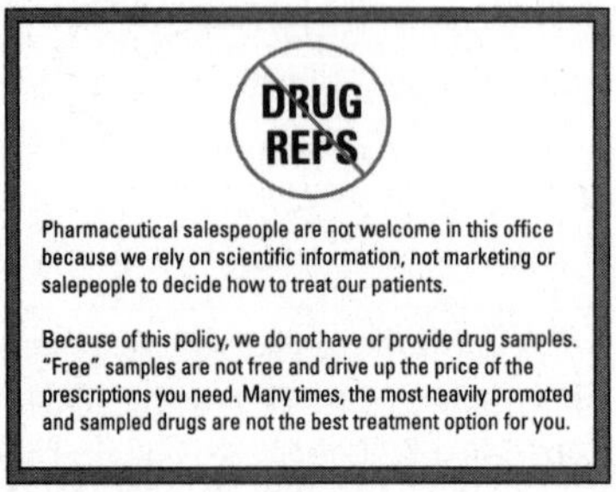

Figure 21-1: A sign from a doctor's office.

Ⓧ DRUG REPS

Pharmaceutical salespeople are not welcome in this office because we rely on scientific information, not marketing or salepeople to decide how to treat our patients.

Because of this policy, we do not have or provide drug samples. "Free" samples are not free and drive up the price of the prescriptions you need. Many times, the most heavily promoted and sampled drugs are not the best treatment option for you.

The curse of the invisible prospect

The Internet has fundamentally changed buyer psychology and methodology. Like it or not, early in the sales process, your prospects are invisible. Just like doctors eliminating their use of drug reps, your prospects now have the power to let you know when your sales team is needed or unneeded.

Stop using the word "value"

A great example of having to fall on the sword is the use of "value" in marketing. Most businesses aren't the low-cost provider, so they sell value. Their claim is that the increased cost of their product over the low-cost provider's is worth the extra money.

Is this how *you* purchase goods and services? When you're the buyer instead of the seller, and you hear the word "value," what immediately pops into your head? Most people say, "Got it. Yours is more expensive." I'm not saying you need to lower your prices. I'm saying that the new buyer psychology created by the ease of performing cost comparisons on the Internet has created a trophy for the lowest price mentality. The buyer wants to win, and the easiest way to feel victorious is to get the lowest price. When you use the word "value," you automatically trigger the thought in the minds of buyers that they won't get their much-desired victory.

Instead, highlight the key attributes of your offering with no reference to price or value. After all, "value" simply means the extra price paid is worth it. Let the buyers decide whether the extra money is worth it to them, and don't you make that claim.

In general, you should assume that your prospects want your sales team to help them as late in the process as possible, if at all. Prospects want to anonymously gather nothing more than helpful information in the early stages of the sales process. If you try to force them out of their anonymity, you may lose the prospect.

Have you ever been to a website in search of information only to be asked for your name, address, phone number, e-mail address, age, birth date, and dog's name? What did you do? You promptly exited the site. This exit was your way of saying, "I was only window shopping, and you yanked me into the store and asked me to count the money in my wallet in front of you. No way!"

If you don't let your prospects protect their anonymity and provide the information they want the way they want it, your prospects could leave your sales funnel without you even knowing it. This is the curse of the invisible prospect.

Falling on the sword

Whenever I talk to businesspeople about the curse of the invisible prospect, their first response is, "Why can't it just be like it used to be?" I'm with you; it was easier to sell in the good old days. Unfortunately, this back-to-the-past plan isn't going to work. The good news is there's a plan that can work — for everyone.

All you have to do is "fall on the sword." Falling on the sword entails sucking it up and selling the way the prospects want, regardless of whether you agree or don't, like it or not. What the prospects want is information how and when they want it. Meeting this need through virtualization of your sales process can be a game-changing improvement to your business model. Some aspects of the process may turn your stomach, especially if you had a well-functioning salesperson-driven system. If you're unwilling to do those uncomfortable or even distasteful portions, the plan won't work. Reconsider the Cadillac example from earlier in the chapter. Over the past 20 years, car dealers have had to shift from a show-and-tell in-person sales system to an Internet virtual showroom and even a virtual test-drive system. Buyers don't want to select fabrics or colors in the showroom. They want to select them in their living room. An auto company that doesn't let buyers purchase a car in the method they desire will lose to a competitor that better emulates the desired process.

These problems present opportunities

Invisible prospects, buyers in control of the sales process, excessive transparency driving down margins — Yikes! All these dynamics can damage your business model. By the same token, these problems can simply be considered shifts in the way you do business. Move with them, and you have the opportunity to outmaneuver your competition. By re-engineering your sales process to better work with 21st-century buying dynamics, you can seize sales while your competitors complain. A virtualized sales process uses methods that are in alignment with this new buyer psychology.

Considering the Benefits of Sales Virtualization

A virtualized sales process lowers your cost of sales, is in better alignment with how the customer wants to be sold, and works better than your current process. Consider these benefits:

- **Sales virtualization lowers the cost of sales.** The prospect wants anonymous information in a sales-free environment. Effectively, this change amounts to the prospect self-selling. By creating informative marketing materials and providing access to them, you eliminate a costly human, one-at-a-time sales machine and replace it with a hundreds-at-a-time marketing ATM called the web.

- **Prospects appreciate a virtualized sales process.** It's nice to be nice, but sales pay — niceness doesn't. In this case, niceness can pay too. Because the prospects are in control of the process and have a variety of vendors to choose from, doing business in a way the prospect doesn't enjoy or appreciate will most likely translate to the prospect shopping somewhere else. Give prospects the buying process and experience they want, and you'll get more prospects and convert more of them.

✔ **Sales virtualization works better.** Forget that it's cheaper. Forget that prospective buyers prefer it. Virtualized sales processes sell more goods and services than the 1985-style, human-intensive sales processes. Look at Amazon versus Best Buy. Sure, buying online is convenient and cost competitive, but who wants to be tormented by the Best Buy salespeople? How much of Amazon's success is because they use a sales process that matches customers' preferences? Plain and simple — virtualized sales processes are the new standard.

Examining the Foundations of a Virtualized Sales Process

If you want to successfully virtualize your sales process, you need to understand the philosophical pillars of the process. Sales virtualization is more than just converting marketing to digital media. Sales virtualization is as much about psychology as sales. Therefore, understanding the philosophical pillars of sales virtualization is paramount to success.

Giving up on outdated methodologies

I've said it before, and I'll say it again. You need to be willing to fall on the sword. A lot has changed in the world of selling since 1985. Buyers are firmly in control, and your process needs to reflect that. If you're using any of the old tried-and-true methods that used to work, they may only alienate your prospects today. Unfortunately, it doesn't matter whether you like this new buyer mentality or not; if you don't follow a process that buyers want, they'll quietly and visibly exit your sales funnel.

Leveraging quid pro quo

Quid pro quo is another way of saying you've got to give to get. By falling on the sword and giving buyers an information-rich, salesperson-free sales process, you're giving them what they want. However, you get to receive a little bit in exchange. If buyers want pricing information, you want their e-mail addresses. If buyers want a deeper level of information on your product, you want them to watch a five-minute instructional video. A strong sales virtualization process incorporates quid pro quo. First you give, then you get.

When designing the process and creating the marketing tools within it, keep in mind what information and actions you want from buyers and what you'll have to give them in order to get what you want.

Educating early in the process

What does a salesperson do? Salespeople don't sell. Buyers won't allow a salesperson to come into their office and do nothing but sell them. Salespeople can do only what buyers will let them do — educate. Ideally, buyer education turns into persuasion, which turns into sales. But make no mistake, salespeople don't sell, they educate.

In the sales virtualization process, you want to educate the client as early in the process as possible for several reasons:

✔ **High-level buyers all need the same education.** What does the product do? How do the features and benefits help customers? How much does it typically cost? You're paying your sales team a tremendous amount of money to answer these frequently asked questions in person to one prospect at a time. A virtualized sales process, such as videos, can answer all these questions 24 hours a day, 7 days a week, 365 days a year. Not only that, videos don't have bad days, get cranky, catch the flu, or lack skills. Videos and other forms of electronic education offer the opportunity to put your best foot forward every time. When you create these electronic education pieces, they serve your organization for years and cost almost nothing to use.

✔ **The ability of prospects to stay invisible requires giving them enough information that they want to expose themselves.** I call this exposure poking their head out of the bushes. Prospects hide in the bushes, gather information, and then poke their heads out if they find the information is interesting enough. Information given early in the process should almost always be educational. The buyer defines what education means, not you. Most companies think educating buyers on the ten reasons they need to buy the product counts as education. It doesn't. Think like a buyer. What questions do you want answered early in the process? You don't want to know ten reasons why you need to whip out your wallet.

✔ **Early education creates an extremely wide funnel.** You now have an unmanned, automated sales process that can accommodate an infinite number of prospects. Rather than spending your time educating and attempting to sell these prospects in person, one at a time, you can let the prospects self-educate and then opt in to the next step in the sales process. This technique provides you much greater leverage and lower cost.

If in doubt, overeducate your prospects. Many businesses have an issue with giving too much information early in the process. They feel if they provide the prospect with too much valuable information, the prospect will make a decision without the company having a chance to sell them. They're right. That's a real possibility. However, the underlying assumption behind this thought is that customers will subject themselves to the sales process if you don't share the information, and they probably won't. They'll just quietly leave your sales process, because you haven't given them enough information to move forward. Don't confuse prospects subjecting themselves to a conventional sales process with success.

Giving away pricing information is a common point of contention for business owners. They feel exposing their pricing information will ruin their chance to sell. Be open to the idea that sharing rather than withholding pricing information in your virtual sales process may be better. For instance, web-based price calculators have been a game-changing tool for some companies. I've never met a business owner who wasn't scared to death of the web price calculator, but I've seen a business owner whose business tripled after she bit the bullet and installed one.

Using a mutual opt-in mindset

When was the last time you did a deal that wasn't win-win? It was probably a long time ago or perhaps never. The days of snake oil salesmen are long gone. Today's prospects are too well informed to make a win-lose deal. Here's the point: When you sell, you try to persuade the prospect to do what you want. As long as what you want is a win for the customer, you have a deal. No matter how well you sell or how persuasive you are, the prospect *will not* enter a win-lose deal.

Therefore, all deals you make must be win-win. You may be saying, "Yeah, I already do that." Yes, you probably have a win-win mindset, but you probably don't have a sales process designed to leverage that win-win mindset. Rather than unsuccessfully trying to persuade prospects to do what you want, switch to a mutual opt-in process.

Here's an example of the benefits of a mutual opt-in process:

1. **Give prospects all the education they need to make an informed decision about whether or not to opt into your sales process.** You're not trying to sell the prospects at this point; you're trying to earn the right to sell them.

2. **Work under the assumption that only prospects with a good fit for your offering turn into buyers.** You have lots of data on what a prospect who

can benefit from your product is like. Don't hide this information. Share it with prospects, so they can decide whether they're a good fit too. This is their opt-in. This is an extremely powerful step in the process. If you do it right, prospects who are a bad fit will voluntarily opt out of your sales process. Rather than spending countless dollars and wasting effort on prospects who will never buy, you get them to leave, which costs you nothing, because the process is automated. This is the biggest benefit of sales virtualization.

3. **Because you've been candid and generous with your information regarding fit, you've earned the right to opt out of the process if you want.** Face it, not all prospects are worthy of investment. You now have an arsenal of education-based marketing tools that you can use to automatically and inexpensively sell the prospect. You should segment prospects and/or use lead scoring to categorize them, only opting into the highest value ones.

4. **Sell, baby, sell.** You now have a well-educated prospect who has voluntarily opted into your sales process. Close the deal.

Walking through the Sales Virtualization Process

In this section, I show you the path to take to create a virtualized sales process. Then I give you a detailed example of a franchise sales operation that successfully implemented this process.

How to create a virtualized sales process

Every company has an opportunity to improve its sales process and lower costs with virtualization. An in-depth discussion of sales virtualization would take an entire book, but here I lay out the nuts and bolts for you:

✔ **Figure out what information the client needs to opt in to your formal sales process.**

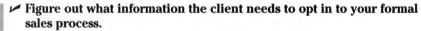

When purchasing an automobile, the client needs to know a significant amount of information before he has any real interest in making a purchase. He wants to know

- Two doors or four. Some people love two-door cars, some hate them. If a person won't buy a two-door car and that's the only option, the sales process is over.

- The approximate cost of the vehicle. If the prospect has only $10,000 to spend, looking at new Cadillacs isn't a good idea.

- What colors are available. A few years ago General Motors came out with a bold yellow color. No other manufacturer had this color. If I'm set on buying a car in this color but want a Toyota, I'm out of luck.

- What options are available on the car. No in-dash GPS system? Sorry, that's a deal breaker.

- What's the standard manufacturer's warranty.

- Where's the nearest dealer who will service the car.

✔ **Figure out what you can receive from the prospect in return.** If you're generous with your information, you can demand quid pro quo from the prospect. For instance, automotive sites gladly share all the information in the previous example without asking for any information from prospects. However, if they want to build their own model or schedule a test drive, the automotive site insists on the prospect providing some information. Start with the information you want to get from the prospect. Then figure out what digital goodies you have to offer in return for this information.

✔ **Create your information ATM.** Keep things as sales-free as possible. Remember the definition of information: data the prospects want — not information you want to give to persuade them to buy. Your information ATM is available to the client 24/7/365 and contains items such as a price list, white papers, digital brochures, FAQs, customer discussion boards, relevant reviews, articles, instructional videos, live webinars, recorded webinars, or anything else the prospect finds useful. I've never had a client tell me they created a digital asset for their ATM that wasn't worth the effort. The shelf life of these digital assets is years, and they could save you hundreds of thousands or even millions of dollars.

✔ **Use lead nurturing campaigns to get prospects to opt in to the formal sales process.** Most products aren't sold on the first interaction. Some products may take dozens of interactions in order to walk the client up the ladder to the sale. Traditionally, salespeople have performed some of this lead nurturing. They take prospects to lunch, call them periodically, drop in to say "hi," and more. You can still use some of these live lead-nurturing techniques, but try to move them to virtual nurturing for cost reasons. My clients have found that virtual nurturing may not be as effective as live nurturing, but a well-informed customer who's allowed to opt in and is a good fit won't leave just because he doesn't get live handholding or a free lunch. The bottom line is that a prospect with a good fit isn't going to leave because you won't buy him lunch.

✔ **Use lead scoring or prospect categorizing to show when it's time to pass the lead to sales.** Lead scoring assigns points for the prospect's demographic fit and the action taken by prospects showing interest. Prospects with good lead scores are more likely to buy than ones with lower scores. When a prospect's lead score reaches a certain level, you stop marketing and start selling. Software company Marketo has a terrific presentation on lead scoring at `http://www.marketo.com/b2b-marketing-resources/best-practices/lead-scoring/the-definitive-guide-to-lead-scoring.php`.

✔ **Insist on better performance from your sales team, because the leads the team is receiving are significantly higher quality.** Your sales staff has now been freed from low-level information providing. Your lead scoring system has allowed the best prospects to bubble up to the top. This process should increase the close rate for the sales staff and decrease their workload. I strongly suggest rethinking commission structures and expectations. I've seen clients take a six-person sales force down to two closers and two support staff and sell more than the six-person sales force did. Whatever you do, insist on better performance from the sales department, because the sales virtualization process is doing a lot of the work for them.

Figure 21-2 shows a visualization of the process. First you use digital media to educate prospects and opt in to marketing. Next you market the prospects and use some form of prospect segmentation, such as lead scoring, to know when they're sales ready. When a prospect is sales ready, you unleash the sales force.

Figure 21-2:
Sales vir-
tualization
process
overview.

Sales virtualization process example: Franchise sales

Sometimes the best way to learn is by example. Here's an example of a franchise sales operation that went from a very labor intensive sales process to a highly virtualized one.

Under the old process, leads were collected from a variety of sources and put into a database. Each day the sales support staff e-mailed a brief PDF of information to the new leads. The next day the prospects were sent an e-mail, attempting to set an appointment with the vice president of sales. Typically, the e-mail wasn't answered. The administrative staff then began chasing these prospects, attempting to set an appointment for their highly skilled VP of sales who would attempt to persuade these people to write the big check.

Even though the first call took a full hour, the franchisor found it took three to five calls just to get a prospective franchisee to attend a franchise open house at headquarters. The administrative staff was perpetually chasing franchise prospects and the vice president's phone calendar was jam-packed.

This process had several issues, including the following:

- ✔ It took five to eight calls to prospective franchise buyers to set each appointment. In order to fully explain the franchise offering, each call with a prospective buyer took the vice president one hour.

- ✔ Franchise lead services are expensive. Average lead cost for a purchased lead was $32, so even if a prospect appeared to be a weak fit, the vice president kept talking.

- ✔ Even with all this effort, they weren't selling enough franchises. The cost of two administrators and one highly paid salesperson was excessive for this small franchisor.

Fortunately, the vice president of sales had an extremely frustrating day and accidentally solved their problem. One fateful day the vice president had five consecutive first phone calls. After five straight hours of explaining what the franchise was, how you can make money, how much you can make, what makes a successful franchisee, and other basic information, he realized the only difference in these five conversations was the person on the other end of the phone listening to him. He felt he could have recorded the conversation and just hit play. The day before, the company had been shooting a video, and the equipment was still set up. The vice president turned the camera on and talked into the camera for conversation number six. He was able to answer 12 frequently asked questions in an hour. They edited the recordings into 12 pieces, creating a video FAQ.

This FAQ video was the germination of their virtualized sales process. Instead of chasing prospects to set up an appointment for a one-hour call, the FAQ video was immediately sent to the lead. The prospect was given two days to watch the video. Then the administrators set an appointment for the vice president to talk to the prospect. The impact of the FAQ video was immediate. The VP was a little reluctant to use a video instead of a live sales conversation, but he was so frustrated, he didn't care. Two of the first three people he spoke with told him how much they appreciated getting the information they desired quickly at a time that was convenient for them. He knew he had stumbled onto something good.

Table 21-2 shows the changes made to the franchisor's sales process over the years to virtualize and fine-tune it.

Table 21-2	One Franchisor's Sales Virtualization
Sales Virtualization Action	*Comment*
Automatically send FAQ video when prospect submits web form	Administrative staff used to manually send information to each lead. Now prospects have instant, on-demand access to one hour's worth of virtual information.
Integrate CRM system with lead capture form on website	80% of leads came from the company website. Switching CRM systems to one that allowed complete integration eliminated data entry.
Cut initial phone call from one hour to 30 minutes	Because each prospect was given a one-hour FAQ video with the basic information, prospects had fewer questions.
Allow prospects to opt in to the next sales step rather than chase them	This was a big step. By falling on the sword and trusting the quality of the initial FAQ video, prospects who deemed themselves a bad fit were allowed to opt out of the process. Franchise leads are notorious for having lots of tire kickers. This step cut the workload of the highly paid vice president in half.
Create a second FAQ video	Prospect feedback indicated the videos were preferred to live phone interaction. It was clear that prospects wanted to deal with a live person, but they also wanted the bulk of their information provided via electronic methods. After the first phone call with the vice president, this second FAQ video with more detailed information was sent to each prospect.
Record candid interviews with existing franchisees at annual convention; send interview videos to prospective franchisees after first phone call	One of the biggest problems for this franchisor was the low number of existing franchises in comparison to the number of prospects. Every prospect wanted to talk to several franchisees in order to get information from a franchisee perspective. It was a reasonable request but was very taxing on existing franchisees. It was so taxing that some franchisees refused to talk to new potential franchisees, potentially causing lost deals. The franchisor made a bold move and strongly discouraged prospects from calling existing franchisees. In order to satisfy prospects' desires to hear the experiences of existing franchisees, the franchisor shot 15 to 20 candid videos of current franchisees. These videos gave the prospects enough information until later in the process when they could talk to existing franchisees.

Sales Virtualization Action	Comment
Create a standardized three-call sales system to ensure the same set of information is sent to each prospect at the end of each call	Research indicated most prospects agreed to attend a franchise open house after three calls with the vice president. Knowing what information a prospect has reviewed and when made the sale easier. The VP needed only to drive the prospect to the next step in the process.
Use client testimonials recorded on video as proof of the franchisor's concept; send them to prospective franchisees after the first phone call	Social proof is an issue when talking on the phone. The VP could make a claim, but at some point he needed to be backed up. Fifty testimonials were videotaped to back up the franchisor's claims.
Automatically e-mail a franchisee qualification document to prospects if they view the franchisee video	Most franchisors send in a qualification form immediately in an attempt to run off the tire kickers. The problem is qualification forms are very detailed and, in the early "discovery" portion of the sale, intrusive. This company decided to use the mutual opt-in process to filter rather than run off potentially good prospects. The trigger of clicking the franchise video was deemed to show significant interest, so the detailed form had a good chance of being completed.
CRM system marks each prospect's record, indicating which FAQ videos have been watched	Administrative staff instructed not to set up calls with the VP if prospects haven't viewed the information. If prospects were deemed uninterested, they were dropped from the funnel.

The end result of the sales virtualization process was dramatic. Before implementing the process, the workload required hiring another highly paid sales professional. After the virtualization process, one of the administrative positions was removed and the VP had enough time to serve in the same capacity for a sister franchise.

Chapter 22

Profiting from the Dynamics of Insurance

. . . .

In This Chapter

▶ Knowing why everyone should be in the "insurance" business

▶ Understanding what you're losing if you're not in the insurance game

▶ Coming up with an insurance plan that increases your profitability

. . . .

*E*veryone should be in the insurance business. If you're like most businesspeople, you probably have a bad taste in your mouth simply at the mention of insurance, let alone at the suggestion of entering the insurance business. I'm being facetious. I don't want you to start an insurance company. In this chapter, however, I do examine the foundation of the insurance business and show you how you can profit from borrowing some of the fundamental underpinnings of the insurance business model.

Defining Insurance

At its most basic level, insurance is nothing more than accepting risk in exchange for money. I can't afford to write a check to rebuild my house if it's destroyed by a tornado, so I pay an insurance company to assume the risk of the destruction a tornado may cause in exchange for an annual payment. The company assumes risk for money. Insurance is profitable. This year's Fortune 500 boasts 35 insurance companies, accounting for more than seven percent of the total profits of all companies on the list.

Most people view insurance companies as stodgy and conservative. To the contrary, insurance companies take massive risks every day. If they don't take risks, they don't collect premiums. The difference between insurance companies and virtually every other company is that insurance companies *want* to take risks and seek them out, whereas everyone else tries to avoid them. Insurance companies are very adept at assessing risk and then selling customers elimination of that risk for more than it costs the companies to do the risk taking — in other words, their profit.

Understanding the Core of Insurance Profitability

Insurance companies do more than accept risk in exchange for money. They pool risk, invest monies at above-average returns, and offer financial products. However, the core of insurance companies' profitability is risk acceptance. Two powerful dynamics power their ability to profit from risk acceptance: insurance companies have the ability to assess risk much more accurately than others, and insurance companies capitalize on customers' misconception of risk.

Accurately assessing risks others can't

I have no idea how someone predicts the likelihood of a tornado, a ship sinking, an athlete's knee blowing out, or life expectancy, but insurance companies do it well. Over decades of data analysis and modeling, insurance companies can predict with some accuracy risks others can't. This ability to statistically assess any risk with the same precision you can rate the odds of rolling a seven in a craps game enables insurance companies to make massive profits. The formula is simple — assess risks as accurately as possible, and then sell the assumption of that risk for much less than the cost of the risk. It's just like Las Vegas with a much higher vig for the house.

For instance, the odds of a tornado destroying a million-dollar building may be 0.01 percent. Statistically, the cost of that risk is $1,000,000 multiplied by 0.0001 or $1,000. The insurance company sells the assumption of that risk for much more than the "true" cost of $1,000.

Capitalizing on misconception of risk

Neuroscientists at the USC Brain and Creativity Institute have identified distinct brain regions with competing responses to risk. A study gave volunteers a task that measures risk tolerance and observed their reactions with functional magnetic resonance imaging (fMRI). The researchers found a difference in brain activity between those with high risk tolerance and lower risk tolerance. No one likes unnecessary risk, but some of your customers may view risk much differently than others.

If a tornado blows down my house, I know it will cost me hundreds of thousands of dollars to replace the house and contents. I have no idea whether the risk of this happening in the next 12 months is one in ten or one in a million, but the magnitude of the loss of my house plays tricks on my psyche. Human nature causes me to fear the loss more than I should and to view the odds as far worse than they actually are. I don't want to accept the risk of tornado and want the risk removed for a reasonable price. I don't really care about the statistical value of the risk. I simply weigh the psychological value of the removal of the risk with the cost of doing so.

If the price to remove risk is reasonable, markup is irrelevant. Take a look at these two examples:

✔ **Example 1: High markup but low cost**

Your daughter, like mine, keeps losing or breaking her cellphone. For $8 a month, you can have the cellphone carrier assume this risk. For a diminutive price tag, you can save family strife, so you buy the policy. This is a low-risk/low-cost combination.

Policy cost: $8/month

Average time before claim: 24 months

Total policy cost over 24 months: $192

Approximate policy payout: $100 (used phone)

Policy markup: 92%

✔ **Example 2: Low markup but high cost**

Your 62-year-old grandmother's health is declining a bit. You realize she may need to enter a nursing home, so you research long-term care insurance. When you find out the cost will exceed $9,000 per year, you decide her health isn't that bad after all.

Policy cost: $500/month

Average time before claim: 120 months

Total policy cost over 10 years: $60,000

Approximate policy payout: $50,000

Policy markup: 20%

Even though the markup on this policy is far less than the cellphone insurance policy in Example 1, the high-cost/high-risk combination reduces the attractiveness of this offer to both the provider and the purchaser.

By removing risks at a price reasonable to customers, insurance companies continue to generate outstanding profitability.

Denying Your Customers Insurance Is Costing You

Your business model can benefit from the same dynamics the insurance companies benefit from — accept risk in exchange for money. Your customers have some risks they want to be reduced or removed. If you deny customers the opportunity to do this, you're costing yourself money.

Ask yourself whether your customers take risks by doing business with you. Most people immediately respond, "No." They're wrong. Customers accept lots of risks for the privilege of doing business with you.

Take the example of a plumber. Many customers ask themselves questions like the ones in the following list. Each question centers on risks the customer is forced to accept.

- ✔ Will the plumber show up at the scheduled time? If you've taken off work to let the plumber in or rearranged your day, the answer to this question is a big deal.

- ✔ Does the plumber have the necessary tools? If not, will I be billed for him to obtain them?

- ✔ If the plumber doesn't have the right tools, will he try to perform the work with the wrong tools and ruin something?

- ✔ How skilled is the plumber? Is this his first day or 20th year on the job?

- ✔ Was the plumber out late drinking with his buddies last night?

- ✔ Am I safe alone in the house with the plumber?

- ✔ How full is the plumber's schedule? Will he rush my work or drag it out?

- ✔ Does he have the parts necessary on the truck or will I be charged for an unnecessary trip to the hardware store?

Wouldn't the customer like to remove some of these risks? Businesspeople tend to focus on excellence delivering their product or service, assuming well-delivered service equates to lack of risk. It doesn't. Look at these questions again. No matter how well the service is delivered, you can't eliminate these risks. *Someone has to take the risk;* it won't just disappear. Generally, businesses push risks onto their customers. The old adage, "The customer comes first" isn't true when it comes to risk assignment.

How many of the risks in the list would a typical customer pay to remove? The answer is several. Think about purchases you've personally avoided simply because you didn't want to assume the risk. For instance, you need a good used car but don't purchase one from your friend because you're not sure it's reliable. Over your lunch break you take your phone in for repair.

The service technician assures you your phone will be fixed within an hour. You need your phone right after lunch so you tell the technician "never mind." In both these situations, traditional business decisions such as price, quality, and brand had nothing to do with making the sale.

In order to make the sale, the risk needs to be removed, or the customer simply won't buy. If you can figure out how to remove unwanted risks, you can increase customer satisfaction, attract new customers, and increase profits. This adds up to a better business model.

I'm going to add a layer to the contention, "Insurance is accepting risk in exchange for money." You could bet $1 on the flip of the coin. I'll give you five-to-one odds on your bet, thus accepting risk in exchange for money. However, I'd be accepting too much risk for too little money. So I change the definition to:

> Profitable insurance is the acceptance of risk for more money than the risk is expected to cost.

Instead of insuring the flip of the coin for $5 when true odds are $1 wins $1, I want to offer you a quarter if you win the flip for a dollar bet. Now the odds are stacked in my favor. Imagine if I made bets like this over and over. True odds for a coin flip value the "insurance" at $1, yet it costs me only a quarter if I lose. This is exactly what a profitable insurance company does.

You have stacked odds like this with your customers. Because your knowledge of your business is vastly superior to your customers', you know the true cost of any risk. The customer is just guessing. You can use this disparity of knowledge as a profit center.

Take the customer's uneasiness about the skill level of a plumber. A poorly skilled plumber costing $150 per hour can run up a bill several hundred dollars more than a highly skilled plumber doing the same job. The customer views this risk from the angle of the worst-case scenario and attaches a several-hundred-dollar risk price tag to the risk. The plumbing company knows the skill level and performance of each plumber quite well and knows that the true cost of this risk is much less. In addition, the plumbing company controls the activities of the plumber and can mitigate some of this risk through training, procedures, and operational plans. The plumbing company has the opportunity to remove this risk for a reasonable fee and make a handsome profit.

You can't remove the inherent risk in a business transaction. The risk doesn't go away. Someone accepts the risk — you or your customer. Instead of forcing the risk onto an unwilling customer, why not profit from it instead?

Consider the following:

✔ Insurance is accepting risk in exchange for money.

✔ Insurance is very profitable if you can properly assess risk.

✔ You have superior knowledge that allows you to assess risk better than customers.

✔ Your customers unwillingly accept risk from you.

✔ Your customers will gladly pay a reasonable sum to remove risk.

✔ The amount the customer will pay to remove the risk greatly exceeds the statistical cost of the risk, thereby creating profits for the company.

Therefore, your secret profit formula is:

Superior knowledge + Risk acceptance = Outrageous profit

Instead of looking for ways to avoid risk, look for ways to accept risk — for a profit.

Charging Insurance in Creative Ways

It's doubtful that a plumber can literally charge an insurance premium. Can you imagine him saying, "For an extra $3 we can guarantee the plumber who shows up will be competent?" Instead, you need to get creative. Charge a fee for what is essentially an insurance premium but not obviously so.

Many companies have profited from creative insurance premiums.

✔ Extended warranties sold by Best Buy and Circuit City in the mid-2000s accounted for 60 percent of Best Buy's profit and all of Circuit City's.

✔ Comcast guarantees on-time service or the customer receives $20. Comcast doesn't charge a premium for this insurance. However, its profitability is directly tied to customer retention. By assuming the risk of timeliness, retention is increased and profitability with it.

✔ Guarantees are a form of insurance. The company knows the quality level of its goods much better than the customer. The company charges more for the product and provides a product guarantee. The additional sales price represents the insurance policy against product failure. The company knows the cost of replacement will be far less than the additional monies generated.

✔ Reputation management is a form of guarantee. A plumbing company spends significant time and money building and managing its reputation. Efforts spent on the Better Business Bureau, Yelp, Angie's List, and an online presence are expensive. Effectively managing a good reputation results in new customers feeling less risk and more business for you. The cost of creating and managing the reputation is less expensive than the next best solution.

✔ Prepaid dental plans accept the risk of the client's bad teeth. However, these plans also ensure the client will use the dentist for the highly profitable cleanings.

✔ Health clubs sell memberships based on their knowledge of average attendance. Large health clubs can have as many as 15,000 members. If 10 percent of these members showed up at the same time, the health club couldn't accommodate them. The health clubs' ability to accurately predict show rates allows them to sell more memberships.

✔ Airlines intentionally sell more tickets than seats available on a flight. Surprisingly, airlines can more accurately predict whether you'll miss your flight than you can. The airline knows that a certain percentage of travelers will miss their flight. Selling phantom seats provides the airline with tremendous profits for an item with no delivery cost. However, if the airline guesses wrong and ends up with more travelers than available seats, the airline must bribe flyers to change flights. When this happens, the airline loses money on the phantom ticket.

✔ Cellphone loss/replacement plans are extremely profitable for cellphone carriers. The carrier will replace a lost, stolen, or carelessly broken phone. In addition, if customers lose their phones, they may have to pay a steep price for a new unsubsidized phone. Only eight dollars a month to avoid this potential pain seems cheap. The customer's perception of the risk is high. The carrier understands the actual risk is much lower. Most likely, most customers won't lose or break their phones. If customers do require a new phone, they receive the same make and model — not a brand-new one. This detail dramatically lowers the cost of replacement and dramatically increases profits from the replacement plan.

✔ Energy management firms assume the risk of rising utility bills for large manufacturers. These firms agree to long-term (five or ten year) contracts that cap gas and electric bills at current levels. This is a great deal for a manufacturer who may be spending $1 million a month on utilities. The removal of the risk of spiraling energy costs entices the manufacturer into the contract. The energy management firm doesn't have superior knowledge of energy prices, but it does have superior knowledge of how to reduce energy consumption by as much as 20 to 30 percent at most factories. The energy management firm evaluates potential customers to ensure savings can be captured and then retrofits lighting and motors in the factory and introduces ways to reduce natural gas consumption. The energy firm accepts the risk of an increasing energy bill, but enjoys the benefits when the bill drops by 30 percent.

✔ An IT firm charges $1,000 per year per workstation for all technology-related services. A company with 20 workstations pays $20,000 annually for everything, including necessary software, support desk, wiring, server hardware, any new hardware needed — including monitors, keyboards, and computer — training, and software updates. The IT company removes all technology risks, allowing customers to focus on their business rather than IT headaches. The customer feels great about not having to purchase expensive hardware and software. The IT company understands that hardware doesn't break often and doesn't need to be replaced often. The difference in the customer's perception versus reality provides a profit opportunity for the IT firm.

✔ Solar companies insure sunshine. Solar firms will pay to install panels on your home and buy back the electricity.

✔ Value-based pricing pushes the onus of a desirable outcome to the provider. Firms like cost consultants have identified areas most businesses can save. These consultants charge nothing for their services other than sharing the savings. The risk of the project being successful is assumed by the consultant.

✔ A medical waste disposal company charges by the week rather than by the industry standard of per container or pound. Customers simply call when they need a pickup. The company assumes the risk of excessive volume. This plan has resulted in 2.3 customer pickups per month versus 4 prior to the plan. The savings associated with 1.7 fewer pickups per customer saves the company on vehicle costs, fuel, labor, and overhead.

✔ Voluntary- or tip-based pricing can yield a higher average sales price. Some organizations allow customers to pay what they want for purchases. The company accepts the risk that customers will grossly underpay. For instance, a training company offers a suggested price per trainee but allows customers to pay whatever they feel is fair. The company's analysis shows the voluntary payment system yields $22 per trainee more than if the company asked for a fixed sales price. The company accepts the risk that customers will underpay and benefits when they don't.

✔ Bumper-to-bumper warranties are a form of extreme guarantee popularized by automotive companies. The reputation gained by guaranteeing everything, instead of just major components, was significant from a marketing perspective but insignificant from a cost perspective, because all the expensive components were already covered under the old warranty.

✔ All-you-can-eat buffets accept the risk that a customer will eat more food than the price charged.

✔ All-inclusive resorts know many guests stay on the beach or in their hotel rooms rather than using cost-intensive services. Guests intend to use these services extensively at the time of purchase, but use them less than intended. The resorts profit from their knowledge of "the eyes are bigger than the stomach" phenomenon.

✔ Zipcar rental has no mileage or gasoline fees. Zipcar assumes the risk that the driver will overuse the vehicle. Because its cars are available primarily in urban areas, the company understands that drivers probably won't drive the cars far. By accepting the risk of long trips that will wear out their fleet, Zipcar can offer an attractive all-inclusive price with a profitable insurance policy bundled in.

✔ Costco sells products at a lower margin than traditional retailers in exchange for a membership fee, essentially making the membership fee a purchased advance discount. The consumer pays $55 to $110 per year to get lower pricing. Costco makes very little profit as a pure retailer due to the reduced margins. Costco makes almost all profits on membership sales ($694 million last quarter). Costco accepts the risk that the customers won't overuse the $55 advance discount.

✔ Some landscaping and snow plow companies sell by the season. They accept the risk of weather. They don't have the ability to predict weather better than the customer, but they do know that the law of averages can lead to better profitability. The customer desires cost predictability, so the company charges for the expected number of mows/plows and adds an insurance premium.

✔ Lawyers' retainers are effectively reverse insurance. The client guarantees the lawyer a certain number of hours will be purchased.

✔ Fixed fees contain an insurance premium. For instance, a logo designer charges $350 for the logo, accepting one primary risk — that the client will require too many redo's. The logo designer may charge only $50 per logo rendering, but the client has no idea how many renderings will be required. The logo designer knows that number to be 4.7 historically, and charges the difference between 4.7 renders and 7 as an insurance premium.

When an hour isn't an hour

I saved the best for last. The best way to capitalize on the dynamics of insurance is through the use of a flat-rate hour. A flat-rate hour redefines 60 minutes.

Here I use the example of automotive repair, because flat-rate hours are commonly used in the industry. When you take your car to the repair shop, you may have noticed a sign showing a $70 per hour labor rate. In the automotive world, an hour isn't an hour. Automotive repair shops use reference manuals like Mitchell's to tell them how long a repair should take. The repair shop charges you the hourly rate times the hours in the Mitchell manual — not the actual time it takes to fix your car.

This system has many benefits for customers. The customer knows the total cost of the repair before work begins. More important, the risk of poor workmanship, bad planning, and cost overruns are shifted to the repair shop. If you think about it, no one wants to buy anything by the hour. Try it. Name something you prefer to buy per hour. When you purchase hours, you always feel the pressure of tick, tock, tick, tock. Almost everyone prefers the removal of that feeling. If you buy by the hour, you accept the risk of time overruns, and it creates a win-lose relationship between vendor and customer. The customer benefits if the repair happens fast. The vendor benefits if the repair goes poorly and takes longer. Fixing this misalignment benefits both vendor and customer.

However, the flat-rate hour system benefits the auto repair shop tremendously. A skilled mechanic can accomplish most general repairs in half the time stated in the Mitchell manual. Highly skilled special team mechanics (engines, transmissions) can complete work in one-third the time. The repair shop is billing two or three "hours" for each hour actually worked.

By redefining an hour as the amount of time needed by an average mechanic to complete a task, the repair shop creates a profit center for mechanics of greater skill. A good mechanic doesn't get paid twice what a bad mechanic makes, but under a flat-rate billing system, the good mechanic bills double.

Example of creative insurance: Enron

Enron is famous for many bad business deals, but the company had an outstanding program that leveraged the power of insurance. Enron would approach large manufacturing facilities with a tempting offer to lock in the cost of their utilities for five or ten years. Large facilities such as automotive assembly plants can spend more than $1 million a month on utilities. Enron wanted to add customers like these to its energy brokerage business.

Fearing uncertainty about rising energy costs, factories were very receptive to Enron accepting the risk of rising electricity and gas costs. Enron used the customer's desire to eliminate risk to its advantage. Here's how:

- ✔ An Enron division specialized in increasing efficiency of large facilities. This division would retrofit lighting to significantly more efficient products; replace old, inefficient energy-sucking motors; install superior insulation; detect and repair air leaks; and more.

- ✔ Typically, these energy retrofits cut the utility bill by 25 to 50 percent.

- ✔ Because Enron accepted the risk of rising energy bills, it also accepted the benefit of lowered energy bills.

- ✔ Due to Enron's superior knowledge in the arena of energy retrofitting, the company was able to accurately predict the amount of energy savings available at the plant. This amount was compared to the potential increase in energy costs. If the comparison was favorable, Enron agreed to hold energy costs constant.

✔ Enron's timeline for payback for the cost of retrofitting the plant was usually 12 to 18 months. When this payback period expired, Enron's profits were significant. Energy costs may have inched up a few percent, but energy savings may have cut the bill in half.

Worksheet: Creating an Insurance Program

Clients always tell me, "I like the concept of insurance and see how it can improve profitability, but I don't know where to begin." Here's how you begin:

1. **Analyze the risks your customers or clients want to eliminate.** Some of these risks will be obvious; some won't be. Customers have been trained by vendors that many risks are nonnegotiable and can't be removed.

   In the 1960s, athletes had to self-insure against a knee injury. Today, they can buy a policy from Lloyds of London paying them if their career ends early. Your customers are still in the 1960s. They haven't considered that some risks can be removed. You may not discover any of these latent risks, but if you do, you may have a game changer.

2. **Think about the possibility of the customer or client paying to remove the risk.** When you go to the car wash, a flock of geese could fly over your car immediately afterward, ruining the beautiful wash. The car wash could insure against this possibility, and you may even value it, but you probably don't value this insurance enough for it to be a viable option.

3. **Consider how much the customer would pay.** Best Buy made a fortune selling extended warranties on $17 calculators for $5. Personally, I don't know how customers justify this math, but people bought these policies. Remember, it's not what the insurance costs; it's what it's worth in the customer's mind.

4. **Decide the logistics of how you'll deliver the insurance.** As you can see in Figure 22-1, some insurance can be a different marketing angle, a pure insurance policy, a guarantee, or another creative vehicle.

5. **Determine what the insurance will cost.** Is the cost-benefit relationship worth the effort? If so, go for it.

Figure 22-2 is a blank worksheet for your use in creating profitable insurance products in your business.

Figure 22-1:
Potential
insurance
opportuni-
ties.

Getting in the Insurance Business

Risks Clients are forced to accept	Would they pay to mitigate?	How much?	Potential insurance policies	Our cost	Additional profit
Is the plumber well-skilled?	Yes, the time needed for a poorly skilled technician could add hundreds to the bill	10% - 20% more	Self-certify plumbers as ABC Plumbing Gurus/Master Technicians. Hire only plumbers with 5 years or more experience and advise accordingly. Have a fix it the first trip guarantee	1/2 or less the additional revenue gained	50% margin on upsell
Will have to take off work and wait on the plumber?	The cost of the inconvenience is significant for some customers	$20 - $50 per job	Do better than the 1 hour windows promised by the other companies. Guarantee the plumber will be there exactly on time. It's simple, under-schedule not over-schedule. Budget slack time so the plumber can be on time. Charge customers if they are not on time too. Companies employing this strategy can command rates 25% -50% higher than market.	30% of additional revenue created	70% margin on business created
Is the plumber honest or will he sell me things I don't need?	Over-selling is a big fear in service industries	5% - 25% more	Gather dozens of video (not written) testimonials with happy customers discussing this issue	$1500	Margin generated by additional sales
Will the plumber be "casing" my home?	May not be reasonable for the customer to feel this way but some have this sinking feeling	A little	Background check all employees, run employee's credit scores every 6 months to ensure they are not having financial issues. Create a "We watch our employees so you don't have to" campaign where employees wear wireless helmet cams monitored by the home office.	$5000 - $10,000	Margin generated by additional sales
Does the plumber have the right tools and parts on their truck?	Customer does not want to pay $150/hour for a trip to Home Depot for a $2 fitting.	5% - 10% more	It's impossible to always have everything on the truck, but it is possible to have everything 90+% of the time. This one is a classic opportunity missed. Because it's impossible to always have everything on the truck, plumbers give up on guaranteeing it. The answer is simple, upcharge for the guarantee and eat the cost of the times you don't have everything. You can have a driver fetch parts so the plumber doesn't have to leave or offer customers a $100 discount if you do have to leave.	10% - 50% of additional revenue generated	This feature could attract new customers or get existing customers to pay more, so the profit potential is significant
Does the plumber have a next job or will they try to drag this one out?	A plumber with a busy schedule probably completes the job with briskness. A plumber wondering where his next gig will come from might stretch this one out.	5% more	Flat rate	Cost of poorly estimated jobs	Improves profitability via more closed sales from comfortable prospects.
Will this repair fix the problem permanently or will I be calling them in 6 months for "round 2"?	Most customers want to understand the total cost to fix the problem, not just the cost today.	A little	Create a "One and done" or "5 year guarantee" to make the customer comfortable that you have completely solved the problem. You don't have to give it on all jobs. If a customer has a 100 year old house, nicely tell them that you cannot guarantee any pipes over 20 years old.	Minimal because our high-quality work already should last 5 years.	Margin generated by additional sales
How long will this repair take at $150/hour?	That feeling of clicking the stop watch and knowing every minute the plumber scratches his head and says "Hum" costs you $2.50 stinks.	Potentially a lot more because the customer has no idea how long the job should take. If the customer thinks 5 hours is reasonable but the job will only take 1 hour, the margin opportunity is significant	Flat rate	Cost of poorly estimated jobs	Game-changing

Getting in the Insurance Business

Risks Clients are forced to accept	Would they pay to mitigate?	How much?	Potential insurance policies	Our cost	Additional profit

Figure 22-2:
Creating
your
insurance
business.

Part V
The Part of Tens

For a bonus Part of Tens list, full of unique business model ideas, visit www.dummies.com/extras/businessmodels.

In this part . . .

- ✔ Explore examples of ten great business models to get your brainstorming juices going.

- ✔ Use top innovation techniques with your model. Innovation is necessary if you want your business to be successful in the long-term, but it isn't always easy. Use these techniques as inspiration.

- ✔ Watch out for this list of one-liners your venture capitalist, banker, or partners never want to hear about your business model.

- ✔ Discover phrases to strike from your vocabulary immediately! A lot of entrepreneurs use these phrases without realizing they're red flags for investors. I keep you from making that mistake.

Chapter 23

Ten Terrific Business Models

- -

In This Chapter

▶ Discovering ten time-tested business models proven to generate profits

▶ Seeing the key business strategy one celebrity entrepreneur uses in every business deal

▶ Leveraging emerging buyer psychology to your advantage

▶ Making billions by creating a must-have brand

- -

Sometimes the best way to learn is by example. In this chapter I discuss ten business models that have proven to be profitable over long periods of time. I discuss high-profile companies that use each of these models as well as detail how they make the models work effectively.

The benefit of studying various business models is they usually spark an idea. As you study these models, think of how you can borrow a piece of their strategy for yours.

Build Once, Sell Many

The world's *worst* business model is build once, sell once. The only way to achieve significant profits with the build once, sell once model is with a very high hourly rate. That's getting tougher and tougher in a flat world.

If build once, sell once is the worst business model, it stands to reason that build once, sell many is one of the best. If you guessed that, you're right. You can leverage the build once, sell many business model in many ways. Consider the following:

✔ Manufacturing was one of the first business models to leverage build once, sell many. Significant effort was made to set up an assembly line and processes, resulting in a product that was produced at low marginal cost per unit, resulting in profits.

✔ Mineral extraction is similar to manufacturing. Significant effort goes into finding the oil, copper, gold, or iron ore, and then purchasing expensive equipment. After the infrastructure is built one time, the resources can be profitably extracted.

✔ Software companies like Microsoft, Intuit, and Oracle are simply modern day digital manufacturers using this model. The software is written once and sold over and over. Software manufacturing has an advantage over physical manufacturing with use of versions. Software has built-in obsolescence created by the company. This use of versions keeps sales coming and the software manufacturing line busy.

✔ Leveraging or selling intellectual property — such as ideas, processes, patents, or trademarks — counts as build once, sell many. Many companies create intellectual property as an aside to their "real" business only to find that the intellectual property is worth more than the "real" business. BlackBerry developer Research in Motion values its intellectual property at $3.37 billion, or nearly 85 percent of the value of the entire company. Nortel Networks sold 6,000 wireless patents in a bankruptcy auction for $4.5 billion in 2012. Eastman Kodak struggled to be profitable as a film company but agreed to sell its digital imaging patents for about $525 million.

✔ Brand building can qualify as build once, sell many. What is it that gets you to pay $4 for a cup of Starbucks coffee? Sure, it's a good location, delicious coffee, and friendly service, but you can get that at a lot of places. Part of your $4 is for the Starbucks brand. The building and leveraging of a strong brand counts as build once, sell many.

✔ The same is true for reputation building. Companies with strong reputations enjoy the build once, sell many dynamic. Take the example of an HVAC contractor. The work is performed and profited from (build once). Because the work is done in outstanding fashion, a reputation is created and leveraged in the form of referrals (reduced sales cost) and the ability to charge premium prices (a form of sell many). The premium price created by the good reputation is a form of sell many.

✔ A large fixed-cost investment can qualify as build once, sell many. Miniature golf courses, Disneyland, cruise ships, hotels, and toll roads all create an asset beyond the financial reach of any one customer with use of the asset sold in small pieces. In many cases, the combination of a large fixed cost investment and first-mover advantage is a powerful business model.

Be careful about too much fixed cost investment. Research shows that too high a fixed cost investment can depress long-term return on investment — witness airlines, the big three U.S. automakers, and shipping companies. Ideally, the scope of your large investment will depress competition, not returns.

✔ Service companies have become more sophisticated in leveraging build once, sell many. Lawyers reuse well-written clauses in contracts for more than one client. LegalZoom has flipped the legal business model by selling standardized forms with a small amount of service included versus a lawyer selling a lot of service combined with a small amount of document standardization. Doctors and dentists record videos with surgery instructions rather than instruct each patient individually.

✔ Franchising is a great way for successful companies to build once, sell many. After the business model is built, sell the rights to use it for a percentage of the revenues.

With an ever-increasing portion of the economy shifting to service businesses, build once, sell many is more important than ever. It's easy for a service business to sell the work, and then do the work — every job a one-time project. This is a good recipe to make a living but not a good business model. If you succumb to this model, you'll always be hampered by pricing pressure and commoditization.

Service companies can leverage build once, sell many in two ways:

✔ First, always be on the lookout for additional uses of the primary job. Professional speakers do a great job of this. Job #1 is getting paid to speak to an audience. The speaker works hard to create presentation content, and then gets paid once to deliver it. Done right, the speaker can use the presentation like a piece of software and deliver the same or similar one to another audience. However, the speaker is still selling her time for money.

The speaker can further leverage her intellectual property by taping the presentation and selling the recording, transcript, workbooks, or other products related to it. The speaker can sell consulting from the podium, thereby eliminating sales cost. Better yet, the speaker can use portions of the presentation during the consulting assignments.

✔ The second method to leverage the build once, sell many dynamic is skill leverage. For instance, a duct company did nothing but large-scale, custom installations (in other words, build once, sell once). Some of the installers noticed that certain elbows were closer to universal than custom, so the company invested in machinery to pre-bend these elbows rather than make them on the job site. By shifting the labor from the job site to the factory, the firm was able to make these elbows in a third of the time. The savings weren't passed on to the customer, because the work was proprietary. The customer was charged the normal time it took to bend the elbows on the job site.

The trick is to never just do the work. Always be thinking about how you can leverage job #1 into savings on job #2.

You can take build once, sell many too far. The robosigning scandal in the mortgage industry is a prime example of over-leveraging.

Create a Must-Have Brand

One of the most profitable business models in history is creation of a must-have brand that goes beyond mere differentiation. A must-have brand is a trump card that allows a company to charge a premium price and generate significant sales.

- ✔ Apple has become a must-have brand for this generation. Japanese sociologists have determined that the Apple brand invokes near-religious fervor in many Japanese teenagers.

- ✔ The Toyota Prius was more than just an eco-friendly automobile. Hollywood stars drove their Priuses as a status symbol to symbolize their environmental consciousness. This endorsement helped propel the Prius to capture more than 50 percent of the U.S. hybrid market, helping Toyota capture more than 70 percent of that market.

- ✔ Beats Audio sells headphones for $199 versus $50 for a comparable pair of Sony headphones.

- ✔ Under Armour and Nike can put their logos on a variety of shoes, clothing, or sporting items and charge double for what the same item would sell for without those logos.

- ✔ How much does a car buyer pay for the Mercedes, BMW, or Lexus emblem on the hood of their car? Sure, these cars have many great features, but so does a Hyundai Genesis that costs $25,000 less. Why does the buyer pay so much more for a BMW? Because it's a BMW.

- ✔ A Patagonia jacket costs twice as much as a comparable one. Patagonia produces high-quality, environmentally friendly garments that cater to outdoor lovers who want to protect the environment and are happy to pay a company aligned with that philosophy.

- ✔ Harley-Davidson sold motorcycles for more than a cheap sedan and had year-long backlogs.

- ✔ Coca-Cola is the proud owner of the world's most valuable brand, estimated to be worth $77.8 billion.

Brand power isn't reserved for consumer products. Companies like Oracle, Cisco, Snap-On Tools, Dungarees, and IBM have built powerful business-to-business brands. Arguably, the greatest brand power of all time was IBM during the "Big Blue" period. Just ask any salesperson forced to sell against "No one ever got fired buying IBM." IBM commanded a significant price premium for its mainframe computers that totaled billions over time.

You don't need to be a Fortune 500 company to create a must-have brand. Lawyers, doctors, landscapers, architects, homebuilders, and any other company can create a must-have brand. This is an oversimplification, but by being first with something spectacular, you too can create a must-have brand.

Get Customers to Create Goods for Free

The rise of crowdsourcing and cheap knowledge transfer via the Internet has unleashed a new wave of business models. You don't need to be a technology company to benefit from these trends. The Internet has created a worldwide meritocracy. As consumers have access to more information and the ability to share their preferences, companies can benefit from giving customers what they want — control, tailored offerings, and speed.

GPS systems offer a valuable feature to navigate via the fastest route based upon traffic conditions. Twenty years ago, this data had to be purchased from a traffic data service and was cost prohibitive. Today, consumers pay to use the GPS and also contribute their own traffic data. The GPS company assimilates customer data to create a traffic map and sells it back to the customers who created it.

Google does the same thing. Users of the Internet vote on the popularity of sites by linking to them and visiting them. Google collects user data, sorts it based on relevancy, and sells it back to users as a search engine.

Facebook is just a software platform. Without 500 million customers voluntarily adding content to Facebook, there is no product. Customers have spent billions of hours building Facebook's content and data set.

Couchsurfing sites connect free hotels (an open couch) with users and are the only party getting any cash out of the arrangement.

Crowdsourced products are everywhere, from Doritos flavors and kid-designed Lego sets to T-shirt designs on CafePress and Super Bowl commercials. Companies have let customers in to the product design process and received free labor plus crowd-approved products in exchange.

You can leverage the customer helping to create products without any technology too. Examples include:

- U-pick blueberries

- Cutting down your own Christmas tree (and paying a premium to do so)

- Cook-your-own-steak restaurants

- Build-A-Bear Workshops allow customers to self-design and manufacture their own teddy bear and charge a significant premium over a mass manufactured doll

- The proliferation of make-your-own frozen yogurt shops, such as Orange Leaf and Yogli Mogli, where the customers create their own treat and simply weigh it

Allowing customers the freedom to help create your products can dramatically lower costs and increase sales. Execute this tactic well and enjoy a profitable business model.

True Competitive Advantage as the Low-Cost Provider

Sometimes businesspeople confuse the low-cost provider with the low-margin provider (in other words, the fool willing to work for the least profit). The ability to create the same product as your competition for a significantly lower cost is a secret weapon. Savvy companies use this cost advantage as a tool. The additional margin generated by lower cost can be used for

- **Penetration pricing.** Standard Oil was famous for pricing gas artificially low at new stations to put competitors out of business. It worked so well that the practice became illegal.

- **Pricing aggressively when needed.** Most retailers have a hard time competing with Walmart on Black Friday, because Walmart's costs are much lower.

- **Passing savings to the consumer in the form of lower pricing.** If the market is exceptionally price sensitive, the lower price can be critical in gaining business.

- **Increasing profits.** Retain the cost savings for the bottom line.

- **Research and development.**

✔ **Marketing.** McDonald's has economies of scale on other burger eateries and uses the extra profits to create a massive marketing moat. McDonald's spends one-sixth of restaurant profits on advertising.

✔ **A combination of the items in this list.** Dell computer used its low-cost provider model to undercut competition and produce superior profits during its heyday.

In this era of price hypersensitivity and information transparency, it's more difficult than ever to generate excellent margins. Low-cost providorship can serve as a critical business model advantage. Many well-known companies possess the low-cost advantage:

✔ Amazon's scale versus other Internet retailers allows it to capture a large share of the market.

✔ Walmart has leveraged logistics technology and scale to deliver its marketing promise of "low prices every day." Walmart's gross margins are still a respectable 24.9 percent. Compare that to Sears, a mall retailer with only a slightly better 26.1-percent margin.

✔ Procter & Gamble has many great brands — like Tide, Crest, Dawn, Gillette, and Ivory — that are not only the best sellers in their category, but also the least expensive to produce due to economies of scale.

✔ Southwest Airlines is the only consistently profitable U.S. airline because of its innovative low-cost model. Southwest keeps costs low by flying only 737s and rejecting the industry-standard spoke and hub system.

✔ Saudi Arabia's state-run oil company can produce a barrel of oil for $3 versus the highest-cost provider (deep sea drilling) of $50 per barrel.

✔ GEICO has grown from the #7 insurance carrier to #3 by leveraging a low-cost direct sales model.

Most of the time, it's difficult to start as the low-cost provider of a similar product sold to a similar market for a similar use (in other words, apples to apples). Economies of scale, superior business processes, and leverage of the value chain create cost advantage for the established players. Without a technological, brand, or value chain advantage, starting as the low-cost leader is most likely going to be starting as the low-profit leader.

Disruption can play a significant role in cost advantage. Radical innovation of the value chain or technology can have a far greater effect than squeezing the blood out of a penny.

Craigslist didn't aim to lower the cost of a classified ad; it aimed to change the value chain of classified advertising. The result was a low-cost model.

United Parcel Service (UPS) was an early adopter of GPS and handheld technology for drivers in the 1990s. This technological advantage translated into lower fuel costs, driver pay, and operations.

Extraction of Natural Resources

It's not the world's oldest business, but pulling diamonds, wood, gold, oil, iron ore, copper, and other natural resources from the earth has produced profits and wealth for thousands of years. It's one of the oldest business models and is still profitable.

There are currently 43 billionaires whose fortunes were created by mineral mining and hundreds more whose fortune was created from oil extraction. More than ten percent of the world's billionaires made their fortunes from natural resource extraction.

During the extended worldwide recession, the Australian economy has grown and prospered. Not surprisingly, their economy is heavily weighted toward mining. The mining sector represents ten percent of Australian GDP; the mining-related economy represents another nine percent of GDP — the total mining sector is 19 percent of the entire Australian economy.

It makes sense that resource extraction is consistently profitable if you think about it from the perspective of Porter's value chain (see Chapter 10 for more on this topic). Nonmining companies work to create value added through a variety of processes and means. However, all these means have a cost. The trick for these firms is to have the added value equal more than the cost to add the value. Mining firms let Mother Nature add the value. Just give those decaying dinosaur remains a few hundred thousand years and they transform into oil deposits — for free. Thanks Mother Nature!

Of course, the cost of removing diamonds, gold, and oil isn't free, but well-run mining operations have been consistently profitable for centuries. Not many business models can make that claim.

Valued Intellectual Property with Legal or Practical Protection

What do Polaroid, Eli Lilly, Adobe Systems, Singer, Ford Motor Company, Microsoft, Xerox, Facebook, Green Mountain Coffee Roasters, Ronco, and

Westinghouse have in common? The origin of their success was valuable intellectual property. Consider the following:

- **Polaroid:** Instant camera
- **Eli Lilly:** Insulin
- **Adobe Systems:** Post script language
- **Singer:** First practical sewing machine
- **Ford Motor Company:** Modern assembly line
- **Segway:** The foundation of the Segway people mover, a computer-controlled gyroscopic stabilization and control system was invented by Dean Kamen for an earlier invention, an all-terrain wheelchair, the iBot. Kamen sold this company to Johnson & Johnson but kept the gyroscopic technology and leveraged it into the Segway.
- **Microsoft:** DOS operating system
- **Xerox:** Photocopier
- **Facebook:** Social networking site
- **Green Mountain Coffee:** Keurig coffee system (K-cup)
- **Ronco:** Ron Popeil's Veg-O-Matic and the infomercial
- **Westinghouse:** Air brake system for trains

A great idea can be the bulk of a great business model. The companies in this list took this powerful idea and 1) protected it from imitation, and 2) leveraged the idea into a long-term viable business.

Of course, all the ideas in the list had some form of protection. Patents, trademarks, or simply knowing how to do something your competitors don't can protect your business model from inevitable copying. For instance, when Crocs shoes were hot sellers, many companies imitated the look and style of the shoes. However, Crocs owns the formulation for the special material used in the shoes, so the imitations weren't quite the same as the real thing. This special material helped Crocs maintain sales for significantly longer.

Technological Destruction of Existing Model

Why compete in a market when you can demolish it instead? Technological destruction of an existing market leverages a differentiated offering and typically creates a new low-cost provider. Many times the market destroyed by the seismic technological shift is exceeded in size by the new market created. Table 23-1 shows several industries that were severely disrupted by new technology.

Table 23-1	Disruptive Technology Examples		
Existing Industry	*Disruptive Technology*	*Additional Disruptive Technology*	*Additional Disruptive Technology*
Horses	Automobiles	—	—
Pony Express	Telegraph	Land line telephones	Cellphones
Postal mail	E-mail	Texting	
Handwritten books	Offset printing	Desktop publishing	PDFs
Newspaper classifieds	Craigslist, cars.com, and others	—	—
Painting	Photography	Digital cameras	Cellphone cameras
Garage sales	eBay	—	—
Records	CDs	MP3s	—
Neighborhood retailers	Big box stores/ malls	Amazon	—
Travel agents	Priceline	—	—
Railroads	Automobiles	Air travel	Skype
Maps	MapQuest	GPS	—
Watches	Cellphones	—	—
Live networking events	LinkedIn	—	—
Restaurants	Frozen dinners	Home delivery	—

As you can see, these new industries and models tend to wipe out the older one but create a much larger one in its place.

Look at the painful process happening in the newspaper industry. One could argue that the Internet and Craigslist helped destroy a multibillion-dollar industry that employed hundreds of thousands of people. From 2001 to 2011, U.S. newspaper industry employment has gone from 414,000 to 246,020 people. Craigslist employs around 30 people. So far, the technological destruction caused by the Internet and Craigslist looks pretty bad. But when you look at all the related technological shifts and companies spawned, the traditional pattern emerges.

Public companies like `cars.com`, `autotrader.com`, `monster.com`, `careerbuilder.com`, `ebay.com`, and `huffingtonpost.com` have multi-billion-dollar collective market capitalization and thousands of employees. Throw peripheral items — like the iPad or Kindle, used to read the digital content — into the mix, and one can argue that the "new" newspaper industry is larger than the old one.

To create a business model leveraging advancement, don't aim to improve the industry or make it better — make it different instead. For instance, many pundits feel that three-dimensional printing has the ability to radically change manufacturing. 3D printing has already radically changed the tool and die business by shifting subtractive manufacturing (carving down a piece of metal into the shape required) to additive manufacturing (using a device similar to an inkjet printer that sprays metal) to build the die. If the pundits are right, you'll have a 3D printer in your home and simply download the blueprints for anything you need — such as a broken dishwasher part, a custom toy, or a dress button. 3D printing won't improve manufacturing; it will replace it.

When you create a disruptive technology, replace the existing ways of doing business rather than simply improving them. When your idea takes hold in the marketplace, be prepared to capitalize on the peripheral opportunities as well. True disruptive innovations always spawn many more business opportunities that are discovered only after the disruption takes hold.

Gold Plating the Current Gold Standard

As the worldwide standard of living increases, the demand for higher quality and more prestigious goods and services is rising dramatically. Many successful companies have used a business model strategy that simply takes the best available offering in a category and dramatically increases the desirability of that offering along with the price.

The most infamous advocate of this business model is Donald Trump. Trump may technically be a real estate developer, but his real business model is simply outdoing the best of what's currently available. Trump has been criticized for overpaying for properties. Whether you like or dislike Trump, he does have a knack to push sales prices past the point anyone deemed possible.

Many other companies have utilized this gold plating the gold standard business model.

- ✔ Häagen-Dazs was the first super-premium ice cream, charging as much as ten times more than store-brand ice cream.

- ✔ Panera Bread charges two or three times more for a sandwich than the Subway down the street. Panera is a good example that products don't need to be for the wealthy in order to be "gold plated."

- ✔ A cup of Starbucks coffee costs two to three times more than one at Dunkin' Donuts or McDonald's, yet Starbucks controls half the U.S. coffee market.

- ✔ Coach bags cost hundreds of dollars, competing in a market where most handbags cost around $50.

- ✔ Godiva chocolates cost up to $60 per pound. A box of Russell Stover chocolates costs around $20 per pound.

- ✔ The cosmetics industry has been involved in a game of one-upmanship for decades, creating $50 lipstick and $5,000-per-ounce perfume. The upscale strategy seems to be working as higher end L'Oreal is the world's largest firm, not Procter & Gamble (Pantene, Olay, Cover Girl, and so on) or Unilever (Suave, Finesse, Ponds, and so on).

- ✔ Automobile manufacturers are constantly aiming higher with features like massaging seats, auto-park technology, and fancy navigation systems.

- ✔ Why buy a $20 Timex when you can purchase a $50,000 Rolex? Watch and jewelry manufacturers literally gold plate the gold standard.

- ✔ Designer dog food and pet hotels have grown nicely in the multibillion-dollar pet care industry.

- ✔ Upscale hamburger restaurants serve $20 Kobe beef burgers.

- ✔ The spirits industry has done well upscaling vodka, bourbon, and tequila.

- ✔ Gymboree sells baby clothes for as much as ten times more than Walmart or Target, yet the chain has grown to nearly 1,000 stores and over $1 billion in annual sales.

- ✔ Yep, even instant noodles can be upscaled. For $43 a cup, you can have one of 100 exclusive Pot Noodle cups from Harrods of London. Each posh Pot Noodle cup includes a hand-flocked gold leaf pot.

- ✔ Bling H2O sells water no different from or better than any other bottled water in an ultra high-end bottle for $50 a bottle.

The gold plated model is always a bit risky, because you'll be segmenting an already defined and finite market. Chances are the market size won't grow in units consumed. However, you may be able to grow the sales volume of the market due to the increased price charged per unit.

The water market is much smaller at $50 per bottle than $2 per bottle. There's also no guarantee the customer will pay for a gold-plated version of the offering. Some examples of failed attempts include:

- ✔ Many airlines (Eos, Maxjet, Legend, Regent, Silverjet) have tried a business class–only approach and failed.

- ✔ Auto repair that comes to your home and/or gives you a rental car has failed everywhere but new car dealers.

- ✔ Bottled water for pets failed despite solid demand for upscale pet food.

- ✔ Even some of Donald Trump's attempts to gold plate have failed.

Playing to Customers' Ever-Increasing Sense of Self

The convergence of unlimited digital customization, improved small-batch manufacturing capabilities, and ever-increasing competition among service providers has created a customer culture in which the sky is the limit.

When I was a kid you went to McDonald's and took the hamburger they gave you. You then proceeded to wipe off the mustard onto a napkin and throw out the pickle. The thought of demanding the burger the exact way you wanted it was unthinkable.

Today, all you have to do is stand in line at a Starbucks to see how empowered consumers feel about getting *exactly* what they want. Here's an actual Starbucks drink order:

> Venti, half whole milk, one-quarter one percent, one-quarter nonfat, extra hot, split quad shots (one-and-a-half shots decaf, two-and-a-half shots regular), no-foam latte, with whip, two packets of Splenda, one sugar in the raw, a touch of vanilla syrup, and three short sprinkles of cinnamon.

Keep in mind this order is for a $4 drink. Imagine this person's order for something expensive. The point isn't to pick on complex drink orderers. The point is that consumers want what they want, and they have now been trained by businesses that they can get it.

The uber-customization is part of a larger trend I lovingly call "me, the world." You're allowed to be the center of your own buying universe with your desires and ego at the center, as represented by Figure 23-1.

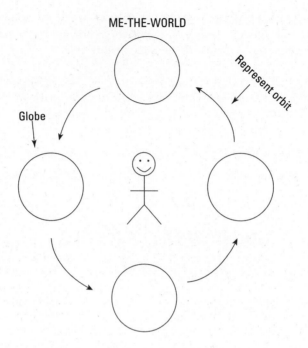

ME-THE-WORLD

Represent orbit

Globe

Figure 23-1:
Me at the
center of my
own world.

Business models that ride this trend enjoy additional profitability by giving customers something they can't get elsewhere. Countless business models cater to this ever-growing dynamic. Here are some recent trends:

✔ $4 cupcakes. Everyone knows a cupcake should cost only 50 cents, but it makes me feel oh-so-special to treat myself.

✔ For around $20, `Skinit.com` will create a custom iPhone or laptop cover or a decal of any picture you upload.

✔ For $149 you can create a custom doll designed to look just like your child at `mytwin.com`.

✔ Spa treatments have become mainstream for many Americans as a way to treat themselves to just a little luxury, as evidenced by the popularity of companies like Massage Envy and Hand and Stone.

✔ Theme parks offer premium tickets for customers who want to skip the lines.

✔ Coca-Cola's Freestyle fountain machine allows consumers to choose among 127 flavor combinations. Companies like Avery's Beverages allow customers to design and bottle their own soda flavors.

✔ Software vendors are allowing customers to pick and choose the features they want to pay for.

Opportunities exist to create business models that stretch boundaries or expand into new categories. Examples may include:

- ✔ Separate VIP lines at Starbucks or a VIP drive-thru lane

- ✔ Predictive grocery buying that analyzes your purchases, computes your estimated usage, creates an order for these items every Friday and has the order bagged and waiting for you to pick up

- ✔ Custom shoes designed from a mold of your feet rather than shoes purchased from store stock

Ultra Niche Player

Twenty years ago, most businesses were constrained by geography — they sold inside a limited geographic radius. Retailers sold to a local-only market. Manufacturers were mostly limited to selling on their continent. The world was not their oyster. Today, improved logistics and transportation systems, combined with the Internet, make the entire world a prospect.

The downside of this improvement is the worldwide competition to match the worldwide market. Ask most retailers about the effect of the Internet on their business, and they'll complain about `Amazon.com` or some other Internet foe in their sector.

The problem with a worldwide marketplace is that the number of offerings is overwhelming. In the good old days, a large hockey store in Minnesota enjoyed being the best option for local consumers to purchase hockey-related goods. Geography protected the store because customers would have to drive hundreds of miles to find a similar offering. The Internet removes the geographical protection enjoyed by the store and puts them in competition with every hockey store in the world.

There is a business model that solves this problem: the ultra niche. This marketing process differentiates your offering by making it very specific and very deep in its offering. Here are some actual examples of an ultra niche offering:

- ✔ Partners & Crime Mystery Booksellers in New York City (`http://www.crimepays.com`)

- ✔ Graduation cap charms (`charmfactory.com`)

- ✔ Vacuum cleaner parts (`vacpartswarehouse.com`)

- ✔ Shoelaces (`shoelacesexpress.com`)

- ✔ Plus-size bridal dresses (`plussizebridal.com`)

- World's largest collection of left-handed scissors (leftyslefthanded. com)
- Custom collar stays (qstays.com)
- Women's hunting gear (hercamoshop.com)
- Yoga sandals (yogasandals.com)

Although most business models for the ultra niche will be Internet retail, the concepts can be applied to service businesses as well by leveraging telephony, video streaming, and the Internet. Service firms are now selecting ever-tighter niches:

- Consultants aren't just smart people who can help. They're now specialists in managing organizational conflict or creating processes for hiring sales staff or implementing RAID storage solutions.
- If you visit the International Coaching Federation website, you'll find hundreds of potential coaching options, including Chinese languages, midlife crisis coaching, and children's website coaching.
- Some construction firms travel the country building only McDonald's restaurants. Similarly, roofing companies chase storms, fixing hail and wind damage to roofs wherever the storm hits.
- Businesspeople who used to work for only one company have become specialty contractors to a handful of companies instead. These businesspeople specialize in anything from telemarketing to seniors to managing problem firings to CRM integration.

Many businesspeople are afraid to chase an ultra niche, because they think they're limiting themselves. This philosophy may have been applicable in 1990, but today a broad market approach can mean an undifferentiated approach. Your business model is far better off with a unique, finely-tuned niche than a me-too niche.

Here's how to make the ultra niche work by using Chris Anderson's long tail framework. Figure 23-2 shows the bridal dress market. As you move to the right on the graph, the market size becomes smaller. Step 1 is to analyze what niche is unserved or underserved.

The majority of the market is already taken by well-established players — stay away from direct competition with them. Step 2 of the ultra niche strategy is based upon carving out a small slice of their market that the big players serve as an afterthought. Figure 23-3 shows the most likely niches for your offer. Research the areas to find the combination of little competition with largest market potential. Keep in mind that many markets look small today because they're underserved. When you serve these markets well, the market may become much larger. Reebok started in the underserved aerobics shoe market only and grew to a multibillion-dollar company.

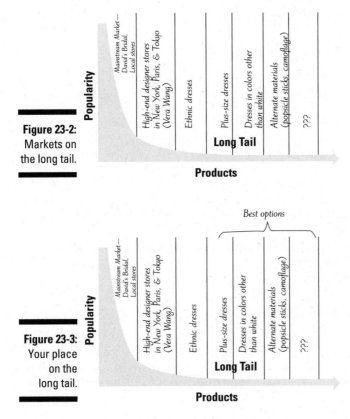

Figure 23-2:
Markets on
the long tail.

Figure 23-3:
Your place
on the
long tail.

Step 3 in the process is to go deep. This means if you're offering black wedding dresses, offer everything imaginable for that market. The mainstream bridal stores don't have what these customers want. Make sure you have everything the customers in this market could possibly want.

The last step in the ultra niche process is to open up to the world. Because your market size is smaller, you must leverage sales across a much wider audience, ideally worldwide.

Chapter 24

Ten Signs You May Have an Issue with Your Business Model

In This Chapter

▶ Spotting symptoms of a faltering business model

▶ Fixing the root causes of common business issues

▶ Realizing why lack of funding is never the real problem

▶ Knowing that hiring a sales superstar never fixes a business model

▶ Discovering a powerful delegation tactic

Sometimes a business issue is just what it appears to be. You need more sales and the sales force is underperforming. Fix the sales force and the issue is fixed. Many issues in business have to do with execution and don't represent an issue with your business model.

Sometimes issues appear to be tactical — like upgrading the sales force, better marketing, or stronger operations — but fixing these issues won't solve the problem. I've seen many businesses spend years tackling these tactical issues only to make minor progress. In situations like these, the impediment to success may not be strategic or tactical, but the business model.

Your business model is the foundation of your business success. If you build a house on a weak foundation, walls can crack, water lines can break, the roof can separate, and bricks can be damaged. Fixing the walls, water lines, roof, and bricks doesn't fix the root cause of the problem. Just like a savvy home-owner recognizes cracking walls and bricks as symptoms of a foundation issue, the business problems I address in this chapter can be symptoms of a deeper business model issue.

In this chapter you see ten common business issues that you can fix by updating your business model. You also discover some potential solutions to these issues.

You Have a Strong Desire to Sell the Business

A client once told me, "If I didn't own this place, I'd quit." Because the business owner can't quit, many business owners use the hope of selling their business as the universal magic wand to fix their frustration. Often, a business owner has been slaying the dragons of his everyday business for years only to wake up the next day and find a different dragon. This fight gets old. Frustrated with the lack of permanent progress, the business owner gets a bright idea — sell the business and push the problems on to somebody else, and get paid to do it. Sounds like a pretty good plan.

Frustration, however, is never a good reason to sell a business. As the buyer performs due diligence, the skeletons will come out of the closet. The buyer will recognize that these problems need to be fixed and demand to get paid to fix them.

The better solution is to stop chasing symptoms and start chasing the underlying problem — the business model. Ask yourself, "If the buyer could pay me only for my business model, what would the company be worth?" Remove all the company's value tied up in human, customer, and physical capital. What's left? If you're Coca-Cola, there's $77.8 billion left — the estimated value of the Coca-Cola brand and business model.

Make a list of all the things that are bugging you about your business, and then write down your proposed solutions. That's a great start, but you're not done. Now move one level higher. How does your solution to each problem fix an underlying issue with the business model? If your solution doesn't improve the business model, you need to come up with a better solution. If you do, you'll improve your business model and improve your payday when you sell the business.

You're Underpaid

The world of entrepreneurial pay is a bit erratic and polar. I've met thousands of business owners. In general, these business owners are either underpaid or overpaid. I meet too many business owners working long 65-hour weeks for $56,000. I also meet plenty of business owners taking $2 million a year out of their business. If you're in this category, congratulations and skip to the next section.

If you feel your talent level and hard work aren't being rewarded by your business, there's a reason. Your business model is letting you down. It's not the quantity and quality of your efforts that's the issue; it's what you're putting your efforts into. It's like driving with the emergency brake on. Pressing on the gas harder doesn't make the car go faster. You have to first release the brake. The same is true if your business model needs adjustment. You can work and work with little reward if your model is acting like the stuck emergency brake of your business.

Nothing against McDonald's, but if you decided your best career move was to drop everything and become the world's best French fry engineer, how far would 65 hours a week of hard work get you? Not very far because hard work doesn't equal rewards — the right hard work does.

Continuing to work hard when you feel underpaid is a bad plan. You need to get to the root of the problem, which is probably a fundamental business model issue. The following sections show you two common scenarios.

Scenario #1: Charlie Cheapskate

Charlie spends 10 hours per week doing the books, 20 hours a week selling, 20 hours a week minding the shop, and 10 hours a week on miscellaneous tasks. Charlie has some long-term employees who could do some of the work, but to move a significant amount of this work off Charlie's plate would require hiring somebody. Charlie already feels underpaid, so the thought of hiring somebody else isn't palatable. After all, this person's pay comes right out of Charlie's pocket.

Charlie has to decide whether a pay cut for himself (hiring a new person) can be leveraged by the business model. That is, can Charlie and the business add more value to the business than the employee costs the business? Just like the earlier French fry example, if the pay of the new person can't be exceeded by the value that person adds to the business, it's a waste of money.

It's disconcerting that Charlie is overworked and won't take the simple solution of hiring more help. Why won't Charlie do this? Most likely, Charlie knows his current business model can't add much more value with the new employee than the cost of the employee. That's why Charlie does the work himself. His model is unable to be leveraged and he knows it. Charlie needs to tweak his business model so the addition of an employee adds value of four, five, or even ten times the employee's cost. This will make the decision much easier.

In the mid-sized and small business world, Charlie's issue is very common. Charlie is the bottleneck of his business, and he's underleveraged. First, Charlie needs to work at his highest and best use to the business. This use isn't bookkeeping or administration. Charlie has unique skills that are quite valuable to the business, and it's a safe bet he isn't doing them often enough. By leveraging other employees, Charlie can work at his highest and best use. I created a detailed step-by-step plan, telling you how entrepreneurs can accomplish this task, in my book *The 51 Fatal Business Errors and How to Avoid Them* (Mulekick Publishing). Check out Error #16 specifically.

You can re-leverage yourself year after year. If this leveraging plan works, your business model is in great shape. At some point, your leveraging plan may not work as well or may fail. Now it's time to look at your business model. For smaller businesses, leveraging the highest and best use of the owner is so vital that I believe it warrants inclusion as part of the business model.

Scenario #2: Habitual Harriet

Virtually every business starts with too little help. There's lots of work to be done and far too few hands to get it done. This dynamic leads to the entrepreneur performing parts of dozens of jobs. This bootstrapping approach is vital to the successful launch of the business. Sometimes though, the habit of doing jobs like deliveries, invoicing, customer service, and other tasks that can be performed well by employees, overtakes the day of the owner.

The result is an under-leveraged business model. Your job as the owner of the business is to fully leverage your skills into the business model. Cranking out invoices isn't your highest and best use. Just like scenario #1, you need to spend money to better leverage yourself.

You Need to Constantly Borrow Funds in Order to Grow

Sales are increasing 30 percent per year. Your accountant informs you that you've produced nice profits for several years, but you never have any money in the bank. In order to fund your growth, you're in constant need of borrowed funds.

Initially, your bank provided you an operating line of credit that helped you grow. Now that line of credit is maxed out and you still need more. You've tapped your IRA, friends, family, and anyone else who can loan the business money — after all, look at the nice profit you're producing.

This cycle can't go on forever. Eventually, sources of new funds will dry up or your bank will want out of the line of credit. Then what? The most likely cause of this issue is insufficient margin — a business model issue.

Imagine your product had a 95-percent profit margin. Would you constantly need to borrow funds? The answer is no. The margin generated by sales would eliminate the need for debt. If you constantly need to borrow funds, the capital needed to grow the business and the margin generated by marginal sales isn't in balance. You need to fine-tune the business model to squeeze out a little more margin.

You have a good business model. Sales are growing, but the excessive appetite for debt will eventually damage the business. You really have only two choices, slow growth or increase margins.

You Feel You Need to Hire Sales Superstars to Fix Your Sales Issues

Here are some of the most common scenarios I see with mid-sized and small businesses:

- ✔ Employing a small sales team that produces mediocre results
- ✔ The business owner is the top performing salesperson by a wide margin
- ✔ A history of hiring salespeople with great hopes they will be the "chosen one" who can sell significantly better than the others
- ✔ Continuing to look for the elusive sales superstar who can outsell the owner

Hiring a sales superstar is rarely the answer to this issue. The issue is in the sales performance model of the business model. Most likely, the company has no proven and repeatable sales process. The owner intuitively knows how to close deals but can't create a process anyone else can duplicate. She can hire all the superstars she wants; without a proper sales process, none of them will succeed.

Within that proven and repeatable sales process is the issue of salability. Maybe there's a reason only the owner can sell the product or service. Maybe under the current set of features and benefits, it's simply too hard to sell, and an ordinary salesperson will have a hard time.

Rather than spend hundreds of thousands of dollars looking for Superman or Superwoman, create an offering and a proven process that allows a salesperson of average skill to sell an acceptable amount of product.

You're Unbankable

If I had a nickel for every time I heard, "I don't understand why the bank won't loan me money," I would have a lot of nickels. Yes, banks can be frustratingly conservative. However, banks are also financially sophisticated and have created many advanced metrics to evaluate the financial viability of a business. Rather than be frustrated and think that the bank doesn't get it, fix the real issue — the bank doesn't like the financial aspects of your business model.

Every banker will tell you, "We don't want to be an equity partner in your business." What the banker is saying is the business model doesn't support the bank as a financial partner and the only way the bank sees getting its money back is to patiently wait for an equity return. That's not the bank's business model.

The root of this issue is most likely your margin. Businesspeople tend to think increasing sales will fix this issue. Yes, increasing sales will help, but increasing margins will probably help more.

Find a way to cut fixed overhead, increase sales, and increase margins, and you'll find many cooperative lenders. If you want a quick acid test for the likelihood of getting a loan, visit www.bankabilityindex.com.

Your Margins Are Lower Than Your Competitors' Margins

Great business models are built upon great margin. What does it say about your business model if your competitors' margins are better than yours? It's not the end of the world, but it certainly means you're climbing at a steeper grade than your competition.

Decreased margin puts you at a significant disadvantage vis-à-vis your competition. Competitors will be able to hire better employees, because they can pay better. They'll be able to hire a better sales staff, because they can pay better. They'll be able to advertise more, because they have more margin enabling them to do so. They'll be able to subsidize one offering with another with the excess margin. The list goes on and on.

If your margins are lower than your competitors' margins, you have two options:

- ✔ **Fix it:** The best option is to fix the problem. Look to innovation for the answer. New, innovative offerings tend to carry higher margins than old offerings.

- ✔ **Live with it:** The second option is to live with it. It's hard to imagine a company creating a higher margin from a coffee offering than Starbucks. If you were stuck competing with Starbucks, you may not be able to fix the margin issue. However, you'd want to design your business model with the presumption of this handicap. Oil companies such as Clark have a large number of old gas stations built around World War II. They're built on lots far too small for today's massive convenience stores. Because of this handicap, Clark's business model is denied access to the high-margin upsell items in the convenience store. Clark uses a minimal cost model and no-frills approach with these stations as a result.

You Put Up with Lousy Customers Instead of Firing Them

Most businesses have occasionally had customers who drive them crazy. These customers constantly complain, always require additional assistance, treat your people poorly, pay their bills slowly, and/or beat you down so badly on price, you can't make any money. You wish you could tell these customers to take a hike, but you need the sales.

Your problem isn't the over-demanding customer; it's your business model. Ask yourself, why won't you fire these customers who clearly deserve it? Consider these potential answers:

- The customers' sales are a significant percentage of your total sales (Root issue: pitfall)

- The margin generated by the customers may be a small percentage, but without it you can't meet your overhead burden (Root issue: profit model)

- Deep down, you know you can't find better customers (Root issue: marketing model or sales model)

Fix these underlying root issues, and you'll be able to enjoy the ever-so-satisfying feeling of telling these customers they would be better off purchasing somewhere else.

You Feel There is No One to Whom You Can Delegate

Most business owners work below their pay grade. They know they should delegate work, but they don't. These are the five primary factors at work:

- **Money:** The work doesn't get delegated because you can't afford to pay someone to do it. You do the work yourself because it's "free." Of course it's not really free to do the work yourself because of the opportunity cost. I sound like a broken record here, but it's probably a margin issue in the business model. The margin generated is insufficient to support the true needs of the business. Rather than fix the margin issue, you artificially subsidize the business with the donation of your "free" time.

- **Trust:** Employees never do the work as fast or as well as you do in the way you want it done. That's a given. This issue may not be a pure business model issue but it affects the business model. By denying your business model the leverage you could provide by delegating work, you're underperforming. Use Figure 24-1 to decide the best work to delegate.

Delegation Checklist

Rank each task from 1-10 (1=least favorable)

Variable	Ranking	Weight	Total	Note
$/hour the activity is worth				Lower value/hour is better
Frequency the task occurs				More frequent is better
Time task takes to complete				Longer the task the better
$/hour the activity will cost to have someone else do				Lower the better in relation to value of task
Ease/difficulty of the task				Easy is better
Ease/difficulty of delegation				Easy is better
Training time (how long before up to speed)				Shorter training time is better relative to value and frequency of task
Workload of delegee (try to push to lowest level in the organization)				Overworked delegee is bad
Impact on customers if done wrong (internal vs. external)				Huge impact on customers may make it not worth delegating
Who will do the training? You?				You=bad
Outside resources available to train? Inside resources?				Fred Prior seminar or New Horizons canned training favorable

Figure 24-1: Delegation checklist.

✔ **Talent:** It's not that you're unwilling to delegate, you're unable to. Your staff simply lacks the required talent to complete the work. To clarify, sometimes it's difficult to tell whether the staff is poorly trained or under-skilled. The symptoms are the same. If the issue truly is the caliber of your staff, the root cause in the business model is insufficient sales or insufficient margin. Of course, you could just be a lousy judge of talent and need to hire better, but in my experience that's rarely the case. If it is, hire someone to do your hiring for you. If the issue is sales related, create a more sellable product or a better sales process. If the issue is insufficient margin, raise prices or innovate.

✔ **Cheapskate:** Sometimes business owners have the money to pay to delegate, but they don't do it. I'm probably the biggest cheapskate of them all, but even I know if I fail to leverage my skills I fail to grow my business. There's smart cheap and there's dumb cheap. Smart cheap is typically achieved when the business is young and requires you to perform many jobs to avoid hiring a full employee for half a job. Dumb cheap is when you make the bad decision to keep the pay of the employee rather than leverage yourself.

✔ **Training:** The traits that make for a great entrepreneur tend to make for a lousy trainer. Entrepreneurs tend to lack the patience and detail orientation required to train effectively. Sometimes employees have plenty of motivation and talent to perform the skills, but the entrepreneur fails to give them the tools they need to succeed. Investing in your employees' training is a wise investment. It's very difficult to over-train someone. *The 51 Fatal Business Errors and How to Avoid Them* (written by yours truly and published by Mulekick Publishing) offers significant guidance on this point. Supplemental to the book, I have plenty of free downloadable tools at www.51errors.com.

Fix your delegation issue and you'll have the ability to better leverage your business model.

Your Best Performers Often Leave for Better Opportunities

Nothing is more frustrating than having a talented performer leave the business. It's harmful to morale and the bottom line. If you find yourself in a situation where your best performers tend to leave for better opportunities, you have a business model issue.

Assuming you're not the world's worst boss, your people are leaving because a competitor's business model extends a better opportunity to the employee. Facebook and Google offer computer programmers a better opportunity than most other companies, because their business models are more profitable. That profitability trickles down to employees in the form of better pay, better benefits, better work environment, and better job security.

Even if you can't assess your business model, your employees can. Employees have a great knack for sniffing out strong business models and flocking to work for those companies. If you want to recruit the best people, you need to have the best business model.

Your Customer Base is Stagnant or Declining

Stability isn't always a good thing in the business world. In the world of business, it's grow or die. Everyone in business is on a treadmill, and it's moving. If you find yourself in a situation where your customer base isn't growing, you may be in for trouble. We all desire stability, but in business, growth is stability.

If you aren't attaining stability through growth, you probably have an issue with your business model. Why can't you attract new customers? Here are some possibilities:

- ✔ You're in a declining market (Root issue: marketability)
- ✔ Your offering is bested by the competition (Root issue: value proposition)
- ✔ Your product is sellable, but you're failing to execute (Root issue: sales performance model)

✔ Your offering is stable (Root issue: innovation factor)

✔ You used to have competitive advantage, but you've allowed competition to catch up (Root issue: ongoing competitive advantage)

Address any or all of these issues and your customer base will grow.

Chapter 25

Applying Ten Sources of Business Model Innovation

● ●

In This Chapter

▶ Finding inspiration for the innovation process

▶ Digging the golden ideas out of everyday activities

▶ Using creativity to find business model innovation from unrelated and competitive businesses

● ●

*B*usiness model innovation is critical to the long-term success of your enterprise. Sometimes it's difficult to assume *The Thinker* pose (from Auguste Rodin's famous statue) and spew forth brilliant ideas. The "think system" didn't work very well for Professor Harold Hill in *The Music Man* when he said, "Come on men, *think.*" Most people need a starting point for some inspiration.

In this chapter, you discover ten potential sources of business model innovation as well as how you can best apply them to your business model.

Business Books

Business books provide an abundant source of ideas for business model innovation. Great business books contain many stories and/or case studies that can provide the seed for an innovation. Here's a list of a few of my favorites:

> ✔ **Business modeling books**
>
>   • *Business Model Generation: A Handbook for Visionaries, Game Changers, and Challengers* by Alexander Osterwalder and Yves Pigneur (Wiley)

- *The Business Model Innovation Factory: How to Stay Relevant When The World is Changing* by Saul Kaplan (Wiley)
- *Seizing the White Space: Business Model Innovation for Growth and Renewal* by A. G. Lafley and Mark W. Johnson (Harvard Business Press)

✓ **Marketing books**

- *The 22 Immutable Laws of Marketing: Violate Them at Your Own Risk!* by Al Ries and Jack Trout (HarperBusiness)
- *The New Rules of Marketing & PR: How to Use Social Media, Online Video, Mobile Applications, Blogs, News Releases, and Viral Marketing to Reach Buyers Directly* by David Meerman Scott (Wiley)
- *Marketing For Dummies* by Alexander Hiam (Wiley)

✓ **Sales books**

- *You Can't Teach a Kid to Ride a Bike at a Seminar: The Sandler Sales Institute's 7-Step System for Successful Selling* by David H. Sandler and John Hayes, PhD (Bay Head Pub)
- *SPIN Selling* by Neil Rackham (HighBridge Company)
- *The New Strategic Selling: The Unique Sales System Proven Successful by the World's Best Companies* by Stephen E. Heiman, Tad Tuleja, Robert B. Miller, and J. W. Marriott (Business Plus)
- *Selling For Dummies* by Tom Hopkins (Wiley)

✓ **Innovation books**

- *The Innovator's Dilemma: The Revolutionary Book That Will Change the Way You Do Business* by Clayton M. Christensen (HarperBusiness)
- *The Innovator's Solution: Creating and Sustaining Successful Growth* by Clayton M. Christensen and Michael E. Raynor (Harvard Business School Press)
- *The Lean Startup: How Today's Entrepreneurs Use Continuous Innovation to Create Radically Successful Businesses* by Eric Ries (Crown Business)
- *Business Innovation For Dummies* by Alexander Hiam (Wiley)

✓ **Compilations**

- *The 100 Best Business Books of All Time: What They Say, Why They Matter, and How They Can Help You* by Jack Covert and Todd Sattersten (Portfolio Trade)

Competitors

Sure, competitors are a perpetual burr in your saddle, but if you're clever, competitors can provide valuable ideas for business model innovation. Jerry Jones may drive other NFL team owners nuts, but he's credited with teaching other owners how to monetize assets they had never considered. PC manufacturer after PC manufacturer failed to make a tablet computer work. Apple's iPad taught them that the market didn't want a tablet computer, it wanted a toy.

Other examples include the following:

- ✔ An innovative funeral home figured out how to monetize their website. Soon, hundreds of other funeral homes copied this innovation.

- ✔ Several years ago, innovative retailers used hiring kiosks to lower their cost structure. Now most retailers use a similar plan.

- ✔ Many large companies are integrating the practice of lead scoring into their sales process. Savvy smaller competitors are creating scaled-down versions of lead scoring to improve their own sales process.

- ✔ Holiday Inn competitor Days Inn understood that its business model required a lower cost structure than Holiday Inn's. Days Inn used a low-tech but effective site selection process — wait for Holiday Inn's proven site selection team to pick a desirable location, and then open up across the street.

- ✔ Extended warranties are a very profitable addition to a business model. When innovative retailers proved this was a viable concept, most other retailers followed suit.

- ✔ Several years ago, a handful of sellers on eBay discovered it was far more profitable to overcharge for shipping and undercharge for the item purchased. Within a year, this best practice had been copied by most eBay sellers. Interestingly, the practice was so profitable, eBay customers revolted and sellers had to reverse course.

- ✔ The Herman Miller Aeron chair pushed the limits of design and price. This innovation taught all office furniture manufacturers that customers would pay $1,000 for a single chair if it was cool enough.

- ✔ And the most famous of them all — Steve Jobs saw the mouse and graphical user interface at Xerox PARC and used the concepts to create the Macintosh. *Note:* Jobs did license these ideas from Xerox, but Jobs monetized what Xerox could not.

Don't assume your competitors are stupid. Don't ask me how many times I've heard a client say, "I can't believe this dumb competitor is . . ." If you assume your competitors are stupid, you may be missing the opportunity to find and copy their innovation. It's more likely that the competitors have stumbled upon something brilliant than that they're behaving against their own best interest.

Consultants

Consultants are like bumblebees. Without bumblebees spreading pollen from flower to flower, none of them would flourish. Business consultants not only help businesses succeed, but also pollinate innovation and best practices among the businesses they serve.

A well-traveled consultant with expertise in your industry or area of need can bring an abundance of quality ideas for your business model.

Great Companies Outside Your Industry

The best ideas for business model innovation can come from companies outside your industry. There's a reason everyone inside your industry is constrained by the thinking of that industry. They say things like, "Everyone knows you can't . . ." or "It's been that way since . . ."

Companies outside your industry aren't forced to deal with the constraints of your industry. If you're clever enough to sift through great ideas, filtering out the irrelevant but keeping the occasional gold nugget, you'll find your best business model innovations.

Companies around the world valued ideas from the Walt Disney Company to such an extent that Disney University was created. Disney charges thousands of dollars to educate companies in every business imaginable on the secrets of its successful business model.

Here are some examples of great ideas coming from unrelated industries:

✓ Most people credit Google with the 10-percent rule — allowing employees to spend 10 percent of their time on unrelated projects. However, Google borrowed this idea from 3M. Since 1948 3M has allowed employees to spend up to 15 percent of their time on pet projects.

✔ Many savvy businesses have followed the lead of franchises in regard to marketing expenditures. Franchises charge a flat percentage of sales to be spent on advertising and marketing. Rather than just spending ad hoc, savvy businesses have adopted a percentage of sales to be spent on marketing regardless of the sales level.

✔ Good or bad, many businesses have adopted Walmart's fanatical "keep costs low" philosophy.

✔ Outsourcing and offshoring was a trend started by a handful of large technology companies.

✔ The toner refilling industry borrowed many best practices from the long-established automotive rebuilding industry.

✔ Inventor Dean Kamen was clever enough to borrow his own best practice. Kamen sold his gyroscoping wheelchair to Johnson & Johnson and used the same core technology in the Segway Peoplemover.

✔ An uncanny number of Vince Lombardi's Green Bay Packer players have become very successful in business. Most of these players attribute their business success to the lessons they learned on the football field.

✔ A business owner was struggling with his manager's productivity. In particular, employees were lingering in the manager's office too long. The owner remembered a story about Ray Kroc wanting his McDonald's managers on the floor and not in their offices. Kroc's solution to the problem was to saw the backs off of the chairs in the manager's office and make it less comfortable to sit. The business owner simply removed the guest chairs from each manager's office. This tactic cut the drop-in meeting time from ten minutes to two minutes and greatly improved productivity.

The Crystal Ball

Using the crystal ball is more than just guessing at the future or daydreaming. Using the crystal ball is a process by which you paint a vivid picture of what the business environment will be three to five years from now. Ask yourself:

✔ What will be the general economic climate?

✔ What will interest rates be versus today?

✔ What will be the general state of your industry?

✔ What new competitors will have entered your market? Who will have exited?

- ✔ What new technology will be commonplace both in the general population and in your market? What competitors will have adopted this technology?

- ✔ What new laws or regulations will affect your industry?

- ✔ What product features will you have added and why?

- ✔ What new products have competitors introduced? How successful are they?

- ✔ What is the economic health of your clients and their industries?

- ✔ What marketing methods will be the most effective?

The purpose of this exercise isn't the same as a five-year plan. A business plan is only about your business and doesn't put much emphasis on what changes happen to the world around you. The crystal ball exercise focuses entirely on the environment your business will be forced to operate in and then allows you to make the necessary adjustments. Your first-hand knowledge of your industry lets you see into the crystal ball and predict what the future will bring.

Many contend that Bill Gates's success at Microsoft was partly due to his ability to read the crystal ball. Gates prognosticated that every home and desk would have a computer on it. At the time Gates said this, most businesses had no computer, and very few homes had one. However, Gates behaved like his prediction would come true. He worked to dominate the critical applications for this army of future computers. Bill Gates was successful for many reasons, but one of them was his ability to predict the future through the crystal ball.

Employees

Companies use employee suggestion boxes for improvements to their business process, but employees can be a valued source of business model improvements as well. Employees have access to the intimate details of customer interactions, business processes, and competition every day. Giving your employees the opportunity and permission to assist with business model innovation is good business.

Here are just a few examples of how employees helped improve a business model.

- ✔ Vendors, customers, and employees were given input into the design of the Ford Taurus. The Taurus not only made billions of dollars in profits for Ford, but also changed the way Ford did business. One of the more interesting suggestions by employees was placing a small plastic nub in the middle of the dashboard assembly. This nub helped balance the dashboard, so one person could install it. Previously, two line workers were needed to install the dash. Imagine the savings Ford has enjoyed since implementing this seemingly small suggestion.

✔ Japanese pharmaceutical maker Eisai Co. got critical input from employees on a jelly-like substance that Alzheimer's patients can swallow easily.

✔ A group of female employees at Best Buy convinced management that women were better customers than men. After analyzing data, management agreed. Store data revealed that women customers tended to return less merchandise than men did, and thereby generated more profits. Best Buy then devised a strategy to target this underserved female market.

✔ J. Willard Marriott started out with a chain of nine A&W root beer stands, including one near an airport. An employee noticed that passengers would purchase meals, stuffing the food into their carry-on luggage. This idea resulted in the store establishing a delivery of prepackaged box lunches directly onto the tarmac. Several months later, the service expanded to American Airlines catering to 22 flights each day. This airport food service has now evolved to more than 100 airports.

✔ Miller Furniture created the first office cubicle unit as the result of an employee suggestion.

Products or Services You Buy

Products and services you already purchase can provide the genesis of a business model innovation. Ben & Jerry's ice cream and its funky flavor collection prompted other businesses to take wild chances on everything from soda flavors to clothing styles.

If you're looking to find creative ideas in existing products, you need to think about the utility the product or feature provides rather than what it is literally. For instance, McDonald's aggregates drive-thru food orders in the equivalent of a call center hundreds of miles away from where you place your food order. You probably can't use the concept of remote drive-thru call centers in your business. However you can use this concept in your business. The important concept of the McDonald's drive-thru is live remote client interaction. Most businesspeople feel that the only way to serve the customer live and in real time is face to face. The McDonald's drive-thru challenges this assumption.

Another potential concept you can copy from McDonald's is the previewing of your drive-thru order on a screen. Before long, the customers will be punching their own orders on the screen. You can extrapolate this idea into your business through the concepts of customer self-service or customer quality control of their own orders.

Be on the lookout for great ideas on the grocery shelf, in your kitchen cabinet, and everywhere else you look.

Travel to Other Countries or Hotspots

Sometimes the best innovation is borrowing other people's innovation. Howard Schultz got the idea for Starbucks while sitting in an Italian café. Plenty of creative product, fashion, and food ideas come from taking a proven product or concept from another area and transplanting it.

Here are some examples:

- ✔ The Kit Kat bar, which was the idea of an employee, was originally launched in London and the South East in 1935. It was then brought to the U.S. where Hershey's began to sell it in 1969.

- ✔ The British hit series *Pop Idol* was copied and brought to the U.S. as *American Idol*.

- ✔ The hamburger is an American invention that's now sold around the world.

- ✔ Italian immigrants in New York created many successful pizza restaurants.

- ✔ Vitamin companies started selling fish oil tablets after discovering Eskimos had extremely low incidence of heart attack despite eating a fatty diet.

- ✔ Payment by cellphone is expected to increase dramatically in the U.S. as a significant number of Asian countries have already adopted use of the technology.

- ✔ Hospitals in India have adopted innovative medical practices that dramatically lower costs. For instance, doctors don't interpret x-rays — professional x-ray interpreters do. These non-physicians do nothing but look at knee x-rays all day, and get paid a fraction of what a physician costs. Many professionals feel a trained technician who reads many more x-rays can do a better job than a doctor. It will be interesting to see whether a similar practice is adopted in the United States.

- ✔ Ryanair has created a successful no-frills airline in Europe. Using the restroom is free, but Ryanair toyed with charging $2, as the airline charges for every add-on imaginable. The flights can cost half of the nearest competitor though. To date, no U.S. airline has copied Ryanair's strategy, but it won't be long until someone does. Ryanair is even considering free tickets and monetizing passengers via in-flight gambling and standup seating.

Whether you're observing the latest Greenwich Village or Hollywood trend or a cool business practice from Asia, other cultures offer great innovative ideas for your business model.

Ignoring other cultures' innovations and ideas can be dangerous for your business. For many years Volkswagen refused to put cup holders into the vehicles it sold in America. The folks at Volkswagen couldn't understand why anyone would want one cup holder, let alone 15 of them. Eventually, Volkswagen gave in to soda-guzzling American consumers and added cup holders. Why did Volkswagen give in? Simple. Americans refused to buy Volkswagen vehicles due to the lack of cup holders.

Daydreaming

If you've seen the movie *Night Shift,* you probably remember the famous line uttered by Michael Keaton, "Note to self, feed the mayonnaise to the tuna." Keaton played a hapless wannabe entrepreneur always coming up with crazy ideas like pre-making tuna salad by feeding the mayonnaise to the tuna.

Hopefully the quality of your ideas will be better than Michael Keaton's character's, but don't underestimate the value of daydreaming. I bet at some time during a long drive, you zoned out and had a terrific idea pop into your head. If you give your subconscious an opportunity to work, it can do great things.

People are so busy and harried these days, they don't give themselves permission to daydream. If you have a history of generating high-quality ideas while daydreaming or zoning out, find a way to do it more often.

A client endured two long flights to China in a four-day period. He jokingly told me, "I do my best work on an airplane." He explained how he completed most of his high-impact work and had several great ideas on the plane trips. I jokingly asked him why he didn't take more plane trips. Rather than laughing off my comment, he bought the cheapest ticket with the longest flight time so he could do this quality work. He literally spent an entire day flying to Los Angeles, sitting in the airport for two hours, and then flying home. He assures me it was the best $400 he spent all year.

Salespeople

Salespeople can be great sources of information and innovation. Salespeople are on the front lines dealing with customers and prospects. Here are some ways salespeople can help you improve your business model:

✔ Salespeople have a great feel for what prospects are and aren't receptive to. They have their finger on the pulse of marketability (see Chapter 6 for more on this concept).

✔ Salespeople have a good feel for what the market will bear regarding your product. For example, can you raise prices, or do you need to lower prices? In this way, they can help with your profit model (see Chapter 8).

✔ Salespeople come up with great ideas for add-on products. These are examples of profit model and innovation factor (see Chapters 8 and 11).

✔ Salespeople can help create a proven and repeatable sales process. (For details about your sales performance model, check out Chapter 9.)

✔ Salespeople can gather competitive data. (See Chapter 10 for more on your ongoing competitive advantage.)

✔ Salespeople help sniff out trends, which can help you with innovation and ongoing competitive advantage (see Chapters 10 and 11 for details).

✔ Salespeople understand what clients will and won't pay for. (See Chapter 7 for more on a unique value proposition.)

Several years ago I was facilitating a CEO Roundtable. One of the participants was frustrated with the performance of his sales force and wanted input for changing his value proposition to help them sell better. One of the other participants gave him one of the best pieces of advice I've heard. He said: "You don't need to figure out how to sell your product because a good salesperson will figure it out for you. If your current salespeople can't tell you how to sell it, they're the wrong people."

Chapter 26

Ten Things a Venture Capitalist Never Wants to Hear About Your Business

*Y*our business may not be funded by a venture capitalist, but it *is* funded by someone, even if that someone is you. Investors demand a solid business model before investing, so it's important you get the model right. Because venture capitalists are the most sophisticated investors in business models, I use them as an example of how you should view your business model and the things you should say about it.

In this chapter, I discuss common ways entrepreneurs describe their business models and how a venture capitalist may interpret these descriptions. How you describe your business model can speak volumes about its potential success or failure.

I'll Figure Out How to Monetize This Later

What do Twitter, Groupon, Solar City, biofuel companies, Webvan, and most blogs have in common? They've all attracted a vast number of customers but failed to profit from them.

The Internet has brought a new mentality to the business world in which users matter more than profit. The concept is to capture a large audience and figure out how to make money from the audience later. For Internet companies, an underlying presumption indicates that free users can be converted to paying users later. For solar, biofuel, and other hot technology companies, the underlying assumption is that customer adoption of technological gains will fix the "make it for $10 and sell it for $5" problem.

For every `Amazon.com` that did move from large losses to large gains, you can find a Groupon that moves from large losses to larger losses. In 2011, Groupon had an impressive $1.6 billion in sales but managed to lose $238 million. That's not impressive for the industry leader selling a digital coupon with little cost. Sure, sometimes you need economies of scale in order to achieve profitability. Amazon proved this to be true. But at $1.6 billion in digital coupon revenue, doesn't Groupon have critical mass?

Your investors don't want to hear that your business model doesn't convert sales into profits. It's simply too big an assumption.

The following list addresses three key distinctions that merit discussion for these "we'll make money later" companies:

- ✔ **Companies that have sales (just not enough of them):** The first group consists of the solar power, wind power, bio fuel, and Groupon-type companies. They have sales, just not critical mass. The key assumption in question is the growth of sales and the decrease in cost per unit sold. Is everyone going to be driving electric cars or just 0.001 percent of drivers? Overly aggressive predictions of customers' willingness to adopt new technologies can doom the business model.

- ✔ **Companies using the audience to monetize through advertising or indirect methods:** The companies in the second group are primarily Internet-related offerings that capture large audiences, and then make money via the indirect model. These companies use the television model — selling advertising or selling access to their audience. Free iPhone apps, technology blogs, Google, Facebook, and Pandora make money not from selling access to their sites/products but by selling access to their audience to advertisers.

- ✔ **Companies using a freemium model:** The third group is the most dangerous. Companies that spend significant effort building an audience or customers and figure the money will come later are following the *Field of Dreams* plan — if you build it, they will come. The problem with this plan is that the customers are trained to think the product is free or underpriced. When the customers are asked to pay fair value, they simply matriculate to the next free provider.

I've heard much chatter regarding Twitter charging a token $5 per month for a service that many users value deeply. To date, it's simply chatter. Twitter has 500 million total users and 200 million active users yet doesn't make a profit. A few million of these users paying $5 a month would make Twitter a profitable business. So why doesn't Twitter flip the switch and go from a money loser to a money maker? They know most of their users would flee, that's why.

The Internet has created the culture of free. This "they'll pay later" plan doesn't work very often. Be careful. It's a better bet to use an alternative monetization plan for the customer base than to charge for use. The profit model portion of your business model may be weak with a monetize-later approach.

Clayton Christensen, author of *The Innovator's Dilemma* (Harvard Business Review Press), wisely recommends "be patient for growth and impatient for profit." If you follow his simple rule, you can avoid this issue altogether.

It's Kind of Like Groupon, Except . . .

You'd be amazed how many times my staff hears an entrepreneur pitch his business model with the first line, "It's kind of like Groupon except . . . it's in Queens, it's for kids, it's for backrubs only, it donates a portion to charity," or simply, "it's better."

There's already a business kind of like Groupon. It's called Groupon. There's a simple rule to know if your offering has solid footing:

Different is always better than better.

Customers don't want or need a better Groupon, but they may be open to a significant differentiation of Groupon. A model without a unique value proposition or "Groupon with a twist" isn't going to cut it. Even if a Groupon-with-a-twist concept works, it's way too easy for Groupon to just copy the idea.

In order to one-up Groupon, you'd need to:

- ✔ Create a meaningful differentiation
- ✔ Make the concept difficult or unattractive for Groupon to copy
- ✔ Go after a segment unserved or underserved by Groupon

A business model meeting these criteria isn't "like Groupon."

I Used to Work for a Company That Did the Same Thing

This plan has a good and a bad aspect. The bad part is the same as the Groupon issue (see the previous section). A successful company is already using this business model. Without significant change to the model, why bother?

The good part is a proven business model and management that understands the model. The critical question is, "What are you expecting from the business model?" If you're looking to simply take a share of the former employer's market, then go for it. If you want to build a business that's bigger and better, you need a bigger and better business model.

The borrow-the-model plan has worked for some. The sub sandwich model has been copied and subdivided by surprisingly similar models. Subway, Blimpie, Jimmy John's, Quiznos, Penn Station, and dozens more have carved out business models that place meat and cheese on bread. The world of construction has many businesses created from a key employee leaving to start his own HVAC contracting, plumbing, or home building company.

Generally, it's a bad idea to simply copy the business model and start a similar business. If you want to copy a successful model, consider differentiating in one of these ways:

- **Move the model to a new geographical location:** When John Hewitt sold Jackson Hewitt tax service, he didn't have a non-compete agreement for Canada. Hewitt moved the business model to Canada, where it eventually became Liberty Tax, the third largest tax preparation service.

- **Capitalize on your talent:** Talent is part of the business model. Superstar lawyers, architects, and doctors can copy a business model outright and still differentiate based upon their superior skills.

- **Move the model to a different industry:** Wayne Huizenga created the Waste Management empire, and then took the core principles of that business model and built Blockbuster video. This is an excellent tactic compared to wholly copying a model. Huizenga's success at Waste Management centered around consolidating a large number of mom-and-pop operators in an industry with no large national players. He used the same magic formula at Blockbuster.

Note: If the former employer went out of business or is struggling for a good reason, copying the model outright may be all right. These reasons may include financial mismanagement, embezzlement, flawed marketing, failed innovation, missed new market opportunities, and more. However, the list doesn't include, "I think I can do it better."

My Business Plan Calls For . . .

This issue is also known as "assuming the hard part." Every business plan calls for rapid increases in sales, low costs, hiring of outstanding employees — a general euphoric state. The real world tends to have finicky customers, hard-to-close sales, problem employees, and more. Particularly in the area of sales forecasts, business plans are nothing more than guesswork.

Be prepared to explain to investors why your business model will work in the worst case scenario as well as the best. A wise real estate investor told me, "I always have six or seven exit strategies for a building." Most investors have only one strategy — sell the building for a profit. This successful investor had Plans A, B, C, D, E, F, and G. He not only had a graceful exit no matter what the circumstances, but also analyzed each deal based upon all the strategies. If he couldn't find enough viable exit strategies, he passed on the deal.

The same holds true for your business model. Of course your model will work well if everything goes as planned, but it won't go as planned. Work to make your business model strong enough to handle a variety of scenarios.

I'll Make It on the Back End

This plan calls for sacrificing today in the hopes of a better payday later. The loss leader concept utilizes this strategy. Get the customers in the store for cheap lettuce, and they'll spend money on other, higher margin, items.

This profit model worked much better pre-Internet. Customers are much more informed today and know what items should cost. Luring them in with loss leaders in hopes of getting them to pay a premium for other items is getting tougher and tougher. Customers simply matriculate to another vendor offering your high margin items as a loss leader.

The Groupon phenomenon is a perfect example of this issue. Retailers deeply discount an item on Groupon in hopes of getting a new customer. The data say that a very small percentage of Groupon users become new customers, leaving the merchant selling items below cost. The hope of making it up on the back end with the business gained from a new customer has never materialized.

Some business models still use this concept effectively. McDonald's, Wendy's and Burger King have used $1 menus to drive traffic and upsell to more expensive meals and high-margin sodas. Gas stations make little or no money pumping gas but have outstanding margins in their convenience stores. Before you use this business model, test your assumption that you *will* make it up on the back end.

Everybody Needs This Product

The Gentle Ear Wax Vacuum Cleaner removes water and gunk from your ears via a battery powered, hand-held vacuum that you insert into your ear. The idea makes perfect sense: everyone has ears, everyone needs to clean those ears, and the existing solution, cotton swabs, can damage your ears. Shoot, everyone needs this product. Do you believe everyone will be buying an ear vacuum cleaner? I don't.

People don't buy what they need. People buy what they want. When investors hear, "Everyone needs this product," they may get the impression that you don't understand your market. Everyone has ears, but everyone doesn't need or want an ear vacuum. Only people dissatisfied with cotton swabs and the inclination to stick a vacuum in their ears are prospects.

The marketability portion of your business model requires you to conservatively define your market rather than broadly define it. Be conservative. Define your market in the narrowest sense and see whether your business model still works. If so, you have a winner. You'll probably gain customers outside this narrow definition. That will only add to your success.

I'll Make it Up In Volume

Sometimes, a business does need additional volume to make the model work. Amazon is a prime example. However, when an entrepreneur looks to additional volume as the magic bullet to fix things, it's a red flag to investors. You can find several unspoken assumptions buried in the "I'll make it up in volume" approach:

- ✔ It assumes additional volume is available. Can McDonald's double the number of hamburgers it sells per store?
- ✔ It assumes additional volume will be as easy to acquire as existing volume. That's almost never the case.
- ✔ It assumes additional sales will be at the same or a better margin. The customers who valued your offering the most are already buying; won't you have to wheel and deal to land the customer with the next worst fit?

Your efforts are better spent assuming sales volume will stay the same and figuring out how to profit from that volume level. Do you believe Groupon can turn profitable by adding volume? If the company can't make money with $1.6 billion in sales, it simply can't make money. More sales isn't the answer for Groupon. The answer is adjusting its business model to make a profit off the $1.6 billion it currently takes in. In the case of Groupon, its profit formula isn't working well.

We Need to Get Only One Percent of the Market

"We need to get only one percent of the market" is another example of a statement that makes perfect sense but doesn't work. Financial projections almost always look great with *only* one percent of the market. But investors cringe when entrepreneurs say so because they wonder

> ✔ **One percent of what market?** One percent of all human beings? One percent of all adults in a 50-mile radius? One percent of all left-handed, non-smoking golfers in town? How you define the overall market you want one percent of matters greatly.

> ✔ **Why one percent?** Face it, one percent is SWAG (scientific wild a*s guess). Why not 32 percent or 0.00043 percent? Entrepreneurs use a small number like *only* one percent in an attempt to make investors more comfortable that the company needs only a tiny percentage of the market for success.

Here's a good concept: Make investors comfortable. SWAG-type guesses don't make them comfortable. Instead, make reasonable projections based upon thoughtful analysis and show the market penetration percentage last.

I've Been Working on This Big Sale for a Year and It Will Close at Any Time

When investors hear, "I've been working on a big deal for a year and it will close any day," what they really hear is, "I haven't been able to get enough customers and the company is in trouble, but we have a Hail Mary that might come through."

What's wrong with the sales model that's keeping this big deal from being closed? Why haven't you been able to close other smaller prospects to validate the model? Rather than pitch the Hail Mary Plan to the investors, wait until you close the deal, and then pitch them.

If you don't close the big deal, look at the marketability, value proposition, and sales performance aspects of your business model for improvement opportunities. (See Chapters 6, 7, and 9 for details on these topics.)

What's a Business Model?

Your *business model* is the core strategy to acquire customers and sell them at a profit. Investors know that the business model is the core foundation of their investment. Great businesspeople orchestrating a great business model yield significant returns for investors. Underemphasizing your understanding of the business model or its importance could hurt your chances with investors.

Index

• **W** •

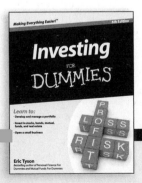
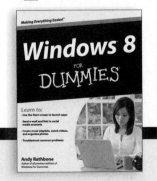

Math & Science

Algebra I For Dummies,
2nd Edition
978-0-470-55964-2

Anatomy and Physiology
For Dummies,
2nd Edition
978-0-470-92326-9

Astronomy For Dummies,
3rd Edition
978-1-118-37697-3

Biology For Dummies,
2nd Edition
978-0-470-59875-7

Chemistry For Dummies,
2nd Edition
978-1-1180-0730-3

Pre-Algebra Essentials
For Dummies
978-0-470-61838-7

Microsoft Office

Excel 2013 For Dummies
978-1-118-51012-4

Office 2013 All-in-One
For Dummies
978-1-118-51636-2

PowerPoint 2013
For Dummies
978-1-118-50253-2

Word 2013 For Dummies
978-1-118-49123-2

Music

Blues Harmonica
For Dummies
978-1-118-25269-7

Guitar For Dummies,
3rd Edition
978-1-118-11554-1

iPod & iTunes
For Dummies,
10th Edition
978-1-118-50864-0

Programming

Android Application
Development For
Dummies, 2nd Edition
978-1-118-38710-8

iOS 6 Application
Development For Dummies
978-1-118-50880-0

Java For Dummies,
5th Edition
978-0-470-37173-2

Religion & Inspiration

The Bible For Dummies
978-0-7645-5296-0

Buddhism For Dummies,
2nd Edition
978-1-118-02379-2

Catholicism For Dummies,
2nd Edition
978-1-118-07778-8

Self-Help & Relationships

Bipolar Disorder
For Dummies,
2nd Edition
978-1-118-33882-7

Meditation For Dummies,
3rd Edition
978-1-118-29144-3

Seniors

Computers For Seniors
For Dummies,
3rd Edition
978-1-118-11553-4

iPad For Seniors
For Dummies,
5th Edition
978-1-118-49708-1

Social Security
For Dummies
978-1-118-20573-0

Smartphones & Tablets

Android Phones
For Dummies
978-1-118-16952-0

Kindle Fire HD
For Dummies
978-1-118-42223-6

NOOK HD For Dummies,
Portable Edition
978-1-118-39498-4

Surface For Dummies
978-1-118-49634-3

Test Prep

ACT For Dummies,
5th Edition
978-1-118-01259-8

ASVAB For Dummies,
3rd Edition
978-0-470-63760-9

GRE For Dummies,
7th Edition
978-0-470-88921-3

Officer Candidate Tests,
For Dummies
978-0-470-59876-4

Physician's Assistant Exam
For Dummies
978-1-118-11556-5

Series 7 Exam
For Dummies
978-0-470-09932-2

Windows 8

Windows 8 For Dummies
978-1-118-13461-0

Windows 8 For Dummies,
Book + DVD Bundle
978-1-118-27167-4

Windows 8 All-in-One
For Dummies
978-1-118-11920-4

Available in print and e-book formats.

Take Dummies with you everywhere you go!

Whether you're excited about e-books, want more from the web, must have your mobile apps, or swept up in social media, Dummies makes everything easier .

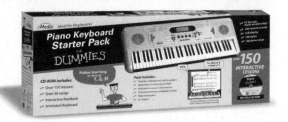